WHY DELUSIONS MATTER

T0269745

WHY PHILOSOPHY MATTERS

Series editor: Professor Constantine Sandis, University of Hertfordshire, UK

Why Philosophy Matters focuses on why a particular philosopher, school of thought or area of philosophical study really matters. Each book will offer a brief overview of the subject before exploring its reception both within and outside the academy and our authors will also defend different provocative outlooks on where the value of philosophy lies (or doesn't, as the case may be). Why Philosophy Matters is accompanied by an ongoing series of free events (talks, debates, workshops) in Bloomsbury. Podcasts of these events will be freely available on the series page.

Books in this series
Why Iris Murdoch Matters, Gary Browning
Why Medieval Philosophy Matters, Stephen Boulter
Why Solipsism Matters, Sami Pihlström
Why Climate Breakdown Matters, Rupert Read

Also available from Bloomsbury
Marginality in Philosophy and Psychology, George Tudorie
General Ecology: The New Ecological Paradigm, ed. Erich Hörl with James Burton

WHY DELUSIONS MATTER

Lisa Bortolotti

BLOOMSBURY ACADEMIC
LONDON • NEW YORK • OXFORD • NEW DELHI • SYDNEY

BLOOMSBURY ACADEMIC
Bloomsbury Publishing Plc
50 Bedford Square, London, WC1B 3DP, UK
1385 Broadway, New York, NY 10018, USA
29 Earlsfort Terrace, Dublin 2, Ireland

BLOOMSBURY, BLOOMSBURY ACADEMIC and the Diana logo
are trademarks of Bloomsbury Publishing Plc

First published in Great Britain 2023

Copyright © Lisa Bortolotti, 2023

Lisa Bortolotti has asserted her right under the Copyright,
Designs and Patents Act, 1988, to be identified as Author of this work.

For legal purposes the Acknowledgements on pp. viii–ix constitute
an extension of this copyright page.

Cover image © societsmartboy10 / Getty Images

All rights reserved. No part of this publication may be reproduced or transmitted
in any form or by any means, electronic or mechanical, including photocopying,
recording, or any information storage or retrieval system, without prior
permission in writing from the publishers.

Bloomsbury Publishing Plc does not have any control over, or responsibility for,
any third-party websites referred to or in this book. All internet addresses given
in this book were correct at the time of going to press. The author and publisher
regret any inconvenience caused if addresses have changed or sites have
ceased to exist, but can accept no responsibility for any such changes.

A catalogue record for this book is available from the British Library.

A catalog record for this book is available from the Library of Congress.

ISBN: HB: 978-1-3501-6330-0
         PB: 978-1-3501-6329-4
         ePDF: 978-1-3501-6331-7
         eBook: 978-1-3501-6332-4

Series: Why Philosophy Matters

Typeset by Integra Software Services Pvt. Ltd.
Printed and bound in Great Britain

To find out more about our authors and books visit www.bloomsbury.com
and sign up for our newsletters.

In loving memory of Claudia Bernabè

CONTENTS

ACKNOWLEDGEMENTS

First and foremost, I would like to thank Constantine Sandis for his friendship. It was Constantine who encouraged me to write this book at a time when I was not sure I did have a book in me. Everybody else at Bloomsbury has been helpful and supportive and this book would not have materialized without them.

Second, I am indebted to my amazing students who have been a constant source of inspiration and have kept me sane during the pandemic. Our Zoom sessions were the highlight of the day. Mostly, we told each other lockdown stories rather than doing philosophy, but I always ended the call happier than when I had started it. A special mention to current and past students Kathleen Murphy-Hollies, Eugenia Lancellotta, Rosa Ritunnano, Rachel Gunn, Valeria Motta, Magdalena Antrobus, Federico Bongiorno, Joe Houlders and Ellie Harris whose work has informed my thinking in this book.

Third, I acknowledge the support of the UKRI-funded Engagement Award on Agency, Justice and Social Identity in Youth Mental Health. Some of the ideas developed with the team have shaped my discussion in chapter eight. I could not have formulated those ideas without the friendship and support of long-term collaborators Matthew Broome and Michael Larkin and the always eye-opening conversations with Rose McCabe, Clara Bergen, Rachel Temple and the inspiring members of McPin Young People's Network.

Fourth, I am lucky to be able to count as friends three incredible philosophers, Anneli Jefferson, Anna Ichino and Ema Sullivan-Bissett, who have shared good and bad moments with me over the past few years, and also enriched my understanding of many of the concepts that are central to the arguments in the book.

Fifth, I want to thank the editorial team at *Philosophical Psychology* for enthusiastically embarking on a crazy adventure with me, renewing one of my favourite interdisciplinary journals ever, and achieving the impossible on an everyday basis. I owe a great debt to long-term collaborators and friends Kengo Miyazono and Kathy Puddifoot, whose philosophical views have informed my understanding of delusions and prejudice, respectively.

Lastly, my family is my rock. My wonderful kids have shown creativity, initiative, resilience and love at a time where the grown-ups all around them felt puzzled and helpless. Before the pandemic spread in Europe and after lockdown ended, my daughter Anna attended conferences with me. She even helped me present a paper on the agential stance at Leuven, demonstrating that you are never too young for philosophy.

This book is dedicated to my cousin Claudia who is no longer with us. This dedication is not coincidental. Here I am advocating interpreting others with curiosity and empathy. Claudia was the most selfless, curious and empathetic person I ever met.

INTRODUCTION

This book is about delusions. It is a matter of controversy, a controversy I want to contribute to in this book, how we should define delusions and how we should think about them. So, I will start with extracts from testimonies of people who experienced delusions, written after they stopped holding onto their beliefs.

In the following extract, Danielle Huggins remembers how she experienced delusions while travelling to London, after discontinuing her medication for mania due to some side effects:

> I hear Lorenzo speak to his mother in Italian. I think: Why are they speaking Italian? Is something wrong? Is this a code? I know that being severely manic can cause the brain to spin webs of conspiracies and make connections that aren't really there. But I no longer ask myself if I am or am not manic. His mom must be an illegal immigrant. We're going to have to smuggle her back into the U.S. I am terrified. I am certain that his mom is not a citizen and that the British police are onto us.
>
> (Huggins 2022)

In the next extract, Jidarth Jadeja recalls how it felt to believe in the QAnon conspiracy theory and how he realized the conspiracy was not true:

> When I found QAnon, I didn't just flirt with it – I fell deep. I internalized the idea that the world was run by the Cabal, a Satan-worshiping child-molesting group of liberal politicians, Hollywood moguls, billionaires and other influential elites. I believed that Donald Trump was leading the fight against the Cabal and that there was a plan in place to defeat them. I couldn't wait for the coming of the Storm, QAnon's version of judgment day that would herald the announcement of martial law and a wave of public executions. I was looking forward to the execution of Hillary Clinton, whom Q portrayed as a pedophile and a murderer. I would have cheered.
>
> (Jadeja 2021)

In the next extract, Susan Weiner remembers experiencing delusions during her graduate studies, and how her beliefs caused her to distance herself from friends:

> Over a period of several months, I began to believe that messages were being left for me in graffiti across campus. I also began to believe that my phone was being tapped. My friends insisted I was mistaken. But no one knew enough to realize anything was wrong. And then one day everything changed. One afternoon I realized the people on the radio were talking to me, much the way one has an intuition about a geometry proof, a sudden dawning of clarity or understanding. This clarity was more compelling than reality. It took me several weeks to put the pieces together. What I had known all my life was wrong. My friends were not real friends: at best they were neutral, at worst they were spies for the CIA.
>
> (Weiner 2003)

In the final extract, Dannagal G. Young describes how she tried to find explanations for her husband's unexpected cancer diagnosis, finally landing on a conspiracy:

> I started searching for information to account for the causes of his brain tumor, which eventually led me down a dark internet rabbit hole. Perhaps there were chemicals at his job that caused the tumor, I thought. One of his 30-year-old coworkers had died of cancer several years prior. That seemed weird, didn't it? And now Mike with this brain tumor? When I mentioned this to his doctors, they pointed out that for a company of more than 300 employees, these numbers were far below average. [...] Each time I landed on a possible culprit, my anger reenergized me. Instead of making me feel hopeless, it gave me a target and suggested there might be some action I could take. If it were from his work or from an old factory site, maybe I could file a lawsuit. Maybe I could launch an investigation or trigger some media exposé. If I could just find the right person or thing to blame, I could get some justice. Or vengeance. Or ... maybe just a sense of control.
>
> (Young 2020)

In such articulate and moving first-person accounts we find many of the features of delusional beliefs that we will examine together in the book. The delusion apparently makes sense of otherwise disconnected events or of tragic moments in the person's life. There is a tension between the stress caused by the delusion's often unsettling content and the feeling of power and control afforded by the mere presence of an explanation. The delusion changes social dynamics: it contributes to social withdrawal and isolation when the belief is idiosyncratic and other people do not understand it, but it gives rise to a sense of affiliation and belonging if the belief is shared, and embraced by a group of people rejecting mainstream explanations of the contested events.

Why do delusions matter?

Delusions are beliefs that we feel are lacking in some important respect, even though people may disagree on what it is precisely that delusions lack. When we call a belief delusional, we suggest that the person who reported that belief should not have done so. This is not merely because the belief does not represent reality as we see it, but because the mere fact that the person spoke with sincerity and conviction indicates that there is something wrong with that person. A concern is that, when a person has an implausible belief and is not disposed to revise the belief or give it up, the belief may stand in the way of the person's gaining a better understanding of themselves and their environment, compromising their capacity to work with others and plan effectively for the future.

Delusions are often considered as a sign of pathology, and reporting beliefs that are described as delusional can cause people to be silenced and excluded from participation in debate and decision making. The use of the word 'delusion' is itself controversial and is often considered stigmatizing: in a recent study, participants rated someone's character based on a description of that person's behaviour. The character rating was worse when the person responsible for the described behaviour was labelled as delusional (as in 'Jessica is delusional') as opposed to when no label was used (as in 'Jessica') (Cuttler and Ryckman 2019). I will use the word 'delusion' in this book, or better: it will be the point of the book to make explicit what we imply when we use that word and to suggest that some of those implications need to be challenged. I will show that, if we adopted a more reflective attitude towards delusions and their role in our mental lives and in the lives of the people around us, we would find that delusions exemplify not merely the weaknesses of human cognition and agency, but also their strengths.

So, why do delusions matter? First, because an analysis of the reasons why we call some beliefs delusional reveals something important about our interactions with the physical and social environment. When we reflect on the formation and persistence of delusional beliefs, we learn about the various factors, pressures and constraints that affect our adopting and maintaining beliefs in general. We learn that we are not passive mirrors reflecting the world as it presents itself to us. Rather, we are folk-scientists on the lookout for causal connections that are never fully apparent to us and that we have a powerful urge to disclose (Gopnik 2000). We are talented storytellers who weave scraps of information together to make sense of even the most surprising events (Coltheart 2017). We are brave explorers trying to find our way in a new, unpredictable, land, without much help from the locals. Because there are gaps in our explanations, stories and maps that we have to fill, we are imperfect mirrors, each of us reflecting a slightly different reality. If we understand that we may all end up with delusional beliefs when we dig for causes and hunt for meaning, we will stop finding delusions so puzzling in other people.

Second, delusions matter because an analysis of the reasons why we call some beliefs delusional reveals something important about our interactions with each other. We are hungry for causes and meanings when we are driven by the desire to know more about the natural world, but we are even hungrier for causes and meanings when we want to explain and predict each other's behaviour. The capacity we have to enter another person's world and reconstruct their reasons for choosing and acting as they do is nothing short of miraculous; after all, we do not share the same life experiences and perspectives on the world, and our representations of the world are all imperfect in slightly different ways.

Interpreting other people's behaviour often comes natural to us, and in most cases it is not even something that we realize we are doing. But occasionally interpretation is harder: we need to assemble various sources of background knowledge about the person whose mind we want to understand and ask ourselves how they experience the world before we can understand their utterances and make sense of the patches of behaviour we get to witness. Thinking about the conditions in which we attribute delusional beliefs to others, and others attribute delusional beliefs to us, can help us become more proficient at the difficult instances of interpretation, exercise the virtues of curiosity and empathy, and coordinate better with each other.

It might be obvious that delusions reveal our *weaknesses*. But maybe it will come as a surprise that delusions also tell us about our *strengths*. I think of delusions as a response to significant events that throw us back and seriously disrupt the pursuit of our projects. Such events could crush us or paralyse us if we did not have the capacity to make sense of them. Delusional beliefs are often imperfect ways to make sense of a threat. When we seek an explanation for an unsettling event, a satisfactory explanation captures some of the actual causal processes that are responsible for the event, enabling us to at least partially understand the events and to predict future developments. For this purpose, we need explanations built on evidence and expert testimony that can be confirmed or disconfirmed as we learn more about the event. But this process of learning, involving flexibility as the relevant evidence becomes available, is sometimes a luxury we cannot afford. The anxiety and stress caused by the threatening event need to be managed before they become overwhelming and uncertainty must be quelled by imposing some meaning onto the event.

So, an explanation is needed, but not all explanations are equally appealing. At times, we are conservative, and prefer those explanations that match our past experiences, existing beliefs, aspirations and values. Adopting those explanations is seamless. They are endorsed already, or likely to be endorsed, by individuals or groups that we are happy to associate with and that we have good reasons to trust. At other times, we are revolutionaries, and prefer those explanations that are bold and break with the past but seem to fit the unsettling event like a glove. The bold explanation often dispels the uncertainty surrounding the event and restores our sense of control but also responds to the need to feel special and unique. If the explanation is not widely shared, but something we conjured on our own, then it may be something that singles us out by showing how insightful or competent we are.

So, we seek explanations, but we are not content with *any* explanation. We want explanations that make sense to us and motivate us, explanations that fit with our current perspective on the world, and explanations that reflect actual causal connections between significant events. It is not always the case that the same explanation can play all those roles. At times, we accept an explanation that does not really make sense to us, maybe because we trust others to do most of the understanding for us. We may not know how viruses spread and how pandemics can be modelled but we are happy to let epidemiologists produce explanations and predictions that we can borrow, make our own and then act upon. At other times, we need to relieve the anxiety caused by the unsettling event before it paralyses us. The need to restore a sense of control can override other needs: we may no longer care about what the experts say. Suppose that I need to have a story about why I failed my driving test. In seeking explanations that help me reconcile an inflated view of my driving skills with the feedback of the examiner, I consider the idea of a plot against me. Maybe I failed the test because the examiner was biased against women drivers. It is easier for me to accept that the examiner is to blame than to acknowledge that I was not well prepared for the test, as this way I do not need to revise the overly positive conception of myself as a competent driver.

Our explanations respond to a number of conflicting psychological and epistemic needs (Bortolotti and Ichino 2020). In the course of the book, we stop and consider some of them. A need is *psychological* if fulfilling it contributes to our well-being; and a need is *epistemic* if fulfilling it contributes to our knowledge of the world and of ourselves. In practice, though, it is not always easy to distinguish a psychological need from an epistemic one: arguably, the need to feel more in control of the environment around us is both psychological, because the illusion of control gives us confidence and comfort; and epistemic, because the illusion of control gives us the sense that we know what to expect.

Delusions may satisfy psychological and epistemic needs but they often lead us astray and also have considerable psychological and epistemic costs. It would be pointless to deny that they prevent us from pursuing and achieving some of the goals we set for ourselves: they stand in the way. But what I want to suggest is that delusions also play a role by enabling us in some critical circumstances to preserve a sense of who we are and sustain our motivation to interact with the environment around us (Bortolotti 2020a). So, delusions can be seen both as *detrimental* and *instrumental* to our capacity to exercise agency. It is this constant tension between what delusions take from us and what they enable us to do that I intend to capture in this book.

Criteria for delusionality

The book offers an account of delusionality (i.e., the quality of beliefs that are considered delusional) in terms of what type of beliefs delusions are, across clinical and nonclinical contexts. I examine the conditions a belief needs to meet to be called delusional, whether the target is a delusion of persecution affecting people with a psychiatric diagnosis or a conspiracy belief entertained by someone who has never used mental health services. We do not typically call our own beliefs delusional, so when I say 'our delusions' what I mean is 'our cherished beliefs that other people do not share and find problematic'. Which *other people*? How *problematic*?

Each of us plays many roles in our social interactions but here I am interested in two basic roles. We are *speakers* – reporting a belief or explaining an event to someone who is listening to us, our interpreter. We are also *interpreters* – making sense of another speaker's belief or explanation when they share that belief or explanation with us. When an interpreter calls a speaker's belief or explanation delusional, the practice suggests that the interpreter is passing judgement over the report, and that the judgement is a negative one. As I said from the start, the very term 'delusion' suggests that, as a belief or as an explanation, the speaker's report is lacking in some important respects. In the book I ask what conditions need to obtain for the interpreter to call the speaker's belief a delusion. I vindicate the common use of the word 'delusion' across contexts, but I also suggest that some of the received wisdom about delusional beliefs or about the people who report them should be challenged.

There are two parts to the book. In Part 1, I focus on those criteria of delusionality that are predominantly epistemic. That is, those features that concern truth and justification, and how the belief reflects reality, relates to evidence and is based on or informs knowledge of the type of person we are. Among other things, I ask why some unusual beliefs are considered delusions while other unusual beliefs aren't, arguing that many definitions of delusions miss the point when they claim that being false or being badly supported by evidence is a necessary condition for a belief to count as a delusion. I also consider an aspect of delusions that is often neglected: how they emerge from and contribute to a person's identity. In Part 1 I want to capture the notion that, when we call a belief delusional, we express a negative judgement about the belief: that it is an implausible and unshakeable identity belief.

In Part 2, I concentrate on the effects of delusional beliefs. In what sense are delusions pathological beliefs? What costs and benefits do they have for speakers and interpreters? Although delusions have significant epistemic and psychological costs, they have benefits too that need to be acknowledged. For this reason, I suggest that not all the assumptions we routinely make about delusional beliefs should be embraced. For instance, it is not obvious that delusional beliefs are pathological: maybe no delusion is strictly speaking the outcome of a dysfunctional process and many delusions are costly in some way to the person reporting them and to others but are not the main cause of the harm the speaker may experience. This also suggests some ways in which we can deal with delusional beliefs in our lives and in our social interactions, as individuals and as societies. Thus in Part 2 I also explore whether we should hold each other responsible for our delusional beliefs and the actions that might emerge from them.

So in the book I aim at capturing the notion of delusion as it is currently used but I am also being revisionist about it, suggesting that we should decouple delusionality from falsity, ill-groundedness and pathology; and that the perceived gulf between delusional and nondelusional beliefs is a myth. The emerging picture is one of reconciliation: the speakers whose beliefs are called delusional are not fundamentally different from the interpreters who attempt to make sense of those beliefs. Speakers and interpreters are all blessed and cursed with some delusions because adopting and hanging onto delusional beliefs is part of how they navigate the world, respond to uncertainty, express identities and exercise agency. As counterintuitive as this may sound, given that philosophers have often described delusions as the most fundamental failure of rational agency, in some special circumstances delusions *support* agency.

The framework

I frame delusions as beliefs of a certain kind and often use examples where the delusion acts as an explanation of an unusual or otherwise significant event. Beliefs are the things we attribute to other people when we want to better understand their past behaviour and we have an interest in predicting their future behaviour. Imagine a situation where two people are talking to each other in a shared environment: two children in the playground, a doctor and a patient at the surgery, two politicians from opposed parties in a public debate, a teacher and a student in the classroom and so on. In each exchange, you have a speaker and an interpreter swapping roles as the conversation proceeds. The speaker says something and the interpreter listens, making inferences about the speaker's beliefs, desires, feelings, hopes and intentions on the basis of the speaker's words, facial expression, tone of voice, previous behaviour and so on. Interpretation is ubiquitous and sounds exhausting when we describe what it entails, but we engage in it all the time, mostly effortlessly. All our social interactions depend on it.

Attributions of delusionality (when an interpreter calls a speaker's belief delusional) occur when interpretation stops being effortless and becomes challenging. In a preview of future attractions, I give you in a nutshell my take on why attributions of delusionality are made: the beliefs the interpreter deems as delusional are those that are reported with sincerity and conviction, are central to the speaker's identity, and are judged by the interpreter as implausible, unshakeable, and costly. In the book, I explain the epistemic conditions for delusionality (what I mean by implausibility, unshakeability and centrality to identity). I also spell out what it means for an interpreter to view delusions as costly, where the costs can affect the speakers themselves or other people, and can be cashed out in terms of a variety of undesirable outcomes, including compromised understanding, decreased well-being, anxiety and distress, bad decision-making, unnecessary risks and health problems. Interpreters rarely see delusions as beneficial, but most delusions have perks for speakers that on reflection interpreters could appreciate. Delusions either let speakers see the world as they want the world to be; make speakers feel important and interesting; or give meaning to speakers' lives, configuring exciting missions for them to accomplish.

A brief synopsis is in order. In Chapter 1, I argue that delusionality involves *belief*. This does not mean that delusions are nothing but beliefs, or are always best characterized as beliefs, because the notion of delusion is heterogeneous and applied widely. But it means that delusions are an investment that we make, something we are committed to and that influences our thoughts, feelings and behaviour more generally.

In Chapter 2, I consider the relationship between the content of the delusion and the world. When interpreters ascribe delusional beliefs, do they do so simply because the beliefs misrepresent reality? Or do delusions need to misrepresent in a particular way, for instance, have a bizarre content as well? Ultimately, falsity and bizarreness are both unsatisfactory as conditions for delusionality. I conclude that the best way to capture the relationship between the belief and reality is to say that delusions are *implausible*, in the sense that, whether true or false, bizarre or mundane, they are difficult to believe.

In Chapter 3, I turn to the relationship between delusions and evidence which for many experts represents the key feature of delusion as an epistemic notion. What makes our beliefs delusional is not what we believe, but how we believe. When interpreters ascribe delusional beliefs, do they do so because the beliefs are groundless, ill-grounded, insensitive to challenges or irresponsive to evidence? All proposals seem to have some obvious counterexample or leave us with a partial picture that applies to some delusions but not to delusions in general. Instead, the most distinctive epistemic feature of delusions across contexts is their *unshakeability*, and I explain how best to understand that.

In Chapter 4, I reflect on the relationship between delusions and identity. Are delusions always self-related beliefs or self-defining beliefs? Neither. Some delusions are about the world and not our role in it. Not all delusions define us. Then why is there this strong relationship between delusions and the self? Why does it seem that, when people relinquish a delusion, they also need to relinquish a part of themselves? Maybe because delusions are fuelled by, and contribute to, aspects of our identities. They act as *identity beliefs*.

In Part 2, I start putting pressure on a major assumption about delusions, that they are a mark of mental illness or mental instability. This is a very ingrained assumption about delusions and indeed according to the psychiatric manuals for the classification and diagnosis of mental disorders some delusions are symptoms of schizophrenia, delusional disorders and several other conditions.

In Chapter 5, I argue that we have no good reason to believe that delusions are the output of a *dysfunction* affecting belief formation or belief maintenance processes. On some views of delusion formation, such as the two-factor theory and the predictive coding theory, a deficit is explicitly invoked in the explanation of how delusions emerge. But I shall argue that it is not clear that there is a deficit affecting cognitive processes as such. Moreover, the surface features of delusions may be satisfactorily explained by appealing to other factors, such as reasoning biases.

In Chapter 6, I maintain that delusions are not always a source of *harm* for speakers even if they are acknowledged to be costly in one way or another by interpreters, and sometimes even by the speakers themselves. I examine different types of costs, psychological and epistemic, and ask whether such costs have an adverse effect on the speaker only, on their immediate or wider social circle, or on society at large. In this context, I discuss health risks, self-harm, exclusion and stigma, and the delegitimization of societal institutions as possible consequences of reporting or spreading delusional beliefs.

In Chapter 7, I turn to the potential *benefits* of delusions, concentrating on the protective role some delusional beliefs can play. Co-existing with their costs, delusions have benefits in that they enable us to give meaning to experiences that can be both upsetting and puzzling. Often the delusion is distressing in the long term but it also relieves us from the anxiety caused by the sense that our experience hides a mysterious and insidious threat. That is because the delusion explains the experience in some way that is meaningful to us.

In Chapter 8, I venture to think about the practical applications of the view of delusions I recommend in the book, drawing from some very recent work in social and political epistemology. My scepticism towards the view of delusions as pathological beliefs and conviction that there are both costs and benefits in adopting and maintaining delusional beliefs lead to a discussion about the best ways to approach delusional beliefs. Can we protect ourselves and other people from the costs of those implausible and unshakeable beliefs? The idea that the presence of a delusion signals that there is something wrong with the person reporting it is a dangerous oversimplification: when speakers adopt beliefs that interpreters call delusions, the problem does not start and does not end with the speakers themselves. Some delusions could be avoided by inhibiting the disinformation affecting our epistemic environments and supporting the exercise of our epistemic agency (Levy 2021). This might enable us to change our habits and patterns of reasoning, promoting those virtues and controlling those vices that affect our vulnerability to delusional beliefs (Murphy-Hollies 2022). If many delusions are rewarding but illusory explanations, then taking away the delusions may address some of the costs caused by adopting or maintaining the delusional beliefs but won't respond to the needs that gave rise to the delusions in the first place. Something else needs to replace the delusion, something that fulfils its role without carrying as many costs.

The knowledge of the precarity of our agency won't by itself provide a solution to the challenges of finding adequate and fulfilling explanations for uncertain events but can make us more discerning explorers of the world and more empathetic and curious interpreters of each other.

Aims of the project

So, Part 1 identifies the epistemic features of delusional beliefs, and in particular those features concerning how we gather, process and revise information. I offer a sketch of what delusionality requires and what is typically associated to. Delusional beliefs are implausible and unshakeable beliefs that a speaker reports sincerely and with conviction and that are central to the speaker's identity.

Part 2 focuses on other features of delusions that are not exclusively or predominantly epistemic: what causes them, what effects they have and how they support and compromise our agency. Together, Parts 1 and 2 tell us also about our practices as speakers and interpreters. What clearly emerges from the analysis of the conditions for delusionality is that calling the speaker's belief a delusion is not merely a neutral description, but a value judgement.

Interpreters who think that the speaker's belief is delusional typically view the belief as irrational and dangerous – and are thus motivated to downgrade the speaker's rights and responsibilities, excluding the speaker from participation in debate and public life.

This dismissal of the speaker's perspective is something we can work harder to avoid as interpreters. An analysis of the criteria for delusionality helps us understand and maybe overcome the polarization that has become a constant in our mutual interactions, where opponents are discredited and pathologized well before their views are heard and their concerns fully understood.

I hope the book will bring home the importance of delusions for our cognition and agency, and the need to explore their nature to enhance social interactions in our public lives. What we need is intellectually curious and empathetic interpreters who care to listen, ask questions and are disposed to see the world from the speaker's perspective – at least temporarily.

PART I

CHAPTER 1
DELUSIONS AS INVESTMENTS

What, if anything, do delusions have in common? What makes them all *delusional* beliefs? In the first four chapters of this book, I investigate the epistemic features of delusions, that is, the features of delusions that concern how we gather, process, report, revise and use information. Based on our linguistic and cultural practices, I argue that we as interpreters describe a report as delusional when it is made with sincerity and conviction and appears to us as an implausible and unshakeable identity belief. Not all delusional beliefs will satisfy criteria for delusionality to the same extent (e.g., some delusions are more implausible than others) and the same belief will satisfy those criteria to a greater or lesser extent over time (e.g., a delusion can be held with fluctuating levels of conviction and become more or less central to the speaker's identity).

In the last four chapters, I investigate those aspects of delusions that are not exclusively or predominantly epistemic, concerning either the causal history of the belief (how it came about), its downstream effects (what consequences it has) or its overall contribution to a person's cognition and agency. Do delusions support our endeavours or hinder them? Part 2 is where I ask whether delusions are the output of dysfunctional processes or have harmful consequences for the speaker or the speaker's surrounding physical or social environment.

In this chapter I offer some further examples of delusional beliefs, including those that are thought to be symptomatic of mental health conditions, and those that are widespread in the nonclinical population. I ask what the main differences are between beliefs occurring in the two contexts, and whether there is substantial overlap between them. On the surface, the differences are striking. Clinical delusions are idiosyncratic to one person and typically cause disruption. Nonclinical delusional beliefs can be shared in well-defined social groups and are not thought of as a cause of disruption. But there is also a substantial overlap which I capture by identifying the criteria that a speaker's beliefs need to meet to be described as delusional by an interpreter: those criteria – I argue – apply across the clinical and nonclinical divide and should be sufficient to persuade us that 'delusion' is an epistemic concept.

I defend a view of delusions *as an investment*, that is, as beliefs that are reported with conviction and sincerity and are to some extent manifest in our feelings, thoughts and actions. When we report a delusion, we make an investment that affects the rest of our mental lives and our behaviour, also powerfully impacting the sense of who we are.

Examples of delusions

The subject of this book is delusions. I take a delusion to be a type of *belief*, something that can influence our other beliefs, affect our mood and drive our actions (Bortolotti 2009a). I am interested in describing what features delusional beliefs share and why calling some beliefs delusional makes a difference to how we interact with the world and with our fellow humans.

Let me introduce and discuss two contexts in which we find delusions. I call *clinical delusions* those beliefs that are delusional and are considered to be symptomatic of mental health issues. I call *everyday* or *nonclinical delusions* those beliefs that are delusional but are not considered to be symptomatic of mental health issues. Clinical and everyday delusions share some important features. In this section, I introduce these types of delusions separately and examine the features that distinguish them. In the rest of the book, however, I mostly discuss clinical and everyday delusions together and use the term 'delusion' or 'delusional belief' to indicate their shared epistemic features. This is going to be a controversial choice which I hope I can justify along the way.

My suggestion is that there is a sense of delusion that cuts across the clinical and nonclinical contexts: delusions are the kind of beliefs that are attributed by an interpreter to someone who reports with sincerity and conviction an unshakeable identity belief that is regarded by the interpreter as implausible. In typical attributions of delusional beliefs, the belief is also thought by the interpreter to have significant epistemic or psychological costs, affecting either the speaker only or their social context more widely.

The clinical context

The term 'delusion' is used in psychiatry to denote a symptom of distress, experienced by people who are diagnosed with schizophrenia, delusional disorder, depression, amnesia, dementia, obsessive-compulsive disorder and other mental disorders.

One example is a young man diagnosed with persecutory delusions who claims that his co-workers intend to get him fired and are spreading bad rumours about him behind his back when such a claim is considered as unsubstantiated by the people around him. Another example is an elderly woman with Alzheimer's disease who is convinced that she is entertaining friends at a tea party in her garden, whereas she is having tea in the cafeteria of a nursing home. Although the report is based on a recollection of previous life events (as the woman used to entertain friends and family in her garden prior to her illness), it is not true of the woman's present situation.

The *Diagnostic and Statistical Manual of Mental Disorders*, published by the American Psychiatric Association, is used by psychiatrists in the United States to diagnose mental health issues. In the Glossary of the manual (DSM-IV 2000, p. 765 and DSM-5 2013, p. 819), we find a popular definition of clinical delusions.

> Delusion. A false belief based on incorrect inference about external reality that is firmly sustained despite what almost everyone else believes and despite what constitutes incontrovertible and obvious proof or evidence to the contrary. The belief is not one ordinarily accepted by other members of the person's culture or subculture (e.g., it is not an article of religious faith). When a false belief involves a value judgment, it is regarded as a delusion only when the judgment is so extreme as to defy credibility.

There are growing concerns about the DSM definition of delusions among philosophers and clinicians, and I will address some of those concerns in the following chapters. One worry is that the DSM definition does not capture satisfactorily what is distinctive about clinical delusions and places excessive emphasis on the belief being false.

Here is another comprehensive definition:

> Delusions are generally accepted to be beliefs which (a) are held with great conviction; (b) defy rational counter-argument; (c) and would be dismissed as false or bizarre by members of the same socio-cultural group. A more precise definition is probably impossible since delusions are contextually dependent, multiply determined and multidimensional. Exemplars of the delusion category that fulfil all the usual definitional attributes are easy to find, so it would be premature to abandon the construct entirely. Equally, in everyday practice there

are patients we regard as deluded whose beliefs in isolation may not meet standard delusional criteria. In this way a delusion is more like a syndrome than a symptom.

(Gilleen and David 2005, pp. 5–6)

It is interesting that the authors express some scepticism about the possibility of finding an adequate definition of clinical delusion that can capture all instances of the phenomenon, due to the heterogeneity of delusions. This leads them to express some doubts about how useful the notion of delusion really is. Maybe focusing on some reports can help us get a better sense of delusions.

In her book about living with schizophrenia, Esmé Wang describes the moment when she glanced at her sewing table and came to believe that she was dead (Wang 2019, p. 126). Wang's is an example of *Cotard delusion*: people with Cotard delusion typically say that they are either dead or disembodied, and sometimes act on that belief too – they may stop washing, refuse food or decide to spend most of their time in the local cemetery. The Cotard delusion has fascinated philosophers for its self-defeating, paradoxical qualities (Campbell 2001): how can the person genuinely believe to be dead, if they can still move and speak and interact with others to some extent? The origins of the Cotard delusion have been sought in the experience of depersonalization, when people feel detached from their experiences, and in the tendency that people with depression have to attribute negative outcomes to themselves (Gerrans 2001; but see also Gerrans 2022). When feeling disconnected from their own experiences, they may be drawn to the idea the world has changed but instead they hypothesize that they have undergone a change, as a result of something like disembodiment or death.

In another compelling memoir, Elyn Saks describes the realization that the houses surrounding her were putting thoughts into her head and sending her messages (Saks 2007, p. 129). This is an instance of a common delusion in schizophrenia, the delusion of *thought insertion*. This consists of people becoming aware of a thought in their head that they do not feel their own and attribute to external sources. The thought often feels alien to them, as if it had been put there against their will. There have been several attempts to explain what the delusion of thought insertion involves and how it can be explained (see, for instance, Bortolotti and Broome 2009; Ratcliffe and Wilkinson 2015; Humpston and Broome 2016). One interesting issue is whether the phenomenon is really distinct from that of auditory hallucinations, and whether it involves the person losing a sense of ownership or agency towards the thoughts they access directly.

Although clinical delusions vary in terms of their content, they all seem to be idiosyncratic to the person reporting them, meaning that, in the person's social context, nobody else reports or shares the belief. As we saw, the *Diagnostic and Statistical Manual of Mental Disorders* captures this by including in the definition of delusion that it is a belief typically rejected by the other members of the person's culture or subculture (DSM-5, p. 819).

The nonclinical context

When we talk about a delusional belief, we do not always have in mind behaviours that are symptomatic of mental health issues. When we say that someone is deluded, we do not always suggest that the person's behaviour should attract a psychiatric diagnosis. Rather, beliefs are described as delusional outside clinical contexts if they have certain characteristics, for instance if they are implausible and strenuously resistant to counterevidence. Everyday delusional beliefs need not be idiosyncratic to the person reporting them and are often shared by groups of people who are committed to similar views or values.

One example of a nonclinical delusion is holistic health guru Jane, coming to believe in June 2020 that the Covid-19 pandemic is not a worse health emergency than the common flu, and that its alleged devastation has been hyped by pharmaceutical companies who have an interest in selling treatments and vaccines (see Remski 2020 for a real-life example). More generally, when we endorse a conspiracy theory, we tend to explain significant events in a way that conflicts with the official version of how such events occurred, attributing responsibility and blame to powerful individuals or organizations (Sunstein and Vermeule 2008; Ichino and Räikkä 2020). As in the case of clinical delusions, we do not easily give up conspiracy beliefs once we have adopted them but, differently from clinical delusions, the beliefs are typically endorsed by more than just us. That is why the adoption of the conspiracy theory may gain us a label that is used to group people together on the basis of their views, and that is usually applied in a derogative way, such as 'Trump supporter', 'anti-vaxxer' and 'flat Earther'. Philosophers and psychologists have developed a sustained interest in conspiracy beliefs, analysing the environmental factors that make such beliefs more likely to spread, such as the presence of a perceived threat and the fear of marginalization, and examining the individual differences that make some people more prone to conspiratorial thinking. As we shall see in Chapter 8, some explanations focus on the individual's limitations, such as ignorance, cognitive biases, epistemic vices or scientific illiteracy, whereas other explanations invoke social and political causes (Uscinski and Parent 2014; Douglas et al. 2017; Cassam 2019; Levy 2021).

Here is another example. British citizen Steve is frustrated. Steve comes to believe during the Brexit campaign that immigration from the European Union is bad for the UK, based on the conviction that his difficulty in finding work is due to a flux of skilled immigrants in the area (see Bortolotti and Stammers 2020 for real-life examples). Steve's belief may also be supported by his personal experience of having to wait for several days for an appointment at his local medical practice. For Steve, the delay is due to the area being swamped by immigrants who require health services and increase demand for services. An external observer may think that Steve's difficulty in finding a job is more likely due to his lack of qualifications, and that the delay in medical appointments is an effect of the austerity measures taken by the government, causing cuts to healthcare provision. So, Steve's belief that immigration is bad may be a prejudiced belief, badly supported by the totality of the evidence available to him. But somehow that belief makes sense to Steve, fits with other beliefs he has about the costs of immigration and multiculturalism, protecting him from several unwelcome truths – such as the acknowledgement that lack of qualifications may be the reason why he cannot secure a job or that the party he voted for at the last general election is not safeguarding his interests by failing to fund health services.

Prejudiced beliefs can take different forms but what makes them all instances of prejudice is that they are not well supported by the totality of the relevant evidence, and they are impervious to counterevidence. There is a growing literature on beliefs characterized by prejudice and stereotyping (Begby 2021; Puddifoot 2021), pointing out their advantages and disadvantages.

Overly optimistic evaluations of ourselves and predictions about our future that are rosier than is warranted by the evidence have also similar features to clinical delusions. In her seminal book on positive illusions, Shelley Taylor explicitly makes the comparison between optimistically biased beliefs and clinical delusions and argues that they are both illusory, although only optimistically biased beliefs have considerable benefits for mental health, and they distort the facts to a lesser extent than clinical delusions (S. Taylor 1989, p. 36). The case of so-called *unrealistic optimism* is a perfect illustration of how the tendency to adopt implausible beliefs that are not responsive to counterevidence is not limited to the clinical context (Jefferson et al. 2017).

Self-evaluations and self-predictions that are not realistic can be due to widespread biases, such as the illusion of control and the illusion of superiority. In the *illusion of control*, we tend to think of ourselves as more efficacious in bringing change to the surrounding environment than we actually are, assuming that we can control events that are independent of us. Due to the *superiority illusion*, we also tend to think of ourselves as more virtuous, talented, and skilled than is warranted by evidence; and as better than our peers in domains as diverse as intelligence, academic performance, attractiveness and generosity. We are also vulnerable to the *optimism bias* when we believe that we are more likely to avoid future crises such as serious illness or divorce than we actually are, and more likely to avoid such crises than our peers.

Our optimistic beliefs resist negative feedback. Suppose Sunita thinks of herself as a talented actress, but she also needs to face the fact that she has been rejected at a number of auditions in a relatively short period of time. If she is optimistically biased, she is more likely to attribute responsibility for those rejections to the incompetence of the evaluators than to revise her positive assessment of her acting skills (Alicke and Sekidikes 2009). However, if her friends complained about being rejected at several auditions in the last few weeks, Sunita would be tempted to think that it is not an accident, coming to the conclusion that they cannot be very talented actors (Zell et al. 2020). Our self-predictions tend to remain rosy even after we are made aware of statistical information about the likelihood of experiencing adverse events. We might know the data about the likelihood of divorce in the country where we live, and still believe that our own chances of getting a divorce are much lower than those predicted by the data. We consider ourselves as an exception to the rule – and this happens also to those of us who should be regarded as experts in the fragility of human relationships, such as divorce lawyers and marriage counsellors.

The beliefs that we adopt under the influence of unrealistic optimism are not always well-supported by evidence and require a fairly creative reinterpretation of negative feedback on our performance. They often require dismissing statistical information relevant to us and our situation. However, such beliefs seem to be *good for us*. They do not contribute to a plausible representation of reality or of ourselves, but they help us maintain our motivation to pursue our goals and react constructively to setbacks. Sunita the unlucky actress will not give up before having attended many more auditions if she believes that at some point her acting skills will be noticed and her efforts will be rewarded. Spouses who experience a crisis in their new marriage will not call their lawyers after the first serious quarrel if they think that their romantic relationship is overall satisfying and will pass the test of time. Optimistic beliefs, even when biased in our favour, or in favour of a more desirable reality than the actual one, can support us in our endeavours and increase the chances of success in a number of domains (Bortolotti 2018a).

Undesirable consequences of delusions

Some garden-variety beliefs are no less implausible or unshakeable than a delusion of persecution, but there are important differences between how delusions manifest in clinical and nonclinical contexts. Delusions of persecution typically cause a disruption in functioning culminating in the judgement that medical attention is required. Moreover, delusions of persecution may be accompanied by other signs of poor mental health, and often bring isolation and stigma.

Conspiracy beliefs may be comforting, at least in the short run, and can strengthen social relationships with individuals or groups who also endorse the same conspiracy belief. Prejudiced beliefs can make us feel better about ourselves by attributing some of our failures or adverse experiences to a convenient scapegoat. As we saw, some everyday delusions such as optimistically biased beliefs have been found to enhance the motivation to pursue our goals and protect us from anxiety and depression. That said, there are circumstances in which these epistemically problematic beliefs (i.e., beliefs that are not plausible or are not given up in the face of counterevidence) are also thought of as dangerous or harmful – and those are typically the contexts in which the label 'delusional' is applied to them.

Everyday delusions can bring disadvantages to the speaker and to society, and they can also be the object of stigma – I return to this in Chapter 6. Let me just mention some of the possible costs. When Jane refuses vaccination due to the belief that it is an intrusive practice orchestrated by the powerful to control people's behaviour, she is at risk of contracting a potentially life-threatening illness and passing it onto others. When Steve believes that he is not finding jobs due to European immigrants offering cheaper labour, he underestimates the role of his lack of qualification which may cause him to make unwise decisions about his future, such as turning down an opportunity to acquire more skills. His beliefs may also colour his interactions with immigrants and cause conflict and misunderstandings. When heavy smokers judge their immune system to be better than average, they fail to take on board the health risks associated to their lifestyle choices and are less motivated to follow medical advice (Bortolotti and Antrobus 2015; Jefferson and Bortolotti 2023). Moreover, when the beliefs are not widespread, there can be social sanctions for reporting or sharing those beliefs. Society can ostracize nonmainstream thinkers and conspiracy believers and exclude them from participation in public debates, more or less openly (Jolley and Douglas 2014; Douglas et al. 2019, pp. 17–21). And when we are overly optimistic to such an extent that our lack of realism is detected, we can be penalized for excessively enhancing our talents and skills, losing the potential advantage that self-confidence or absence of self-doubt gives us in social exchanges (Bortolotti et al. 2019).

Outside the clinical context, beliefs tend to be described as delusional when they are strongly held by the speaker but unpersuasive to an interpreter. There is also some further negative connotation attached to beliefs regarded as delusional, the idea that they are undesirable beliefs to have, in some sense. An atheist may think that believing in God is a delusion. The belief in God that is shared by communities of religious people may be compared to a comforting fairy-tale or blamed as a source of bigotry. A climate change activist may think that denying that global warming is caused by human activity is a delusion. Climate change denialism may be criticized for leading to inaction and complacency in the face of present and future challenges for human societies and the planet.

There are important differences between clinical and nonclinical delusions, in how they manifest, in how they come about and in which effects they have on us when we endorse them (Bortolotti et al. 2021). This might suggest that it is foolish to pursue the project of identifying a common concept of delusion that is predominantly epistemic. Can I really offer an answer to the question why delusions matter that applies to delusions across the board, clinical delusions, conspiracy beliefs, prejudiced beliefs and optimistically biased beliefs, and beyond? With the right qualifications in place, I think an answer can be attempted. Given that the term 'delusion' is already increasingly used outside the mental health context and, as I argue in Chapters 5 and 6, delusions are not necessarily pathological beliefs, it is worth investigating the possibility of developing a meaningful and useful epistemic notion of delusion that partly vindicates this broader use.

Triangulation disrupted

When an interpreter calls a speaker's belief delusional, the attribution of delusionality is not a *neutral description* of the speaker's report. Rather, it implies an evaluation of the belief and expresses the interpreter's *disapproval* towards it (Wilkinson 2020). The interpreter who calls our belief delusional, or calls us deluded, often implies that we are not in our right mind or that we don't know what we are saying. The claim that a belief is a delusion often aims to discredit the speaker as a source of reliable information. It says something about the interpreter's attitude towards the content of the belief, but it goes beyond a mere attribution of falsity or irrationality.

Interpretation

Beliefs are the sort of things we attribute to ourselves and others in a process that helps us explain and predict our own and other people's behaviour. This process of interpretation enables us to coordinate and collaborate with each other, and also control and manipulate others. It has been described by the philosopher Donald Davidson as a form of *triangulation* (see for instance Davidson 1973). The triangle has three elements: an interpreter, a speaker and the environment that is shared between the speaker and the interpreter. The three elements are supposed to interact causally, so the sides of the triangles are possible ways in which interpreter, speaker and environment affect each other.

Suppose that your colleague Kamala (*the speaker*) tells you (*the interpreter*) that she is very tired. She rubs her eyes and yawns, repeatedly looking at her watch. Based on what she says and how she behaves, you infer that she is indeed tired and can't wait to go home. You move from the observation of Kamala's verbal and nonverbal behaviour to attributing to her mental states that you cannot directly observe; in this case, a desire to go home. At times, triangulation does not go smoothly. All sorts of things may happen to make your job as an interpreter difficult. You may not fully understand what the speaker says, or you may fail to make sense of the speaker's behaviour in the light of what they said. Or the way the speaker describes the environment may be different from how you would describe it, even if the environment is supposed to be shared between you and the speaker.

Suppose that Kamala meets the office manager in the corridor just before the end of her working day and instead of asking to go home early she asks for more work. Kamala's request somehow does not fit with what she said earlier about being tired and with her yawning and looking repeatedly at her watch. Was it a mistake to believe that Kamala is tired? Was it wrong to attribute to her the desire to go home? Maybe Kamala is tired but does not want to go home after all. In our everyday interactions with other people, we are indefatigable interpreters, always observing behaviour and scanning the environment for clues to be able to coordinate effectively with others. When the speaker says or does something unexpected, we call into question our initial attribution of mental states to them. It is possible that we lack some of the relevant background information that would enable us to understand the other person's behaviour. Maybe Kamala is tired and yet does not want to go home, because she desperately needs more money this month and is hoping to be paid extra for working overtime.

Breakdowns of interpretation

In a small number of cases, there is a serious breakdown of interpretation that cannot be resolved with a simple revision of the initial mental-state attribution. It is on those occasions that as interpreters we may be tempted to think that speakers are *deluded* about themselves or the environment. What factors drive the attribution of *delusional* beliefs? For Wilkinson, the attribution of delusionality expresses the interpreter's disapproval, it is an expression of epistemic aversion. In Wilkinson's own words: 'To call something delusional is to express your folk-epistemic disapproval, to flag it as suspect.' According to Wilkinson, this understanding of attributions of delusionality, not as factual descriptions of the speaker's belief but as negative evaluations of such a belief, explains many interesting features about delusions. It explains why people have found it really challenging to define delusions and every time a new definition is proposed objections and counterexamples materialize. It also explains why delusions are not always charged with the same epistemic sin: some of the beliefs described as delusional are badly supported by evidence, some are irrevisable, some are inconsistent with other things the speaker believes, and so on. They are all epistemically problematic but there is no single reason why it is so. And, finally, expressivism is supposed to explain the interpreter's perplexity at the speaker's endorsement of the delusional belief, what many psychopathologists characterize as the 'un-understandability' of the delusion and what can be exemplified by the interpreter telling the speaker, 'Why would you say that?'.

Wilkinson's account of our practice of delusion attribution as evaluative is spot-on. However, I want to resist the idea that there is nothing more we can say about the folk-epistemic disapproval that interpreters express in attributing to speakers delusional beliefs. We can further unpack this sense of disapproval and identify the epistemic sins delusions are guilty of, without denying the heterogeneity of the phenomenon of delusions. We can think of delusions as having a core and a periphery. At the periphery variation occurs. But the core is shared and is epistemic in nature: the core is what I aim to unveil in Part 1 of this book. There is something special and unique about the epistemic disapproval that delusions, but not other irrational beliefs, provoke. Interpreters may be moved by an emotional reaction to the speaker's report and be unable to fully articulate the reasons for their disapproval or use an unlikely shorthand as when they associate delusions with irrationality or pathology. However, attributions of delusionality track some features of the speaker's belief that contribute to our understanding of why some beliefs merit the title of delusion and others do not.

In the rest of this chapter, I argue that delusions are investments: the speaker reports them sincerely and with conviction and acts on them in at least some of the relevant circumstances. Delusions are not 'just talk' or 'as if' speech. People mean what they say when they report a delusional belief. In Chapters 2 to 4, I explore a range of options in the hope I can identify further epistemic criteria for attributions of delusionality. I suggest that interpreters are driven to attribute delusional beliefs when interpreters find the speakers' beliefs implausible (*implausibility*), when speakers engage in reason giving and respond to challenges but ultimately do not give up the beliefs in the face of counterarguments or counterevidence (*unshakeability*) and when the beliefs seem to be important to how speakers see themselves in relation to their environment (*centrality to the speaker's identity*). In Chapters 5 to 7 I ask whether delusions are the output of a dysfunctional process, whether they are costly either to the speaker or to others, and whether they do have a positive role to play as well. Although the costs of adopting or maintaining delusions can be other than epistemic, affecting well-being, socialization and active participation in public life, the costs often derive from the beliefs' dubious epistemic features.

Some of the core features are related. Maybe one can only explain the tenacity of an implausible belief by the fact that it contributes to the person's identity and thus it cannot be easily discarded. Maybe the implausibility and unshakeability of delusions are due to a dysfunction in belief formation and belief revision processes – and this explains why delusional beliefs are often regarded as pathological rather than merely irrational. For now, our task is to unpack the specific terms of the interpreter's *epistemic* disapproval.

Sincerity, conviction and action guidance

Let's consider the first condition for delusionality: interpreters ascribe a delusion to speakers who report a belief with sincerity and conviction, as opposed to speakers who are joking, deceiving, expressing a hope or an aspiration, or considering a hypothesis without committing to it. Delusions, as all beliefs, are an investment – and some beliefs are a bigger investment than others.

Belief status

In the psychological and psychiatric literature, clinical delusions, the endorsement of conspiracy theories, prejudiced attitudes and some instances of unrealistic optimism are standardly defined and described as *beliefs*. But in the philosophical literature, hundreds of articles and several books have been dedicated to debating the question whether clinical delusions are beliefs (e.g., Bortolotti 2009a; Radden 2010; Gerrans 2014; Miyazono 2018). There is also widespread scepticism about the belief nature of our religious and political convictions, our prejudiced attitudes and our attitudes towards conspiracy theories, and the overly optimistic predictions we make about our future (see, for instance, Hannon 2021 on political 'beliefs', Ichino and Räikkä 2020 on conspiracy theories and Flanagan 2009 on positive illusions).

Don't political convictions turn out to be expressions of our preferences, more akin to an act of cheering for our preferred candidate or party than a judgement about the relative merits of individuals and policies? Aren't conspiracy theories more like hopes than beliefs, in the sense that we wish them to be true, but we realize at some level that they cannot be? And isn't the thought that we won't divorce from our spouses, and we won't contract lung cancer later in life an aspiration rather than a belief, or maybe a declaration of our intention to do everything in our power to avoid those undesirable events?

Questions we can ask about delusions include whether they really are beliefs rather than instances of imagination, hope, aspiration, desire or wishful thinking, whether they wouldn't be more aptly described as perceptual experiences or mere expressions of how we feel, and what hangs on their being beliefs anyway. Arguments put forward against the belief nature of our mental states can get very sophisticated, but the basic intuition is that none of us can be so irrational as to *genuinely believe* the content of a delusion.

Thus, the thesis that delusions cannot be beliefs stems from the conviction that we cannot be so irrational as to have such implausible beliefs, or from the idea that beliefs are by necessity constrained by reality and responsive to evidence so they cannot go so wrong as to be both as implausible and unshakeable as delusions happen to be. However, psychological science and everyday experience give us plenty of reasons to doubt both the rationality of our belief formation and revision mechanisms and the idealization of belief as a mental state that is always, or even just generally, constrained by reality and responsive to evidence. We are vulnerable to the effects of biases when we process information, and it is not uncommon for many of our beliefs – not just delusions – to distort reality and resist counterevidence (Bortolotti and Miyazono 2015). Moreover, our social and physical environment is sometimes genuinely difficult to understand, and the information that we can gather about it, for ourselves or via the testimony of others, is unreliable (Levy 2021).

Against belief status

For the philosophers who claim that clinical delusions are not beliefs, delusions are different from garden-variety beliefs in the way they develop and manifest. For instance, beliefs are revised in the light of counterevidence whereas delusions are not. However, we know that not all our beliefs are promptly revised in the light of counterevidence. Even when we focus on beliefs in scientific theories – which may be attained and reviewed with a more rigorous methodology than other beliefs due to their subject matter – it is clear that scientists are resistant to abandoning a theory when they have invested time and energy in developing it. When they are faced with counterevidence, they prefer to slightly amend their theory to neutralize the objection than to start from scratch and acknowledge that the errors run deep, as the literature on the irrationality of scientific change has amply demonstrated. This tendency to maintain the beliefs we already have is a well-known feature of our cognition, called *doxastic conservatism*. When it comes to our beliefs, we tend to be conservative, and more so if those beliefs matter to us.

There is another alleged difference between garden-variety beliefs and delusions that motivates scepticism about the belief nature of delusions. Beliefs are supposed to shape behaviour and drive action, whereas delusions are often described as 'just talk'. Hugo Mercier argues that conspiracy beliefs are only apparently endorsed but do not really make a difference to how we behave. The fact that they are so bizarre means that they may have no practical consequences for our lives (Mercier 2020). Neil Levy discusses the example of the Pizzagate conspiracy theory (Levy 2021) – a theory spread in 2016 according to which officials of the Democratic Party in the United States and restaurant owners were involved in human trafficking and a child sex ring. Pizzagate might not have had any special consequences for the lives of the people who shared the conspiracy theory on social media and merely 'claimed to' endorse it. But some people acted on it. A man who wanted to investigate the theory and was looking for evidence used a firearm to open a locked door in a restaurant. The owner of the restaurant and the staff also received threats and were harassed as a result of the conspiracy theory spreading. In the opinion polls at the time, a considerable percentage of voters who were asked about Hillary Clinton's possible involvement in Pizzagate said that she had something to do with it or that they could not be sure – and this was the time when she was a candidate for the US presidential elections. At least in some cases, people are motivated to behave in ways that are consistent with the conspiracy theories they claim to believe, even when such theories are wildly implausible.

What I have described in the case of conspiracy beliefs has been dubbed *double-bookkeeping* or 'the co-existence of two disjoint ways of orienting oneself to reality' (Parnas et al. 2021) in the literature on delusions in schizophrenia. Whereas a man with delusions of persecution in hospital may protest that the nurses are trying to poison him, he never misses a meal. One may be tempted to say that the patient is split between the delusional reality (where the nurses want to poison him) and the actual reality (where the nurses want to feed him), and this fluctuation is responsible for the gaps and apparent inconsistencies between his reports and his actions (Gallagher 2009). The delusion of persecution manifests in the patient's verbal protestations, but the patient's actions tell a different story.

Some philosophers endorse a metacognitive account of delusions, according to which to have a delusion is to misattribute to oneself an act of imagination as a belief. Philosophers drawn to that sort of anti-doxasticism about delusions (e.g., Currie and Ravenscroft 2002; Ichino 2020) want to explain the gaps and inconsistencies found in people who report delusions but do not always act on them. The delusion that the nurses are trying to poison the patient is something he has imagined but now he mistakenly thinks that it is true that the nurses want to poison him. Acts of imagination are not expected to drive action in the same way as beliefs are, so the delusion shares some of the features of imagination (by not driving action), and some of the features of belief (by being endorsed as something that the person believes). If delusions are originally things we imagine and later misattribute to ourselves as beliefs, this might explain why we do not always act on our delusions, and why we tolerate some tension between our delusions and our existing beliefs.

How would this work in the case of conspiracy theories and other bizarre delusions? We merely *imagine that* some Democrats are running a child sex ring in restaurants, but we take ourselves to *believe that* that's actually the case. We merely *imagine that* there is a nuclear reactor inside our bodies, but we take ourselves to *believe that* the reactor is indeed inside us. This misattribution may be invoked to explain why our mental states share some features with acts of imagination. It may explain why we are not seeking evidence confirming that the restaurant is covering up a child sex ring, and we are not overly preoccupied by the fact that nuclear reactors are usually much bigger than the devices that could fit into our bodies.

However, the problem of double-bookkeeping is not such a serious threat to the belief status of delusions as anti-doxasticists suggest. Although it is true that some delusions fail to drive action, it is also true that none of our professed beliefs are *consistently* manifested in behaviour. As the literature on cognitive dissonance abundantly shows, we routinely express commitments that do not convert into actions, especially when the actions are somewhat costly to us. US college students endorse safe sex but do not always use condoms. Responsible citizens who think that water is precious and worth saving take long showers (Aronson 2019). Political leaders profess humility and acceptance but are fractious when their views are challenged. These examples tell us that we often lack consistency, but also suggest that delusions are not qualitatively different from garden-variety beliefs in the way they drive (or fail to drive) action. The patient may be seriously concerned about the nurses' intentions but he also needs to eat. As hospital food is what is available for him to eat, that is what he eats. When we consider the consequences of our beliefs on our behaviour, we should remember that beliefs do not drive action in isolation from other beliefs and other mental states we may have. Our behaviour is often shaped by our beliefs but also by the extent to which we are motivated to act on those beliefs and by other constraints that apply to the physical and social environment where we are situated (Bortolotti and Broome 2012).

Belief or experience?

The arguments against the belief nature of delusions highlight important aspects of the experience of being deluded, including the sense that the imagined and the actual reality can get blurred to some extent. But my impression is that those insightful observations about how delusions manifest in some circumstances are compatible with the view of delusions as beliefs. They do not motivate a complete overhaul of the intuitive belief-view of delusions. Whether attributions of delusionality in triangulation are a convenient folk-psychological fiction or capture real patterns in our mental lives, delusions are attributed to explain and predict behaviour, just like (other) beliefs. To help us support and coordinate with fellow agents, but also manipulate, control and deceive others, we must assume that their belief states to some extent interact with their other cognitive or affective states and shape their behaviour. And the arguments offered to challenge the belief view of delusions do not succeed in showing that the features of delusions that grab our attention are discontinuous from those of the beliefs we encounter in our everyday experience as speakers and interpreters. Garden-variety beliefs can distort reality, resist counterevidence and be locally ineffectual too.

Some phenomenologists argue that at the very core of clinical delusions there is no strange or irrational belief, but a powerful experience that affects our entire conception of ourselves and reality: following Karl Jaspers, the delusion brings a 'transformation in our total awareness of reality'. Although recent contributions to the debate do not explicitly deny that clinical delusions involve beliefs, they raise powerful objections to *intellectualizing* delusions, that is, understanding delusions primarily as false and irrational beliefs. One concern, for instance, is that the emphasis on the belief component of delusions leads to developing causal theories of delusions focused on establishing whether reasoning is faulty, invoking either deficits or biases affecting information processing. This approach risks to neglect other possible causal factors implicated in the adoption and maintenance of delusions (Feyaerts et al. 2021).

Philosophers who defend the idea that delusions are beliefs tend to have a broad, non-idealized notion of belief, where something can be a *bona-fide* belief, and yet be resistant to counterevidence, in tension with other beliefs, and inconsistently reflected in behaviour. That is also my approach, but I recognize the risks of focusing on the belief nature of delusions. First, if the focus is on belief, we put the relationship of delusions with evidence and reality under close scrutiny, but may neglect the relationship of delusions with life experiences and emotions. As delusions are things we really care about, the way they emerge out of our experiences of the world and feed into elation, anxiety, anger and fear matters to the type of mental state they are and to how they impact our lives. Second, if the focus is on belief, when we have delusions we may be seen as isolated agents facing a passive world that just waits to be deciphered by us, whereas human agency is predominantly social and both constrained and supported by the surrounding physical and social environment. We are not atoms and we do not do any believing in the void.

Here is an example about how examining moods and emotions and perceptions and inferences can deepen our understanding of how delusions come about. Paranoid thoughts and persecutory delusions are often attributed to a problem with belief formation – for instance, with how we grow suspicious of other people's intentions because we misinterpret cues in our environment due to perceptual and cognitive biases. But recent empirical work has emphasized how the role of emotional stability is just as important: when we have mood swings, we provoke negative responses from others. As a result, people may appear hostile to us and we may come to think that they are 'against us', prompting a state of paranoia. The world itself may appear unpredictable and threatening when we are emotionally unstable: this unpredictability makes us feel ill at ease and may lead us to worry about potential threats (Broome and Bortolotti 2018).

The case of paranoia teaches us an important lesson: neither clinical nor everyday delusions involve *just* beliefs. Delusions encompass ways of seeing the world and ourselves; they reflect ethical, political and epistemic values; and they are as tied to emotions and moods as they are to a multiplicity of experiences and other beliefs. Indeed, the fact that a delusion arises at a specific point in our lives may be explained by radical changes in our emotional and affective landscape. We interact with the world based on patterns that are partly due to our cultural background, and partly due to our previous experiences. When something inexplicable or potentially threatening happens to us, our existing model of the world is challenged, and we need to revise it in order to account for the changes. This may result into behaviour that attracts the attribution of delusional beliefs. Fascinating examples come from the narratives of people who developed psychotic symptoms after a significant change in their experience (Gunn and Larkin 2020).

Barbara comes to believe that she is the only child of God, and God loves her above everybody else, after coming to terms with a painful breakup from an abusive relationship and a strong sense of guilt derived by some of her previous life choices. Andrew comes to believe that God is giving him power over who can be saved and who deserves to be punished in the afterlife, following a difficult time at work, when he suffers from loneliness, isolation and bad experiences of abuse by his managers. In both these cases, and in many other similar stories, an adverse event transforms the person's life for the worst and the delusion emerges as a response, usually as an attempt to re-establish the person's sense of self-worth and empowerment that was severely compromised (Gunn and Bortolotti 2018).

Believing as investing

The focus on belief may bring about explanations of how delusions emerge that are one-sided and simplistic. But this problem can be solved without claiming that delusions are other than beliefs. It can be solved by broadening our understanding of what matters to beliefs and believers. It is urgent to acknowledge that attributing beliefs in isolation from other mental states and seeing agents as islands is futile. In particular, feelings and emotional reactions to significant events have a powerful effect on how we perceive the world and interpret it. Factors that determine how and what we believe include the influence of the environment in which we operate and the role of other people not just as interpreters but as co-believers and as sources of information that we can either trust or mistrust.

Talking about delusions as beliefs as I do here is not an attempt to simplify, intellectualize or trivialize delusions, but to draw attention to one aspect of what it means to have a delusion or to be deluded which is both important and fascinating. The delusion is an *investment*, as all beliefs are. We commit to seeing the world or ourselves in a certain way and we talk and act (most of the time, not invariably) as if the world is in that way. Considering delusions as beliefs brings the investment to the fore. It is not unusual to have strange thoughts, imagine impossible scenarios, engage in wishful thinking. We do so all the time. But the visions of the world delusions conjure persist and make a difference. We do not easily disavow delusional states; we defend them against challenges; we elaborate on them; we make (not always successful) attempts to integrate them in our complex view of the world. It is that personal investment in the delusion that makes the delusion the extraordinary phenomenon that it is.

Calling a belief delusional is to express a negative judgement about it, starting from the mere observation that delusions are attributed when triangulations get disrupted and an interpreter finds it difficult to explain and predict the speaker's behaviour (Murphy 2012). Often, calling a view delusional is a way to downgrade it to something that should not be taken seriously, equivalent to suggesting that speakers do not know what they are saying or are not in their right minds. Part of my job here, the *descriptive* part, is to properly unpack what the negative judgement involves, across clinical and everyday contexts. But another job of mine, the *revisionist* part, is to challenge the idea that the negative connotations associated with delusional beliefs tell the full story. What if instead of being merely distortions of reality doomed to disrupt communication, the inevitable causes of triangulation breakdowns and other innumerable forms of harm, delusions were imperfect responses to an existing crisis?

The implications of this more balanced reading of delusions are multiple. Let us suppose that interpreters did have the background information required to see delusions as the speakers' imperfect way to manage some aspect of the shared environment that they can no longer control or understand. Then communication would not need to be so severely disrupted and triangulation could be restored, albeit with some effort. With empathy and curiosity – listening carefully to speakers' reports, observing their present behaviour closely and learning about their previous experiences – interpreters could start to see the shared environment through the speakers' eyes, not permanently but long enough to realize that the delusion may serve as a relief and a protection (Gunn and Bortolotti 2018).

Delusions as maps

This project of description and revision also brings to the fore why delusions matter. Delusions matter because they illustrate at the same time the strengths and the weaknesses of human cognition and agency, telling us something important about our role as speakers and interpreters in an environment that keeps changing and surprising us. Frank Ramsey famously described beliefs as 'the maps by which we steer' (Ramsey 1931). Are delusions also maps?

As speakers, we react to setbacks by constructing a desired reality or developing an explanation of a puzzling experience that helps us retain some control over a world that we were never given a fighting chance to understand. We need causal maps to guide us through an environment that is especially difficult to navigate; and delusions are our fallible and faulty attempts at drawing those maps. As interpreters, we also love predictability, transparent causal connections and meanings that effortlessly reveal themselves. When dealing with speakers in our environment, we abhor not knowing what will happen next, and our fear of losing control turns into prejudice against those who find meaning in different things or learn to cope with threats in ways that are unfamiliar to us. Interpreters need causal maps too, to coordinate with fellow travellers; speakers' delusions are the bits of the map that are difficult to read.

CHAPTER 2
DELUSIONS AND THE WORLD

In the Introduction and Chapter 1, I started with some examples of delusions and made a case for considering delusions as reports that we make sincerely and with conviction. What types of beliefs do interpreters take delusions to be? A key feature seems to be that delusional beliefs *distort reality*. Clinical delusions are described as a *failure of reality testing*. Conspiracy beliefs offer an explanation of significant events that systematically and predictably differs from official (more plausible) explanations. Prejudiced beliefs are often straight-forward and yet illusory ways to find scapegoats for the bits of reality that we do not like. Optimistically biased beliefs inflate the speaker's talents, skills and future prospects.

This means that, from the interpreter's point of view, delusions convey how speakers take things to be, but do not contribute to speakers understanding how things are. Although it is common to assume that delusions are false, in this chapter I will argue that neither bizarreness of content, nor falsity as such is likely to be a key criterion for attributions of delusionality. However, *implausibility* is a better candidate. Interpreters find beliefs delusional when they consider them implausible, that is, when the beliefs are not likely to be true given the interpreter's (and often also the speaker's) existing beliefs.

Bizarreness

It is common to associate clinical delusions, and delusional beliefs in general, with a bizarre content. The prototypical delusion in popular culture is something almost absurd, something like 'I am the reincarnation of Albert Einstein and have advanced mathematical abilities' (Isham et al. 2021), that requires no detailed investigation to be revealed as false. But bizarreness is not a feature shared by all delusional beliefs.

Stranger than fiction

There is no denying that *some* delusional beliefs are bizarre. Here are two examples from a study on schizophrenia patients in India (De et al. 2013):

- 'Some rays are there in me, which create magnetic field and I have the power to affect TV signals. Body is producing charge; whenever I touch anything I get electric current. Some heavenly body comes and makes me powerful and communicates with me';
- 'I have some special power, if I call the Sun then it will come to me, whenever I look at the Sun, it smiles back at me'.

Some conspiracy theories also involve bizarre beliefs. Here are some examples (The Week 2020):

- 'Earth is hollow and that there might even be a whole other civilization of advanced beings living in it';
- 'Reptilian humanoids live among us with the intention of enslaving the human race.'

What makes a belief *bizarre*? In the clinical literature, delusional beliefs are regarded as bizarre when at least one of three conditions obtains (Cermolacee et al. 2010):

a) the facts reported are judged to be not merely false, but logically or physically impossible;

b) the claims are incomprehensible within the speaker's culture;

c) the situations talked about do not seem to be ordinary life situations.

In the sense of bizarreness captured by (a)–(c), a bizarre belief content may alert an interpreter to the possibility that the belief is delusional but is not a very promising necessary or sufficient condition for delusionality. The claim that it is sufficient for the interpreter to regard a belief bizarre to call it a delusion is a nonstarter. Some of the beliefs that interpreters find bizarre are not deemed as delusional because, although the interpreter does not share the beliefs or finds them difficult to understand, the source of the discrepancy can be explained by the speaker being at a different developmental stage or having a different cultural background from the interpreter. That Santa Claus can reach all households across the world in one night, travelling on a sleigh pulled by reindeer across the sky, is surely bizarre and yet we do not think of it as a delusion (but see Vines 2007).

Would the interpreter call a belief delusional if it were not bizarre? It would seem so. Delusions of persecution and delusions of jealousy simply convey some of our worst fears, that we are not loved and respected, that we are vulnerable and that the people closest to us deceive us or intend to harm us. There is nothing bizarre in those beliefs, although the beliefs may not be well supported by the evidence available to us. Consider someone who believes that their romantic partner is having an affair: it is neither impossible nor highly unlikely that people in apparent monogamous relationships have affairs; the thought of people having affairs is not incomprehensible to others; and having affairs is a fairly ordinary life situation. However, a man's belief that his wife is unfaithful to him because the fifth lamppost on the left is unlit (a classic example from Sims 2013, p. 119) may still be regarded as delusional due to the tenuous relationship between the belief and what the man takes to be evidence for the belief.

Examples of beliefs about persecution and jealousy present key features of delusions without being incomprehensible or having a physically or logically impossible content. According to the report of a case study of delusion of persecution (Lebelo and Grobler 2020), when Mr X was hospitalized for injuries he inflicted to his scrotum, it became clear that his self-injuries were motivated by his belief that there were people following him around intending to rob him of his testicles. Mr X was not depressed and had no intention to die. He said he just wanted to get rid of the constant preoccupation over his tormentors' intentions by anticipating their moves. It is unusual that people want to rob someone of his testicle, although it is not difficult to imagine a situation where Mr X's reports make sense. Persecutors *could* mutilate the genitals of the person they intend to harm.

In the report of a case study of delusional jealousy, Mr B had the belief that his wife was being unfaithful to him with several men, including his daughter's husband, although no evidence could be found of any infidelity (Silva et al. 1998, pp. 608–9). This belief drove Mr B to take action on some occasions (e.g., washing the bathroom all the time for fear of sexually transmitted diseases) and exhibit hostile, often aggressive, behaviour towards his wife (e.g., threatening and pushing her). The beliefs reported by Mr B are not characterized by impossible contents and they are not incomprehensible. Romantic partners *could* have multiple affairs.

What suggests that Mr X's and Mr B's beliefs are a sign of mental distress is not *what* the speakers believe but *how* they believe: how the beliefs conflict with other things speakers know, how the beliefs come to monopolize the speakers' mental lives and how difficult it is for the speakers to relinquish the beliefs. Important in the cases above is the judgement that the belief is somehow really disruptive – Mr X's persecutory belief causes him to injure himself and Mr B's delusion of jealousy brings chaos and violence into his family life.

Out of the ordinary

One might argue that, although Mr X's and Mr B's beliefs are not physically or logically impossible, they are however out of the ordinary. I started this section on bizarreness with some interesting reports, a person claiming their body was producing electric charge and another saying that they had a special power and the Sun would smile at them whenever they watched it. I already offered examples of unusual beliefs in the Introduction and in Chapter 1. If you remember, Wang believed that her co-workers had turned into robots and Saks was convinced that the surrounding houses were talking to her – or rather inserting thoughts into her head. In some science-fiction scenarios, there are robots that appear human, such as cyborgs, or hybrid beings created by combining human and artificial parts, but we do not encounter such cases out of fiction. Arguably, it is physically impossible for inanimate objects such as a building to communicate with humans unless they have been somehow programmed by humans to do so – we may encounter talking trees or living houses in fairy tales but not in ordinary life. So, it would seem that in several delusions we experience distance between the content of the belief and ordinary life situations.

But does this feature of delusion, being about situations that are not ordinary life situations, present obstacles to triangulation? Does it make the speakers' reports un-understandable? One proposal would be that interpreters call delusional those beliefs that are *impossible* for them to understand. Un-understandability is often discussed as a feature relevant to diagnostic criteria and some beliefs we call delusions are indeed difficult to understand. There is a long tradition in psychiatry and in philosophy according to which at least some clinical delusions are deemed as un-understandable (Kendler and Capmpbell 2014; Kiran and Chaudhury 2009). This starts with Karl Jaspers's claim about what he called *primary delusions,* delusions emerging out of nowhere that are like direct experiences not mediated by thought:

If we try to get some closer understanding of these primary experiences of delusions, we soon find we cannot really appreciate these quite alien modes of experience. They remain largely incomprehensible, unreal and beyond our understanding.

(Jaspers 1963, p. 98)

Capgras and Cotard delusions are often mentioned as examples of beliefs that are incredible or hard to understand, but they do not come out of nowhere. In Capgras delusion we believe that a loved one has been replaced by an impostor, and in Cotard delusion we believe that we are dead or disembodied. The Capgras delusion reminds us of science-fiction stories where clones or cleverly disguised aliens gradually replace the people around us – and none is the wiser apart from us. It then becomes a challenge to persuade everybody else that the gradual substitutions are indeed happening. As we saw in Chapter 1, the Cotard delusion is almost a self-defeating belief, that is, you cannot have the belief without undermining the plausibility of the belief itself. That is because, if it is really true that I am dead, how can I have thoughts (e.g., thinking that I am dead) and share such thoughts with others (e.g., talking about being dead)? When delusions threaten understanding, what is it about them that causes the problem? One promising idea is that, if the beliefs are difficult to comprehend, that is because unusual experiences give rise to them. The nature of our experiences at least partially *explains* why our beliefs have the content they do. It may seem impossible for the interpreter to understand the speaker's reports because the interpreter is not acquainted with the speaker's experiences.

According to an influential explanation (starting with Stone and Young 1997), in the Capgras delusion we fail to receive the affective response to a familiar face that we expect to receive, and this compromises our capacity to recognize the person in front of us as, say, our mother, spouse or co-worker. We see a person who appears identical or almost identical to the person we know but we do not feel what we usually feel when we look at them. The hypothesis that the person in front of us is an impostor is implausible (more implausible than the realization that something is amiss in our facial recognition system) but not impossible to understand given the nature of the experience. Moreover, it is also possible to make sense of the fact that we tend to hold on to the delusional hypothesis. We are likely to reject other people's view that the alleged impostor is not an impostor but the real thing because we claim a special bond with the person who has allegedly been replaced. Surely, we know our mother or spouse better than anybody else and can tell the subtle differences between the original and the impostor while the people around us are more likely to be fooled by the clever substitution.

In the Cotard delusion, the quality of our experience of the world changes dramatically. People describe it by saying that everything feels flat and detached, and nothing bothers or excites them as much as it used to (Thomson 2013). A person with Cotard who was interviewed when she was no longer actively delusional described her experience at the time as an extreme form of jet-lag, when everything feels grey and numb (Freeman 2018). Because the change is undergone by the totality of our experience and not by just some of our experiences, the hypothesis is that the cause of the change is in ourselves and not in the world outside us. In the extremely unusual circumstances, it makes sense to believe that there is something wrong with us: we may have died or lost our attachment to our bodies.

Some authors have argued that a better appreciation of the scientific explanation of how delusions come about can help facilitate the form of understanding that an interpreter needs in order to make sense of a speaker's utterances (Kendler and Campbell 2014), and I think I am making a similar point here. Understanding does not need to be an immediate connection that is either present or absent but can be the result of the application of a skill that interpreters work hard to improve and refine. Some knowledge about what the speaker is going through can help the interpreter make sense of the speaker's reports, even when these initially appear incredible or seem to arise 'out of nowhere'. Given the unusual nature of the experiences that often give rise to clinical delusions, it is not surprising that the delusional beliefs themselves have an unusual content. An interpreter's curiosity about the speaker's experiences could be enough for the speaker to share information that makes their beliefs more understandable.

Alien abduction

Does the claim that an unusual experience is at least partially responsible for puzzling beliefs apply to nonclinical contexts? The content of many nonclinical delusions is mundane: such delusional beliefs may concern ourselves (as in the smoker's positive illusion that they are immune from lung cancer) or events significantly affecting our lives (as in forms of denialism, such as the claim that Covid-19 does not exist or the claim that climate change is a hoax).

There seems to be no unusual experience backing up such beliefs, and we can definitely imagine a world slightly different from ours where the beliefs are plausible and evidence can be gathered to support them. However, there are some nonclinical beliefs that are bizarre and difficult to understand even if they are not considered as symptoms of mental disorders. These have a content that interpreters regard as physically or logically impossible, incomprehensible or detached from ordinary life situations. As in the case of the delusions that are treated as symptoms of a mental disorder, unusual experiences may be partially responsible for the formation of nonclinical bizarre beliefs. Such beliefs may have other features in common with clinical delusions, for instance they can be reported by the speaker with a degree of confidence that, in the eyes of the interpreter, does not match the objective evidence available for the beliefs. Different from clinical delusions though, nonclinical bizarre beliefs are not typically idiosyncratic to the speaker, and are shared by groups of people with similar views or values.

Alien abduction beliefs are a very interesting case in this regard: some people report that they have been temporarily abducted by aliens. The reason for the abduction is often attributed to aliens who allegedly want to examine or conduct experiments on humans. Alien abduction reports are upheld with conviction, can be accompanied by preoccupation and distress and are very resistant to counterevidence. When people claim to have been abducted, they look for confirmatory evidence but are not moved by objections to their claims – for such reasons, at least some alien abduction beliefs can be plausibly described as delusional (Sullivan-Bissett 2020). What is the origin of alien abduction beliefs? One explanation is that the people affected experience Awareness during Sleep Paralysis: they gain consciousness at a time when their bodies are immobilized (REM sleep) and are subject to hallucinations of there being intruders in the room, having difficulty breathing or feeling like they are flying, floating or being out of their bodies (Kinne and Bhanot 2008). Not many people are aware of the possibility that hallucinations accompany paralysis, and thus some other explanation is sought to make sense of the puzzling experiences (Sullivan-Bissett 2020). For those who have already come across alien abduction narratives and are disposed to believe in the existence of aliens, it is not such a big step to conclude that the experience is caused by aliens wanting to know more about humans. This case suggests that people can come to the adoption of an unusual belief in the light of an unusual experience even when their behaviour does not attract the diagnosis of a mental disorder.

It is fair to conclude that bizarreness of belief contents in general and un-understandability of the beliefs in particular are neither sufficient nor necessary criteria for delusionality. Across the divide between clinical and nonclinical delusions, there are some beliefs that are bizarre in content and threaten understanding, although no delusion seems to be entirely incomprehensible. Often, the experience leading up to the belief is unusual and the belief merely reflects that – this is a point often attributed to Brendan Maher to which I come back in Chapter 5. The delusion is an unusual explanation for an unusual experience.

Falsity

Although we tend to assume that delusions are false, being false seems to be neither a sufficient nor a necessary condition for delusionality. A belief can be false and lack some of the other key features of delusion, and a delusion can happen to be a true belief. That being false is not sufficient for a belief to be delusional seems obvious. We have many false beliefs due to ignorance, misremembering, fallacies of reasoning, unreliable testimony, partial consideration of the evidence and so on, that we would not call delusions. If I believe that the train will leave the station at 5 pm today because I misremember the timetable I checked yesterday, my false belief will not be described as a delusion. It is the kind of belief that I am happy to give up or revise when I gain new evidence – for instance when I glance at the departure screen at the station and I realize that the train left at 4:45 pm. That the train will leave at 5 pm is not a belief whose adoption or revision will impact significantly on my sense of self or sense of reality, although I can feel frustrated about missing the train and be a little concerned that my memory is not as good as it once was.

Accidental truths

It is common to assume that delusional beliefs must be false and to expect falsity to drive attributions of delusionality. Most definitions of delusions in the literature mention falsity as a key feature of delusions: on the site of the UK National Health Service (2019), a delusion is described as 'where a person has an unshakeable belief in something untrue'; and introducing their *History of Delusions* programme, the BBC (2014) describes a delusion as 'a belief that is impossible, incredible or false'. As we saw already, in the glossary of the most authoritative source for the diagnosis of mental disorders, the *Diagnostic and Statistical Manual of Mental Disorders* (APA 2013, DSM-5), often half-seriously called the *bible of psychiatry*, delusions are defined as 'false beliefs' based on 'incorrect inference about external reality'. There are several aspects of the DSM-5 definition that are problematic and the necessity of delusions being false is one of those that have been most vehemently criticized. That is because beliefs do not need to be false to be regarded as delusional.

Some of those who openly reject falsity as a criterion for delusionality, such as Max Coltheart and Martin Davies, point to other key criteria, such as the fact that the speaker has no evidence or little evidence supporting the belief (Coltheart 2007) or the fact that the belief is sustained in the face of powerful counterevidence (Davies et al. 2001). Both proposals subscribe to the general idea that it is not *what we believe* but *how we believe* that determines whether our belief is delusional: an idea I explore further in the following chapter. How we believe may include how we have come to endorse the belief, that is, whether the belief is grounded in the available evidence; and how we hold onto the belief in case of challenges, that is, whether the belief is responsive to new evidence.

The approach I am describing is one where a belief is a delusion not due to its being false or bizarre but due to its peculiar relationship with evidence. Such relationship with evidence can be captured by a number of distinct but related notions, the idea that a delusion is an unsupported, unsubstantiated, ill-grounded belief or that it is a belief that is hard to shake and resistant to counterevidence. It is also important to remember again that, in a clinical context, delusions are diagnosed on the basis of our overall behaviour, such as whether we are preoccupied and anxious about the content of the delusion, whether we experience lifestyle changes, and whether other symptoms are present. Whether the belief is true or false does not seem to be the only or even the most central concern.

True *delusions or* fake *delusions?*

This idea that a delusional belief can be true is reflected in some high-profile cases where people were disbelieved but subsequent evidence revealed that their claims had some truth in them: as Vaughan Bell says, 'Just because they're out to get you doesn't prove you're not paranoid' (Bell 2013).

One such case is that of Martha Mitchell, the wife of John Mitchell, US Attorney General in the Nixon administration. Martha was called delusional when she complained to the press about the White House. She claimed among other things that she had been medicated against her will. In the investigations prompted by the Watergate scandal, some of her claims were later proven to be accurate. White House officials did not want her to divulge some events she had become aware of, and so they had an interest in silencing her and questioning her mental health.

This case is interesting because, as Bell explains, Martha did have a number of mental health issues at the time, including paranoia. She was in the care of a psychiatrist and was experiencing suicidal thoughts, which might have affected how people first received her claims. The question is of course whether we are inclined to consider Martha's claims as nondelusional now that we know that they did not completely distort reality or we are still happy to think of them as delusions but recognize that they were partially true beliefs. Were they 'fake delusions' or 'true delusions'? The answer may depend on other features of Martha's beliefs apart from their being true, including how she reported them and argued for them, and what role the beliefs played in her mental life as a whole.

One may think that rejecting falsity as a criterion for attributions of delusionality may be easier in clinical than in nonclinical contexts because clinical delusions present additional features that distinguish them from other problematic beliefs, whereas falsity seems central to the lay conception of conspiracy beliefs and other everyday delusions. However, attributions of delusionality outside the clinical context also support the idea that the relationship between the belief and the evidence is more central to the enterprise than the truth of the belief.

For instance, when climate change denial is referred to as a delusion, it is not because climate change denialists have false beliefs but because they are *unmoved* by the scientific evidence that undermines their position (Shearman 2018; Ingram and Schutz 2019). The rejection of the role of scientific experts in settling the dispute as to whether humans are responsible for global warming insulates the belief from doubt and can turn the belief into a conspiracy belief. A reason is postulated to explain why the scientific community willingly misleads the public by fabricating or exaggerating the risks of human-caused climate change.

Something similar happened with Covid-19 denialism in the initial stages of the pandemic. The belief that Covid-19 did not exist or that Covid-19 was just like the common flu was false, but in the commentaries where people described such beliefs as delusional the emphasis was on the beliefs clashing with, but not being abated by, statistical information about infection rates and excess deaths worldwide. A common explanation for disregarding evidence was that the scientific community and the authorities who produced that evidence had an interest in persuading the public that the disease posed a genuine threat – for instance, one conspiracy theory suggested that political leaders had an interest in spreading panic and fear in order to control citizens' behaviour to their advantage (Romano 2020).

Establishing the truth of a belief about climate change or Covid-19 may actually be even more difficult than establishing the truth of a belief that is considered, erroneously or appropriately, the symptom of a mental disorder. In the Martha Mitchell's case, ascertaining whether she had been medicated against her will was not something difficult to do. Her experience was sufficient reason for her to adopt the belief, and other people could gather independent evidence, listen to witnesses, fact-check her statements. However, in the case of climate change and Covid-19 denialism, the reality that is being misrepresented by the delusional belief is not easily accessible without technical knowledge or scientific expertise.

That is because establishing the truth of claims about the factors contributing to the warming of the planet and about the nature of viral infections often requires technical knowledge and cannot be done without specialized scientific expertise. How do we know to what extent carbon emissions impacted increasing temperatures on Earth if we do not understand how to weigh the evidence available to climate scientists? How can we be sure about the nature of Covid-19 if we do not rely on the work of virologists, epidemiologists and immunologists? It makes sense that what leads us to describe denialist views as delusional beliefs is not that the views are obviously false, because we do require technical knowledge and expertise to evaluate the truth of those claims, but that people endorsing them do not trust the testimony provided by the experts in the relevant fields. Reality distortion seems much less central to delusionality claims in this context than being irresponsive to counterevidence and dismissing the testimony of experts who we would expect to be credible and authoritative.

Moreover, in the literature on conspiracy theories as well as in the literature on clinical delusions, it is widely acknowledged that some conspiracy beliefs are true or could have easily been true. At the early stages of the Covid-19 pandemic scientists disagreed about some aspects of the nature of the virus, including the details of how the virus was transmitted. For instance, there was a lively debate about whether using face masks would be an effective means for people to protect themselves and others from infection. Before robust evidence could be gathered about the way

Covid-19 was being transmitted and the effects of wearing face masks on transmission, it was an open question whether face mask mandates were justified. Arguably, a belief such as the denial that Covid-19 was airborne could have been at the start a hypothesis to be weighed up among many, and not something that people were particularly invested in. However, when evidence for Covid-19 being airborne accumulated and nonetheless people ignored this, making it a question of personal freedom whether citizens could be asked to wear masks to access public spaces and transportation to limit the spread of the infection, the denial of the airborne nature of Covid-19 became the kind of belief that attracts the 'delusional' label (Jefferson and Bortolotti 2023).

In some cases, a theory that is considered a conspiracy theory for quite some time may be at least partially vindicated. David Coady discusses as an example the claim that American government agencies were complicit in drug smuggling and especially cocaine trafficking in the 1990s. The theory was proposed by investigative journalist Gary Webb and initially regarded as a baseless conspiracy. Webb's work as a journalist was discredited and he died by suicide in the aftermath. But when Webb's investigation inspired some thorough reports into the behaviour of government agencies, some claims concerning such agencies tolerating drug trafficking were proven to be at least partially true ten years later (Coady 2006; Coady 2021; Schou 2009).

I imagine we all have some examples in mind of beliefs that were considered obviously false and turned out to be at least partially true. How the change impacts our willingness to call the beliefs delusional tells us about how we conceive of delusionality. Independent of the details of any particular real-life case, if we concede that genuine delusional beliefs can be true, falsity cannot play the role of a necessary criterion for attributions of delusionality.

Implausibility

It is appealing to think that the defining feature of delusions is their being false, because we tend to think of delusional beliefs as false and we tend to infer from something being called a delusion that it is false. But a closer look at how delusional beliefs behave and how delusionality is attributed in clinical and everyday contexts suggests instead that the claim that the belief is false is at best a shortcut for the claim that the belief has a difficult relationship with evidence. What transpires from the examples we considered is that, although delusional beliefs are typically false, their being false does not determine their status as delusions: is there some other feature of the content of the belief that drives attributions of delusionality?

'Hard to believe'

Before I move to consider how delusions relate to evidence in the next chapter, I want to consider another feature of delusionality that captures well the sense in which interpreters find delusions 'hard to believe'. So far, I have argued that:

a) not all the beliefs that attract the label of delusions are bizarre;

b) not all the beliefs that attract the label of delusions are false – they can be true 'by accident'; and

c) even the beliefs that have an unusual content can be made sense of when knowledge about the speaker's current or previous experience becomes available to the interpreter.

I observed how judgements of bizarreness can track how difficult it is for an interpreter to comprehend the belief, and thus may depend on there not being sufficient common ground between speaker and interpreter on the specific content of the delusion. For instance, the interpreter might not be aware of the unusual experiences on which the speaker is basing their beliefs. Some belief contents are then judged to be physically or logically impossible or detached from ordinary life experience. The delusional statement 'There is a nuclear reactor inside me' is difficult to believe because we know that nuclear reactors are simply too big to be hidden within people's bodies. The delusional statement 'I have given birth to an infinite number of Messiahs' is difficult to believe because we know that no woman can have infinite pregnancies (Bortolotti 2018b).

In cases such as those of the nuclear reactor and the infinite pregnancies, the things that are believed sound as physically impossible. But often incredulity is triggered by mere *unfamiliarity*. Which beliefs are unfamiliar may be dictated by a number of considerations, including how often interpreters heard those beliefs reported before, which in turn is determined by the social context. Judgements of familiarity are not always a good guide to either rationality or truth. There are many beliefs that are sadly not unfamiliar in this statistical sense, such as prejudiced beliefs about certain individuals or groups, and these are just as resistant to counterevidence and against our best science as textbook cases of delusions. However, we have grown accustomed to hearing them and they are no longer unusual: 'Girls are too emotional', 'Black men are violent', 'Gay people are promiscuous'. It is important to recognize how certain features attributed to beliefs depend on the interpreter's particular standpoint, and willingness to accept or challenge stereotypes.

Although bizarreness is not a very promising condition for attributions of delusionality, un-understandability is too strong and unfamiliarity does not tell us much about the beliefs themselves, the intuition that interpreters call a report delusional when they find it hard to believe persists. This idea can be cashed out in several ways, but my proposal is that one necessary condition for beliefs to be called delusional is that the reports are judged to be unlikely to be true given the interpreters' (and often even the speakers') existing beliefs. In other words, the report stands out for its content because it is does not fit with the other things we accept as true. This is consistent with some accounts of how delusions come about. As I discuss in Chapter 5, one influential view is that when we adopt delusional beliefs we do so because we prioritize *explanatory adequacy* over doxastic conservatism (McKay 2012). What does that mean?

The power of the experience

When faced with an unusual experience or a puzzling event, we endorse an explanation that makes good sense of the experience or event even if such explanation requires a substantial readjustment to our model of the world. Another way of making sense of this lack of inhibition in accepting explanations that are not constrained by common sense is to describe it as a *liberal acceptance* bias. This bias consists in the tendency not to rule out explanations that are implausible when considering options and has been studied in people diagnosed with schizophrenia:

> A core disturbance associated with schizophrenia is that initially more explanations are taken into consideration when interpreting complex events, whereas healthy participants are more selective, and rule out improbable hypotheses more quickly.
>
> (Moritz and Woodward 2004)

Imagine you are at a party and had too much to drink. To get some fresh air, you step out in the garden and see something that looks to you like a green man. You have a choice. You can explain your experience by saying that there is a green man in front of you (adopting a hypothesis that perfectly fits the experience) or you can discount that hypothesis on the basis that you have never seen green men before or heard about them (discounting the hypothesis as implausible given your existing beliefs). In option one (call it *explanatory adequacy*), you are so impressed with the vividness of your experience that you choose to revise your model of the world because of it, conceding that there must be green men. Needless to say, people who did not share your experience will find your belief hard to believe. In option two (call it *doxastic conservatism*), you refuse to change your whole model of the world just to be able to make sense of one unusual experience: you tell yourself that green men do not exist and that you must have hallucinated. Other people will agree with you and add that what you think you saw may have looked unusual because you were intoxicated, it was dark outside, etc. In the case of unusual experience, or an event that is unusually threatening or puzzling, the tendency to endorse an explanation that fits well that experience or event will lead to adopting a belief that others may find implausible – and that you may also recognize as implausible.

This behavioural tendency has been explained by appealing to the *liberal acceptance* bias. When thinking to ourselves that it looks like there is a green man in front of us, we should realize how implausible the scenario is and immediately dismiss the idea, looking for alternative explanations that are more compatible with what we already believe. But our 'delusional selves' are more liberal in accepting unusual hypotheses, hypotheses that are unlikely to be believed by others. So, instead of ruling out the possibility that there was a green man in the garden, we consider that hypothesis as a serious contender. In a recent study considering the relationship between proneness to delusions and Covid-19 themed conspiracy beliefs, the authors remarked that 'delusion proneness is not only associated with a resistance to change of beliefs […] but also to an increased propensity to incorporate *novel beliefs that are not common* (such as specific Covid-19 conspiracy ideas)' (Acar et al. 2022, my emphasis). So, this tendency to accept a belief that is considered to be implausible for the purposes of explaining something unusual cuts across clinical and nonclinical contexts and is a good candidate for a criterion for attributions of delusionality.

My proposal then is that, if we want to know whether there is anything in the content of a belief that might trigger attributions of delusionality, our best bet is to settle for implausibility. Not all delusions are thought of as bizarre, false or un-understandable, but all delusions are regarded as *implausible* by the interpreter. 'Implausibility' has an interesting etymology: it comes from the Latin *plaudere* which means *approve, applaud* or *praise*. When something is plausible, it is worthy of acceptance or approval, it is *easy to believe*. In other words, a plausible report has the appearance of truth. When something is implausible, it is not worthy of acceptance or approval, it is *difficult to believe*. An implausible report has the appearance of falsity. In this sense, implausibility can be considered a central factor in attributions of delusionality.

The interpreter calls a speaker's belief delusional when the speaker's belief is difficult for the interpreter to believe: this difficulty may have a number of sources. The belief may be difficult to believe due to the logical or physical impossibility of the belief contents, to the detachment of the belief contents from ordinary life situations or to mere unfamiliarity. Underlying all the sources of judgements of implausibility is the acknowledgement that the belief does not fit well with the other things the interpreter (and often even the speaker) believes. In some reports, the speaker acknowledges the implausibility of their own delusions and claims candidly that if another speaker had reported a belief with the same content, they would have found the belief incredible (Alexander et al. 1979).

Different from bizarreness and falsity, but similarly to un-understandability, implausibility does not quite capture something about the relationship between the belief and the world, but something about the relationship between the belief and the interpreter's and speaker's existing beliefs. Whether true or false, delusions are difficult to believe.

CHAPTER 3
DELUSIONS AND EVIDENCE

Beliefs are what interpreters ascribe to speakers in order to understand and predict their behaviour. Based on this idea, in Chapter 1 I suggested that we can make sense of the nature of delusions by considering what conditions a belief needs to satisfy to be ascribed to a speaker as a *delusional* belief. I started by arguing that the delusion is an investment for the speaker, a way of seeing the world that matters to the rest of the speaker's mental life and behaviour.

In Chapter 2 I asked whether delusions accurately represent the world. Are beliefs called delusional when they are bizarre, false or un-understandable? None of these is a necessary criterion for delusionality, even if interpreters often assume that delusions are false. In the end, I suggested that one of the necessary criteria for the ascription of delusionality is that the interpreter finds the beliefs implausible, that is, hard to believe given the interpreter's (and often the speaker's) existing beliefs.

While exploring the notion of delusion and its uses, we saw that the relationship between the speaker's belief and the evidence available to the speaker appears more central to delusionality than the relationship between the belief content and the world. In this chapter, then, I turn to evidence and examine four interrelated features that are often ascribed to delusions: groundlessness and ill-groundedness, irresponsiveness to evidence and unshakeability. Which of these features can play the role of a criterion for delusionality?

Evidential support

Many would agree that what is central to beliefs being delusional is the fraught relationship between the content of the belief and the evidence available for or against it. This reflects a common slogan in the ethics of beliefs literature that I also mentioned in the previous chapter: what matters is not *what* you believe, but *how* you believe (e.g., Stapleford 2012). I argued that falsity and bizarreness are not necessary conditions for delusionality, although delusional beliefs tend to be false and some delusions have bizarre contents. At best, delusional beliefs are implausible, in the sense that it is difficult for interpreters to share those beliefs given their current understanding of reality.

But other factors can contribute to judgements of implausibility. Maybe interpreters find delusional beliefs implausible because such beliefs do not seem to be well-supported by evidence or they do not seem to budge under the pressure of external challenges. Are poor evidential support and insensitivity to evidence promising criteria for delusionality? Delusions have drawn philosophers' attention because, from an interpreter's perspective, it is not clear *why* the speaker endorses the delusional content. Calling a speaker's belief delusional is equivalent to asking the speaker: 'How can you believe *that*?' In the case of delusions, one might say, the problem is that evidence fails to support and constrain the belief.

Ill-groundedness or groundlessness?

One sense of the claim that 'evidence fails to support the belief' is that delusions are groundless or ill-grounded, which means that there is no evidential support at all or no good evidential support for the beliefs at the time of their adoption.

We know that beliefs that are well supported by evidence at some stage can turn out to be false at a later stage, as the succession of competing scientific theories through history of science illustrates. The theory that electrons were tiny balls moving in elliptical orbits around the nucleus of the atom, for instance, had excellent predictive success for a while but was then disconfirmed by quantum theory. It would have been epistemically rational to believe that electrons were orbiting around the nucleus at some point, but when further scientific research revealed that the belief was false, the rational thing to do became to abandon the belief and replace it with another, better supported by the evidence. Conversely, some beliefs that are poorly supported by evidence can turn out to be true: evidence for them can become available only after they have been adopted. Suppose I come to believe that it will snow on Saturday after consulting the most accurate weather forecast app on my smartphone. Indeed, on Saturday it is snowflakes all around. My prediction is confirmed. But later I realize that, by mistake, I had checked the forecast for Sunday, not for Saturday. So, I actually had no evidence on which to base my prediction that on Saturday it would snow. At the time of adopting the belief 'It will snow on Saturday', my belief was ill-grounded. There are also beliefs for which it is a real challenge to gather supporting evidence. For ideological, metaphysical or religious beliefs, no empirical evidence may play a supporting role with respect to the content of the belief.

Other beliefs may start out as hypotheses to entertain, acts of imagination or thoughts we merely wish to be true, and then turn into full-blown beliefs. One example is that of 'implanted' memory beliefs in pre-schoolers. When young children are repeatedly asked to imagine an emotionally significant event in all details – such as being taken to hospital for an injury or getting lost in a mall – they end up believing that the event actually happened to them and make sincere but inaccurate reports of that event (Loftus et al. 1996). In the case of implanted memories, the belief is ill-grounded and will remain so because the past cannot change – if the child never got lost in a mall, their report that they did does not have empirical support.

However, some beliefs that are ill-grounded to start with need not be delusional and need not remain irrational either. We can continue to gather evidence for our belief after we adopt it and the accumulation of evidence may determine our level of commitment to the belief content or the extent to which the belief influences our behaviour – in other words, to what extent the belief is an investment for us. For instance, we might be considering the merits of a certain anti-bullying policy after we hear that our good friend whom we greatly respect defends that policy. We may think to ourselves: 'That may be a good a policy, it may work' and speak in favour of the policy next time we are asked for an opinion. Later, we learn of robust evidence supporting the efficacy of the policy – that it has been applied in some contexts with good results – and our initial inclination towards the policy solidifies into a firm commitment. This sort of cases, which are not uncommon, suggest that beliefs are not always (maybe not even typically) supported by evidence at the time of their initial adoption. It is not the pedigree of the belief that determines whether the belief is rational or justified because good reasons for holding onto the beliefs can become available after the belief has been adopted (Bortolotti and Sullivan-Bissett 2019).

My point in offering examples of everyday beliefs that are groundless or ill-grounded, irrespective of the truth of their content, is to suggest that groundlessness and ill-groundedness are not sufficient conditions for delusionality. Delusions are not the only type of beliefs that may be adopted without evidential support or without carefully weighing up the available evidence. But are groundlessness and ill-groundedness necessary for delusionality?

Experience as evidence

Groundlessness and ill-groundedness do not seem to be *necessary* conditions for delusionality either, unless our conception of evidence is particularly narrow and excludes unusual perceptual experiences and adverse life experiences – as these often count as grounds for delusions. In a broad sense of 'evidence', we do have some evidence for our delusional beliefs and thus delusions are not entirely groundless. Even in the case of delusions with bizarre contents, as seen in the previous chapter, there is usually a puzzling experience that demands an explanation, and the delusion is an explanation that fits that experience – although the explanation may not be plausible all things considered, and alternative explanations may be overall preferable. The experience of feeling numb and detached from everything is (not very good) evidence for the claim that we are dead. The experience of seeing a woman who looks almost identical to our mother but not feeling like we are seeing our mother is (defeasible) evidence for the claim that the woman is not our mother but an impostor. To what extent such unusual experiences can be known to, and understood by, interpreters who have no clinical experience is hard to say, which means that beliefs that are called delusional may have the appearance of groundlessness in the eyes of interpreters, even when they are explanations for ways of feeling and being in the world.

Delusions of persecution are partially grounded in adverse experiences of abuse: such past experiences offer inductive evidence that we should be mindful of the intentions of others and expect trouble. Past adversities may partially explain why we develop suspicion towards certain individuals or groups (e.g., Li et al. 2012). For instance, there is emerging evidence suggesting that experiences of bullying and sexual abuse in childhood are powerful risk factors for experiencing symptoms such as hallucinations and delusions later in life (Broome and Bortolotti 2018). If we experienced a situation where the people who should have taken care of us exploited us and prevented us from flourishing, then it is not a surprise that we have become hypervigilant and tend to assume that the people we meet have evil intentions. A measure of suspiciousness may even be adaptive in the circumstances. Again, as the past adverse experience motivating an attitude of suspiciousness may not be something the interpreter has access to or can reconstruct, that attitude may seem unjustified to the interpreter.

Similarly, when we accept a conspiracy theory, we may be prone to do so because we have had experiences that justify an attitude of mistrust towards the alleged conspirators or towards the sources proposing a different explanation of the relevant events. The slogan 'conspiracy theories are for losers' (Uscinski and Parent 2014) conveys the sense that those of us who are on the losing side of history, the minorities, the marginalized, the forgotten, are more likely to accept a conspiracy hypothesis because they have no reason to trust the elites. The suspiciousness towards the intentions of the authorities is a way to protect ourselves from further exploitation by those who are more powerful and have not had our interests at heart in the past. The conspiracy hypothesis may have the added advantage of helping us gain a sense of control over reality that we rarely experienced ('Now I know what is going on'; 'They won't fool me this time'). In the words of Neil Levy (2019), 'accepting bizarre conspiracies is the price agents pay for being alert to real dangers'. Thus, entirely lacking evidential support is not a necessary condition for delusionality – some delusions make sense in the context of a person's life experiences. Mostly, the issue is that delusionality is attributed to beliefs that are not sufficiently supported by what interpreters consider as *good* evidence for those beliefs, and that is where ill-groundedness may come in.

Good and bad evidence

The term 'ill-groundedness' suggests that there is a third option between being grounded in evidence and not being grounded at all. The third option is to be grounded in some evidence that is not however sufficient to support the belief or is not considered to be good evidence for the belief overall. This brings it home that not all evidential support is the same. The judgement of ill-groundedness carries a negative evaluation of the relationship between the available evidence and the belief. Some of these negative evaluations will be based on assumptions about what counts as good evidence for a certain type of claim and those assumptions may differ from individual to individual or from group to group depending on their epistemic and methodological commitments. For instance, interpreters will find that a speaker's belief is ill-grounded if they can determine that *there is* information available to the speaker that is taken by the speaker as evidence for the belief, but the evidence is insufficient or partial. In other words, in the light of the interpreter, the information is not good evidence for the belief. But it is worth noting that there may not be a common, neutral standpoint from which interpreter and speaker judge the quality of the evidence and, if their judgements about the quality of the evidence are based on their experiences and values, then they can come apart.

Data from climate science may be the gold standard of evidence for an interpreter who is inclined to respect and value the credibility and authority of scientific experts. However, the same data may not be considered as good evidence by a speaker who suspects climate scientists of being biased and ideologically corrupt. Here is another example. In the debate on the safety and efficacy of electroconvulsive therapy (ECT) for depression, there is strong disagreement about the effects of the medical intervention, ranging from the thought that ECT causes lasting brain damage to the thought that it is life-saving as a last resort for cases that are resistant to other forms treatment and more efficacious as a whole than other interventions that are less controversial, such as anti-depressants. Evidence for and against the safety and efficacy of ECT is routinely challenged in mental health debates, and there are explicit discussions about the appropriateness of admitting certain forms of evidence in the debate, comparing different types of review of the available data in the light of their objectives and methodologies (Meechan et al. 2022). Thus, judgements of ill-groundedness may partially depend on whether interpreter and speaker have similar epistemic commitments and value the same methodologies – I return to this in the next chapter, where I address the contribution of some of our beliefs to our identity and the impact of identity on the adoption and maintenance of beliefs.

What have we established so far? When speakers endorse beliefs that an interpreter calls delusional, speakers may have some reasons for their beliefs based on their experiences, so delusions are not typically *groundless* and do not come out of nowhere. Yet, delusions may sound like they have come out of nowhere to an unskilled or uninformed interpreter who is not aware of the speakers' experiences. It is important to distinguish the view that delusional beliefs relate to significant events in the speakers' lives from the view that delusions are the best explanations of those events. A nuanced view of delusion formation acknowledges both the costs and the benefits associated with the adoption of the delusion. Suppose that there is some evidence for a belief that explains what is for us a significant event. The event is that while lying in bed we become aware that we are unable to move and that we see movement in the room around us. The belief is that alien beings have kidnapped us to experiment on us. The explanation addresses the significant event but has some features that attract a judgement of delusionality (e.g., it is implausible given the other things that we happen to believe). Now suppose that there is far better evidence for an alternative explanation that also accounts for the significant event. This alternative belief does not have features that attract judgements of delusionality (e.g., it is plausible given the other things that we happen to believe). This alternative explanation could be that we are subject to hallucinations and experience awareness during sleep paralysis. We will be able to move when the paralysis stops, and the movements we see are mere hallucinations.

Ideally, if we recognized the relative merits (e.g., in terms of plausibility) of the two explanatory hypotheses available to us, we would prefer the latter (nondelusional) hypothesis. But in some contexts, it is difficult for us to accept the nondelusional belief and this may be due to a number of reasons. Maybe we have some reasoning biases which render the nondelusional hypothesis unattractive to us at the time of adoption. Alternatively, or in addition to that, there may be some powerful motivational factors that speak in favour of accepting the delusional hypothesis. In the example of the alien abduction belief, we may be already inclined to believe in the existence of aliens and thus we do not find the alien abduction hypothesis much less plausible than the sleep paralysis hypotheses; or we have a preference for explanations that have entertainment value and make us feel special and unique.

This model can be applied more widely. If we have a Capgras experience, to believe that our spouse has been replaced by an impostor is less plausible than to believe that something has gone wrong with us and we can no longer recognize our spouse. But a consequence of accepting that the affective component of our face recognition system is impaired and gives rise to impostor experiences is that we are losing our mind, which is not a particularly uplifting prospect. So, we may prefer the impostor hypothesis.

When faced with a conspiracy theory, we may prefer the conspiracy belief about the significant event because the alternative is unattractive to us in the circumstances. Maybe the alternative to the conspiracy theory is more difficult for us to understand, due to our limited knowledge of the subject matter, our gaps in scientific literacy, the comforting effects of positive illusions or ingrained assumptions about which sources of information we should trust and which people we should agree with. The consequences of rejecting a conspiracy belief can sometimes amount to seeing our world as a more uncertain and less hospitable place. In the climate change denialism case, if we admit that humans are at least in part responsible for global warming, we also need to recognize that climate scientists were right all along about their predictions, and we need to trust them. This may be difficult for us to do if we harbour anti-science beliefs. We would also need to start worrying about our future, the future of our children and the future of the planet as a whole and the acknowledgement of the climate crisis would sit uncomfortably with our desire to live our lives care-free.

In the case of Covid-19 denialism, if we accept the official theory that there is a pandemic negatively affecting the lives of many citizens worldwide, we also need to accept that political leaders are telling us the truth and we may find that difficult because we know that they lied to us before and we have come to distrust them. Moreover, as in the case of climate change denialism, if we accept the 'official' theory about Covid-19, we must also acknowledge that we have very limited control over threatening and distressing events such as the spread of a deadly virus – and this would carry further psychological burdens (Bortolotti and Ichino 2020). For instance, in the case of Covid-19 denialism, a consequence of accepting that the pandemic is a genuine health threat is that we should be concerned about our safety and the safety of the people we love and change the way we live to stop catching the virus and spreading it.

In sum, delusions are not typically groundless and are not obviously ill-grounded. When we consider a hypothesis that other people may think of as delusional, we do often have some evidential support for that hypothesis, or some reason to find it attractive. The hypothesis may not be as well supported by the evidence as other hypotheses that are also to some extent available to us – and that is why judgements of ill-groundedness may be rife. But I raised two issues: one is that ill-groundedness presupposes an evaluation of the evidence and the criteria of evaluation may not be shared between interpreters and speakers. So, when the interpreter judges a delusional belief as ill-grounded, they may do so on the basis of epistemic commitments and values that the speaker does not share. The other issue is that the desirability of the delusional hypothesis may trump its poor evidential support. Alternative hypotheses to the delusional hypothesis may be something we are aware of, even something we actively considered adopting as beliefs, but we rejected on grounds that are not merely or predominantly epistemic. The alternative hypotheses may be either difficult to understand or difficult to accept, carrying with them psychological costs as well as those epistemic advantages that we forego when we adopt a delusion. The alternative hypotheses might fare better than the delusional ones in terms of how well supported by the totality of the evidence they are and how plausible they sound in the light of the interpreter's existing beliefs. However, they may also force us to come to terms with our inadequacies and our inevitable reliance on society's division of epistemic labour. They may conjure an undesirable reality, potentially undermining our self-esteem, motivation or sense of control.

Responsiveness to counterevidence

I showed that delusions do not need to be groundless and that judgements of ill-groundedness are relative to a certain standpoint. But is there anything else then that we can tell about the relationship between delusions and evidence? For instance, aren't delusions famously irresponsive to counterevidence?

Responsiveness to evidence refers to how we behave when information that is relevant to the content of our belief becomes available to us. The belief is responsive to evidence if we acknowledge new information as evidence for or against our belief content and 'feel the force' of that evidence – this is practically demonstrated by some change in behaviour with respect to the belief. There are several ways in which we can respond to counterevidence and counterarguments: our conviction in the truth of the belief may decrease; we may revise the belief to accommodate the counterevidence; we may reject the belief altogether; or we may discount the counterevidence, leaving our conviction in the truth of the belief unscathed.

Elaboration

Delusional beliefs are rarely dismissed in the face of counterevidence. It is very common for us to acknowledge that the belief is being challenged but also to neutralize the challenge or elaborate the belief so that the challenge is no longer fatal to it. A challenge is almost never considered a sufficient reason to give up a delusional belief and that is why delusions are often described as *fixed* beliefs or as beliefs that are particularly resistant to counterevidence. As already argued in the philosophical literature on clinical delusions (Bortolotti 2009a; Flores 2021), delusional beliefs can be responsive to evidence. We do not typically give up such beliefs on the basis of counterevidence, but we are prepared to defend them and elaborate them, thereby showing that we recognize that others are offering evidence against our beliefs and that our response is needed. Even when we are 'in the grip of a delusion', we are in a position to understand the significance of a challenge to our reports due to new information becoming available, we see that the new information is presented as evidence against our belief, and we are willing to engage. For instance, we may point out that the challenge involves a misunderstanding of our position, we may attempt to discredit the source of the conflicting information or we may react to the challenge with further arguments in favour of our belief.

It is important to establish that delusions are responsive to evidence, because responsiveness to evidence in the weak sense I described here is one of the core features of beliefs, a feature that distinguishes beliefs from other attitudes and applies across different types of beliefs. Responsiveness to evidence does not predict exactly *how* we will react to the challenge but predicts *that* the challenge won't leave us indifferent. When we report a belief sincerely and with conviction, we commit to a certain way of seeing the world and also realize that in the future further information can either strengthen or weaken our belief. Even when we think that the challenge is misguided, we realize that people expect us to react to it and explain why we think so.

What is a typical response to counterevidence like in the case of delusions? An example of engagement with challenges can be found in a reported case of erotomania, the belief that there is someone of higher status who is romantically involved with us. A woman who used to work as helper at a school started reporting that the school headmaster was in love with her. He would ask her to go and see him at a temple but never met her there. She gave reasons why she thought he was in love with her ('he arranged their school annual function on the seventeenth which also happens to be her birthday') and explained his failing to meet her by his being 'a very busy man' (Sowmya et al. 2021). It is interesting to read in the case report that the woman did not ignore potential challenges to her belief: she acknowledged for instance that she had never met the headmaster in person but also attempted to find reasons for the headmaster to miss their appointments. This move (adding further detail to the story to neutralize a challenge) counts as a further elaboration of the delusion that makes sense in context – it is sensible to suppose that the person in charge of the running of a school is too busy to meet their date regularly. Effectively, the move protects the belief from external doubts.

These elaborations in response to challenges are observed in other delusions that are symptomatic of mental disorders – they are called 'secondary confabulations' to highlight that they are a reaction to what other people say as opposed to something that we would spontaneously offer without prompting. In mirrored-self misidentification, we do not recognize our reflection in the mirror and come to believe that a stranger is looking straight at us, as if through a window. When people try to persuade us that we are looking at our reflection after all, because the person in the mirror looks just like us, we might reply by finding subtle differences between the way we look and the way the person in the mirror looks, such as: 'He looks *a bit* like me, that's true, but his eyes are smaller' (Breen et al. 2000; Bortolotti et al. 2012). In this way, we neutralize the challenge by offering an additional reason to believe that 'the person in the mirror' is not us. It is someone with smaller eyes.

The capacity to defend the delusion from challenges by elaborating it further is sometimes explained in terms of the *elasticity* of delusions.

> There is more to delusion maintenance than persistence in the absence of supportive evidence: delusions persist even when there is evidence that directly contradicts them. When confronted with counterfactual evidence, deluded individuals *do not simply disregard the information.* Rather, they may make further erroneous extrapolations and even incorporate the contradictory information into their belief. So, while delusions are fixed, *they are also elastic* and may incorporate new information without shifting their fundamental perspective.
>
> (Kiran and Chaudhuri 2009, my emphasis)

Immunity to evidence

In the case of conspiracy theories, there are also mechanisms in place to ensure that the conspiracy belief is protected from counterarguments.

> [T]he very arguments that give rise to [conspiracy theories], and account for their plausibility, make it more difficult for outsiders to rebut or even question them.[...]
>
> Direct attempts to dispel the theory can usually be folded into the theory itself, as just one more ploy by powerful machinators to cover their tracks.
>
> (Sunstein and Vermeule 2008)

Sunstein and Vermeule talk about the *self-sealing* quality of conspiracy theories: evidence against the conspiracy belief is interpreted as evidence for the conspiracy belief. Consider the conspiracy belief that the attack on the Twin Towers on 9/11 was not a terrorist attack but an inside job. Whenever the government reacts to that belief by denying responsibility for the attack and provides evidence for the claim that the attack was planned and executed by others, the government's denial of a third party's involvement is dismissed as an attempt by the government to deceive citizens and hide the truth.

Conspiracy beliefs are as resistant to counterevidence as clinical delusions, but they are not irresponsive to evidence either. In an interview on Covid-19 related conspiracy theories, cognitive scientist Stephan Lewandowsky explains that the relationship between belief and evidence is one of the factors that help distinguish a real conspiracy from a conspiracy theory: 'conspiracy thinking is immune to evidence' (Allen 2020). Immunity to evidence is not the same as irresponsiveness to evidence. What Lewandowsky means is that no evidence for the pandemic being a real phenomenon will persuade a Covid-19 denialist that there is no cover up. This does not mean that denialists pretend that everybody agrees with them, or that they do not recognize arguments against their position. But their belief is immune from those arguments in the sense that they are not going to change their minds under pressure from those arguments.

Our examples show that delusionality is not characterized by irresponsiveness to evidence, but can we explain how responsiveness to evidence coexists with fixity? There is still a strong intuition that something in the relationship between belief and evidence holds the key to delusionality. In the next section, I attempt to vindicate this intuition by suggesting that, despite our recognizing challenges and responding to them, we do not typically give up our delusional beliefs after coming across counterevidence or counterargument – and it is the *unshakeability* of our beliefs that is central to delusionality. I also discuss an interesting feature of delusional beliefs that is related to their unshakeability: giving up a delusion brings about a sort of self-transformation.

Unshakeability

Before I abandon the search for a criterion for delusionality that reflects the relationship between belief and evidence, I want to examine a more promising candidate than either groundlessness, ill-groundedness or irresponsiveness to evidence. I am proposing to call this 'unshakeability', a term often used to describe delusional beliefs in clinical and nonclinical contexts. Delusional beliefs do not need to lack empirical support or to remain unchanged in the face of external challenges. However, delusions are not typically relinquished just because evidence or arguments are offered against them. It is how our commitment to the beliefs resists pressure from counterevidence and counterargument, together with the implausibility of the beliefs, that characterizes the epistemic notion of delusion.

Playing the game

Think of a child who is learning to play competitive games but does not contemplate the possibility of losing, such as five-year-old Pablo playing Snap. Pablo has learnt the rules and understands the objectives of the game. He can shuffle the cards, deal, wait for his turn and he keeps track of what is happening in the game – for instance, he knows that the person who has the most cards is ahead. But Pablo does not accept the idea that the game can end with his defeat. If someone else is declared the winner of the game, Pablo is going to shout that it is not fair, and he is not going to play anymore. Playing Snap with Pablo is analogous to participating in a debate where the other speakers do not contemplate the possibility that they may be wrong and so do not concede anything or almost anything to their opponents. Participants who are not prepared to give up their beliefs may be happy to participate in the game of exchanging reasons, considering evidence for and against the content of their beliefs, receiving challenges, and responding to them. But the exchange will not end with their acknowledging that they should give up their beliefs due to the pressure of counterevidence and counterarguments.

When we have a belief that interpreters call delusional, the unshakeability of the belief does not mean that we fail to participate in the game of exchanging reasons altogether but predetermines the outcome of the game. As seen in the previous examples of clinical delusions and conspiracy beliefs, we often defend the belief by either discounting the challenges against it or elaborating the belief further. The same happens with optimistically biased beliefs about ourselves: no amount of negative feedback will result into our confidence being shuttered if we feel that we are better than average at some skilful performance. If we were not offered the job, it is because that job did not really interest us. If we failed the driving test, it is because the examiner was biased against us. If we lost the tennis match, it is because we had an injury preventing us from playing at our best. Offering narratives that serve as excuses is part of a strategy for preserving a positive self-view – what psychologists name *self-protection* (Alicke and Sedikides 2011). The proposed narratives can be *reparative*, mending the potential damage of negative performance or feedback on positive self-views ('I didn't play well because my knee was injured'); *pre-emptive* ('I did not want the job anyway'), describing the world in such a way that if failure occurs it does not feel like failure; or *redemptive*, integrating the failure as the low point in a sequence of events where the person then overcomes difficulties and obtains success and recognition in the end ('I failed the test the first time because my examiner was biased but then I took the test again and passed') (Costabile et al. 2018). Self-protection is a broad phenomenon.

> Any desired and important self-views that can be compromised by internal (e.g., conjectures, memories, projections) or external (e.g., criticism, poor performance, declining social or financial status) events are subject to self-protection.
>
> (Sedikides 2021)

No matter how convincing the evidence or argument against our belief in our proficiency or superiority is, or how robust the evidence of failure, we will find a way to protect the belief.

Conversions and revolutions

There are some cases where people give up their delusion although these are not the norm. An interesting case where the challenges to the delusional belief are to some extent taken on board by the speaker is the neuropsychological assessment of LU, a young woman with Cotard delusion. She claimed to have died, probably of the flu, a few days earlier and that the hospital where she was staying was heaven.

> LU was asked whether she had ever seen a dead person before, and if so how she had known that the person was dead. LU responded that after her grandmother's death she had viewed her grandmother, and that she knew her grandmother was dead because her eyes were closed and she was motionless. LU acknowledged that the fact that she herself was moving and talking was inconsistent with the typical characteristics of dead people, and she subsequently expressed some uncertainty about her beliefs.
>
> (McKay and Cipolotti 2007)

In this case, LU seemed to be responsive to the challenges made to her delusional beliefs, to the point that the conviction in her Cotard belief significantly decreased and she gave up the belief altogether a week after her psychological assessment. Are delusions really unshakeable?

One way to cash out unshakeability is to claim that, in order to give up a delusional belief, the person's whole world view needs to undergo a change. How precisely the process of rejecting the belief unfolds depends on the details of each case, but some examples can help flesh out this idea. The fact that an ingrained belief can be overcome only by a radical change in the way we think about ourselves or reality is not new. It is well-known to scholars who study religious conversions and paradigm shifts in science as those are cases where for an individual or a group to give up the belief a whole system of values and commitments needs to change. For Thomas Kuhn, science progresses via paradigm shifts: when a dominant theory in a scientific field is overthrown by a new theory, a scientific revolution takes place. What is interesting about the shift is that which theory is accepted by the relevant scientific community is not the only thing that changes (Kuhn 1962). As a result of the dominant theory being replaced, new problems are considered central to the scientific field, what counts as good evidence may also change, and textbooks have to be re-written. Although the change is radical enough to be termed revolutionary in Kuhn's account, this does not mean that it needs to be sudden: rather, the process by which scientists distance themselves from a dominant theory might take years. Abandoning a theory that has been fruitful in the past and had led to significant achievements is not something that can be done lightly or painlessly. There are several similarities between the paradigm shift as described by Kuhn and the process by which people with schizophrenia describe their distancing themselves from their delusions: it is a transformative and yet gradual process (Stanton and David 2000).

Such process is often described in first-person accounts of people living with schizophrenia as *life changing*: maybe the right prescription is found, or a strategy is learnt that helps cope with the symptoms more effectively. Despite culminating in nothing short of a revolution, or something very close to recovery, the process of change can be still long and tortuous.

> As the weeks passed and the medication began to take effect, the world became saner. The voices stopped. Things started to seem ordinary.
>
> (Herrig 1995)

> Ultimately, I believe that recovery can be described as a process, as a vision, and as an outcome. For me, the process of recovery involves changing roles and life goals – it is an intensely personal transformation. My recovery vision is a vision of a life that meets my needs to feel competent, valued, and connected to others. But I acknowledge that recovery as an outcome may not be a symptom-free

outcome. My ideal recovery outcome is a life transformed into which I can integrate new meaning and purpose as well as my decades of lived and professional experience.

(Anonymous 2018)

Giving up a delusional belief in the nonclinical context, such as a belief in a conspiracy theory, may also count as a transformative experience. This is because, as I suggested in the section on evidential support, a belief in a conspiracy theory is accompanied by firm guidelines about how to evaluate evidence and testimony, such as 'I cannot trust the government', 'I won't be fooled by pharmaceutical companies' or 'The press is corrupted so I cannot believe that they say'. For the belief to be given up, those guidelines need to be revisited too: when we start questioning the conspiracy theory, we may also change our mind about how best to gather information about the world and whom to trust. If we have long been sceptical of the role of human interventions in climate change and have argued against the reliability and objectivity of climate science for years, we will not accept the latest climate science projections as evidence against our beliefs, unless something has caused significant parts of our belief system to change, including those relevant to determining which type of information counts as genuine evidence in a given context. The scientific data we dismissed earlier as a fabrication or a piece of propaganda are now evidence for the claim that humans contribute to climate change. Arguments that were previously brushed off are now given credit to.

Moreover, as I discuss in the next chapter, reporting a delusion and defending it against challenges are often accompanied by some sort of tacit or explicit acknowledgement of our superior epistemic status in a specific context. With clinical delusions, conspiracy beliefs and optimistically biased beliefs alike, we feel we have a special claim to knowledge in the domain of the belief. We may see ourselves as the only ones who realize that their co-workers have been replaced by robots. We may think that our social circle is the voice of reason issuing warnings about the unsafety of vaccines to the gullible majority. We may believe that when it comes to assessing our character, we know better than other people what we have done in the past and what our motivations have been. For the delusion to be ultimately given up, this claim about our superior epistemic status needs to be set aside to make room for the possibility that we made a mistake. In the case of delusional beliefs that are shared in well-defined communities, abandoning the belief does not merely force us to enter a different epistemic landscape but also has powerful implications for our social life, political and religious affiliations, and interpersonal connections (Harford 2022).

To sum up then, when it comes to the relationship between delusional content and evidence, it would be wrong to think that all delusions are groundless, ill-grounded or irresponsive to evidence. Instead, what seems a potentially central and distinctive feature of delusions is that delusions are unshakeable. They are not typically given up under the weight of counterevidence and counterargument. The most common outcome of a delusion being challenged is that either the challenge is dismissed, or the delusional belief is elaborated to neutralize the challenge. Various strategies are adopted to 'protect' the belief from revision or rejection while engaging in the game of exchanging reasons. When a delusional belief is given up, it brings a revolution in the sense that a number of epistemic commitments and assumptions need to be revisited and the conviction in the belief is not the only thing to change.

CHAPTER 4
DELUSIONS AND IDENTITY

I started sketching an epistemic notion of delusion: in Chapter 1, I suggested that delusions can be seen as, among other things, beliefs that we report sincerely and with conviction; in Chapter 2, I considered the relationship between belief and reality and argued that implausibility is a promising criterion for delusions; and in Chapter 3, I focused on the relationship between belief and evidence and proposed that unshakeability is another promising criterion for delusions.

Here I discuss the relationship between belief and the self. Not dissimilar from the relationship between belief and reality, and belief and evidence, the relationship between belief and the self can be captured by a number of interrelated notions. The same belief (e.g., 'I prefer homeopathic products', 'I believe in reincarnation', 'I am Norwegian', 'I am a ballerina') can be merely a belief about ourselves or something more: for instance, a belief that defines what kind of people we are, or a belief that reflects our values and commitments (Jones 1999).

In this chapter, I ask what type of beliefs delusions are with respect to identity and make two claims. First, how we form and maintain delusional beliefs depend on testimonial and outsourcing practices (or lack thereof) that are influenced by our self-conceptions and groups affiliations. So, our identity contributes to delusion formation. Second, the delusional belief itself, once it has been adopted, tends to dominate our mental lives, integrating with other beliefs we have, arousing strong emotional reactions, and affecting our actions and decisions. So, delusions contribute to our identity.

One potential explanation for the fact that delusional beliefs are unshakeable despite their implausibility is that, as many other identity beliefs, they contribute to our sense of ourselves and lose the precarity that characterizes many of our more peripheral beliefs. Once they assume the status of identity beliefs, delusions are no longer dispensable. They become so central to our identity that giving them up requires changing how we see ourselves in relation to other people and to the world.

I propose that another criterion for delusionality is that the belief reflects and shapes our identity. First, it emerges out of processes that are affected by our sense of self and group affiliation, reflecting those aspects of ourselves that make up our identity. Second, it moulds the interactions we have with the world, other individual and groups, contributing to how our identity evolves.

Gathering evidence and borrowing beliefs

In Chapter 3, I discussed the relationship between the content of our delusions and the evidence available to us. Can the failure of the belief to be supported or constrained by evidence explain its implausibility? What are we doing wrong (if anything) when we adopt a delusional belief? Do we fail to gather all the information relevant to the content of the belief? Do we fail to properly weigh up the evidence in favour and against the belief? Or is something else going on? Maybe one part of the answer is that when we form delusional beliefs we do so because we trust unreliable sources of information, or we mistrust reliable sources of information.

What needs examining is the role of expertise and testimony in the processes by which we adopt and revise (or fail to revise) our delusional beliefs. Here I suggest that whose testimony we trust and who we consider to be experts in the domain of the delusion are issues that help us understand how the acts of adopting and maintaining delusions reflect, and contribute to, identity.

Expertise

Who is the expert in the context of a delusion? In general, speakers reporting delusional beliefs – whether these are shared beliefs such as conspiracy beliefs or idiosyncratic beliefs such as clinical delusions – claim a special access to the truth in the domain of the delusion. When we report a belief that interpreters label as delusional, we tend to think of *ourselves as the experts*.

For instance, in a report by Roberta Payne on her persecutory delusions involving alien beings, she says:

The Alien Beings were from outer space, and of all the people in the world, *only I was aware of them*. The Alien Beings soon took over my body and removed me from it. They took me to a faraway place of beaches and sunlight and placed an Alien in my body to act like me. [...] I also saw that the Aliens were starting to take over other people as well, removing them from their bodies and putting Aliens in their place. Of course, the other people were unaware of what was happening; *I was the only person in the world who had the power to know it*. At this point I determined that the Aliens were involved in a huge conspiracy against the world.

(Payne 1992, pp. 726–7, my emphasis)

In the passages I have emphasized, Payne makes a special claim to knowledge of the specific events which are the subject of her delusional beliefs. She claims to be the only person to be aware of the alien beings and she claims to be the only person to have the power to know that the alien beings were removing people from their bodies and replacing them.

The kind of attitude that is expressed by Payne is by no means an isolated instance. Claims to expertise or special access to the truth are found in many delusional reports. Those claims also help us realize why the delusion tends to be *elastic* when it is challenged: the attitude of the speaker who claims expertise or a special access to the truth is consistent with the unshakeability of the belief. From Payne's perspective, the interpreter doubting the existence of the alien beings or their evil intentions does not share Payne's awareness of the situation or her understanding of the alien beings' gradual take-over.

In the case of the Capgras delusion, the claim that other people have not noticed the substitution of our family member with the alleged impostor has no force against the delusion. In response, we are likely to say other people have not noticed the substitution because they are not close enough the allegedly substituted person to fully appreciate the differences between the original and the impostor. The thought is that we have a better chance of detecting the impostor, because we can be sensitive to minor physical or psychological inconsistencies that may be lost to mere acquaintances ('He is not as tall as my son').

The case of conspiracy beliefs is also one where we often claim to have special knowledge of the events. For instance, some empirical work has recently shown a strong correlation between the tendency to endorse conspiracy theories and something called 'the need for uniqueness'. This is the idea that we need to feel special and unique:

All humans share not only the need to belong and affiliate with others but also to be different and stick out from them, to be an identifiably unique individual.

(Imhoff and Lamberty 2017, p. 732)

In a situation where is a threat characterized by uncertainty (Tilner et al. 2022), the need for uniqueness is more pronounced because it serves as a means to restore some sort of control over the situation. The sort of uniqueness we claim when we endorse a conspiracy belief is distinctly *epistemic*. We are different from others by being the ones who have a special access to the truth of the matter: 'conspiracy theories place people in possession of *unconventional and scarce information* that allows them to feel unique compared to others' (Lantian et al. 2017, p. 170, my emphasis). This claim to epistemic superiority was evidently manifested among people rejecting safety measures during the pandemic and arguing against the need to wear masks in public places. Common statements were: 'I don't fall for this' or 'It's not what they say it is' (McKelvey 2020), suggesting that denialists believed to be wiser and less gullible than citizens trusting the government and observing safety measures.

The capacity to arrive at a conclusion by ourselves, without relying on other sources of information, is something like a badge of honour, described as a superpower:

Some people are unwilling to wait for the authorities – scientific experts and health officials – to handle the situation. They feel a need to draw on their inner power and solve the epistemic problem through sheer force of cognitive will. They hunt for data in obscure journals (despite having no background in medicine) and recalculate the statistics offered by public authorities (despite not understanding sampling correction techniques). Most of all, they brave the sneering of 'sheeple' who simply accept conventional wisdom. They seek to become an epistemic superhero, a person who can single-mindedly unravel conspiracies and rescue the truth.

(Buzzell and Rini 2022)

Testimony

The need for uniqueness manifested via claims of epistemic superiority is counterbalanced by another need, the need to rely on other people as sources of information. We all have to obtain some information from our *social* environment, by testimony. Testimony is 'an umbrella term to refer to all those instances where we form a belief, or acquire knowledge, on the basis of what others have told us' (Gelfert 2018). Via testimony, we take what other people believe as evidence for what we should believe. How speakers relate to testimony can be crucial to delusionality. On some occasions, we show disregard for testimony as a source of evidence for our beliefs. For instance, Vaughan Bell and colleagues state that delusions 'show a reduced sensitivity to social context both in terms of how they are shaped and how they are communicated' (Bell et al. 2021).

What does it mean? When we have a delusion, we have reasons to discount sources of conflicting information or, as the previous examples have shown, we have more confidence in our epistemic status than in that of other speakers. This leads us to adopt beliefs irrespective of whether other people share them with us and to reject other people's testimony in order to hang onto the beliefs to which objections are raised. The problem is that we trust nobody but ourselves: Kengo Miyazono and Alessandro Salice argue that the adoption, maintenance and elaboration of delusional beliefs can be explained by the fact that we lose testimonial interactions with other people and discount the evidence they offer. Various possible reasons can be found for these behaviours: people with a diagnosis of schizophrenia may experience paranoia and thus mistrust the testimony of others, thinking that others want to deceive them; and people with grandiose delusions may overestimate their own competence, thinking that others are less competent and should not be listened to (Miyazono and Salice 2021).

Although this account of 'testimonial abnormalities' is mostly an attempt to understand the phenomenon of clinical delusions, some of the discussion can be applied to conspiracy beliefs and optimistically biased beliefs as well. Just like people affected by paranoia, those who are attracted to conspiracy theories may not believe explanations of events that are different from theirs. This may be due to their suspecting that official sources of information (such as the government, the press or the scientific community) have evil intentions and aim to deceive. Just like people with grandiose delusions, people who overestimate their own skills, and especially their epistemic achievements, will tend to see themselves as more competent and knowledgeable than the average. This will lead them to discount views that conflict with their own as less informed or less authoritative.

As Miyazono and Salice argue, feeling that we are part of a group is important to our testimonial behaviour, and the effects of group identification are key to understanding what I call delusional beliefs. In general, the evidence reviewed by Miyazono and Salice suggests that we tend to find the members of our in-group more cooperative and sincere than out-group members. Moreover, we tend to trust the judgement of our group members on topics that are not relevant to group membership. For instance, we may trust the testimony of another person concerning which party to vote at the next general election just because they have the same taste in art or adopt the same style of parenting as we do. If group identification affects testimonial practices, this sheds some light on the relationship between different forms of delusional beliefs and testimony.

People with clinical delusions often feel as if they are different from others and they do not belong to any group. This may explain why they do not rely on other people's testimony. If they are without a group, then they have nobody whose testimony they can trust. For people with nonclinical delusions, group identification matters too, but typically they belong to a minority group rather than to no groups. People who are attracted to conspiracy beliefs feel they have a lot in common with those who share some of their values and beliefs and, as a result, they are more likely to trust those who are like-minded when searching for information and assessing viewpoints.

Neil Levy talks about the adoption of conspiracy theories as requiring a *low-trust* condition and a *high-trust* condition (Levy 2019). When we refuse to vaccinate our daughter because we fear that she might become autistic as a result of the immunization, we show low trust for the health authorities who deny the link between immunization and autism; but we also show high trust for anti-vaccination groups who campaign against the safety of immunization. How we distribute our trust seems to depend at least to some extent on group identification: we identify with anti-vaccination groups and fail to identify with people who trust the health experts on this issue.

In some cases, trusting others is necessary. Suppose we are rational agents who carefully evaluate the evidence available to us before we adopt a belief. Sometimes the information we need is something that we can gather ourselves. Our belief that there are ten students in the classroom can be easily supported by what we see when we get to the classroom if we have no visual impairments, no student is hiding behind furniture and the lighting is good. But not all beliefs are like that. Our belief that climate change is caused by human activities is based on information that other people have gathered and analysed, information that (unless we are climate scientists) we do not have the competence to gather and analyse on our own. So, when adopting a belief, we sometimes *have to* rely on evidence that we do not fully understand; and when we have already adopted a belief, we often come across new evidence that is in tension with our belief and have to decide whether to accept or ignore it.

In most cases, our reliance on other people's expertise and our rejection of other people's views are uncomplicated. We trust so-called experts whose credentials and authoritativeness we do not have reasons to doubt. We mistrust so-called experts whose credentials and authoritativeness we have reasons to challenge or whose motives sound dubious to us. So, we come to believe that we have gingivitis after a visit to our dentist because we trust them to provide the correct diagnosis for our health problems. But we do not come to believe that today is a very fortunate day for us even if our horoscope says so because we do not trust astrology to deliver accurate daily predictions of our life events.

Outsourcing beliefs

So far, I talked about the case where we trust or mistrust other speakers as sources of information and thus either rely on or dismiss their contributions when making up our minds. A more interesting case is when we just 'borrow' their beliefs. This is a more direct process, which Neil Levy calls 'belief outsourcing', and can explain the spreading of some delusional beliefs in nonclinical environments. It is also powerfully linked to the effects of group identification I already introduced. Not only are we more likely to rely on the testimony of group members than non-members and we consider group members as more cooperative than non-members, but we also outsource our beliefs to group members. In a way, it makes sense to assume that members of one of our groups (e.g., people in the same religious community; people who vote for the same political party; citizens of the same country) must have similar views and values to ours. If we need to borrow beliefs from someone, why not them?

When delusional beliefs are adopted and maintained, it is easy to blame speakers for following the lead of unreliable sources and identifying with groups who are not well-informed. But Levy takes a different approach, highlighting the role of society in influencing our testimonial and outsourcing practices. On his view, the problem does not lie with how we interact or fail to interact with others – we do not have outsourcing 'abnormalities' – but with how the world from which we gain information is structured. We are victims of 'epistemically polluted' environments where we are systematically misled about whom we can trust.

Levy argues convincingly that our 'bad beliefs' – which overlap with what I am calling here delusional beliefs in the broad, epistemic sense – may well be the product of environments where markers of authoritativeness and credibility do not track genuine expertise and trustworthiness. For Levy, our practice of outsourcing beliefs to other agents explains some of our epistemic problems. For instance, our beliefs may undergo sudden shifts because we realize that someone prominent in our group endorses a belief that we originally did not share, and we just 'switch' to believing what they believe. An example Levy discusses in his book is that of members of the Republican party who initially declared themselves firmly opposed to Trump's presidential nomination and then changed their minds when other members of their party started supporting Trump. Although we tend to think of those sudden shifts as a sign that beliefs are shallow, Levy argues that the outsourcing of beliefs as opposed to thinking things through by ourselves is the way to go – unless we really do have a claim to expertise in the domain of the belief.

Outsourcing beliefs is not only compatible with, but also required by, our nature as social beings – and counts as rational and adaptive. According to Levy, it is *ecologically* rational because, notwithstanding our limitations, it enables us to overcome our ignorance and acquire knowledge by exploiting features of our environment. But it is also *directly* rational because when we are sensitive to what other people believe (especially people we trust, people who have been benevolent to us, or people we perceive as being like us) we are sensitive to evidence, that is, to reasons for believing in a certain way. Without outsourcing, Levy says, we could not do science. In science, we often need to ask other scientists, machines and tools to do the believing for us – e.g., in interdisciplinary endeavours and in cases where machines and tools are required to gather and analyse data. But we also rely on individuals and groups within the scientific community to help us maintain our beliefs and remind ourselves which beliefs we have. The maintaining and the reminding are necessary because we do not have fixed views on everything and, even when we do, we cannot always recall those views effortlessly. Rather, we interpret ourselves as having certain views based on the evidence most readily available to us and existing cues from our environment. We do so in the making of science and in almost everything else, including when we are asked to report our attitudes and preferences on things that matter to us (Bortolotti 2009b).

In many current approaches to delusional beliefs – even those that take into account social influences on belief – researchers look for faults and defects to be identified in individual speakers. We are *ignorant* if we do not know enough science to reject climate change denialism. We are *biased* if we jump to conclusion or seek confirmation for our current beliefs rather than weigh up new evidence carefully. We are *epistemically vicious* if we fail to exercise intellectual honesty or open-mindedness. And we reveal our *impaired* testimonial and social processes (concerning affiliation, group identification and relationship management) if we trust nobody or trust the wrong people.

However, the problem of believing badly or delusionally may not lie, or not lie exclusively, in one of our impairments or deficiencies or in their combination. It may instead derive from the mechanisms governing the division of epistemic labour, testimonial trust and outsourcing which depend on, and are affected by, our individual and group identities. The practices of trusting other people's testimonies and even outsourcing beliefs are not themselves problematic; they are both necessary and adaptive. They are necessary because we need to make up our mind in order to be able to know how to act and what to decide when we have limited time and limited subject knowledge. And they are adaptive because in many cases they enable us to adopt beliefs that serve us well. However, in some circumstances those practices contribute to adopting or maintaining delusional beliefs, possibly in combination with some of the faults and deficiencies that the literature had already identified as causal factors for the formation of delusional beliefs before the rise of social cognition. I return to these alleged reasoning deficits in the next chapter.

In sum, in this section I pointed to interesting research showing that our sense of self and group affiliation affect the information on which we base our beliefs, including our delusional beliefs. Limited sensitivity to, or engagement with, testimony contrary to our beliefs may be a factor in the adoption and maintenance of idiosyncratic delusions. Sensitivity to and engagement with the testimony of people in our in-groups accompanied by lack of sensitivity to and engagement with members of out-groups may be a factor in the adoption and maintenance of shared delusions. In general, a sense that we are the experts, or that we know who the real experts are, seems to be a widespread feature of speakers who report delusional beliefs.

Cheering and booing

So far, I considered whether sense of self and group identification affect the adoption and maintenance of delusional beliefs and suggested that they do so via our testimonial practices. Now I want to ask how delusional beliefs affect our individual and collective identities. What role do beliefs have in shaping our sense of ourselves? The value of good beliefs is not exhausted by their capacity to convey accurate representations of how things are, as captured by the norms of belief that have traditionally interested epistemologists, such as truth and justification. Beliefs can have other roles as well, and some of these roles are connected to our personal and group identities in multiple ways. Here I want to focus on the potential expressive and signalling roles of beliefs, an issue that interests social and political epistemologists. Do delusions play those roles?

Expressing approval

Some of our reports do not (just) convey things that we believe to be true, but rather *express our approval* or *disapproval* towards certain ideas, states of affairs, people or groups. In Chapter 1, we discussed Wilkinson's idea that calling a belief delusional is an expression of an aversion towards the beliefs that is motivated by epistemic disapproval. Wilkinson's view is that calling a belief delusional is not a neutral description of the features of that belief but an expression of a negative judgement: the interpreter disapproves of the belief. Expressivism is an influential view, and some find it especially compelling when applied to ethical judgements. When we state that murder is wrong, the view goes, we are not pointing to some feature of murder that all wrongful acts share and that is objectionable on objective grounds, but rather we express our disapproval of murder.

Michael Hannon argues that, in the context of political beliefs, when we claim that Obama is the founder of ISIS or that global warming is going to be catastrophic, we do not (just) report what we take to be the case. Instead, we do something equivalent to 'badmouthing' Obama and 'cheerleading' for the environmentalists (Hannon 2021). By making those claims, we express our feelings and values: we assert our identity and let others know what we care about and what we stand for. Hannon argues that this explains why political opponents may agree on matters of policy and yet appear to be divided: their actual beliefs about how the world should be like converge but their allegiances differ.

> Whatever the exact causes of polarization might be, it is widely acknowledged that the strengthening of partisan identities has little to do with the issues and almost everything to do with group loyalty and party identity. Once we identify with a particular party, we are

highly motivated to protect and advance our group's status. This is identity politics at its worst. Democrats and Republicans tend to hate each other but this hatred has almost nothing to do with their opinions on the issues. They dislike the other team simply because they are the other team. As a consequence, we have an electorate that is increasingly divided and raring to fight, yet there is a lack of any substantive policy reasons to do so.

(Hannon 2021)

It is plausible that some of our sincere reports have this expressing role: they let other people know about our preferences and values. Expressivism would explain why some Trump supporters do not give up the claim that there were more people attending Trump's inauguration than Obama's even after being shown pictures of the events that conflict with their claim. Surprisingly if the role of the belief were merely to represent reality accurately, but unsurprisingly if the role of the belief were also to express approval, their beliefs do not change when faced with counterevidence but are even more strenuously defended. More generally, if reports were primarily a way to express preferences and values rather than to make a commitment to how things actually are, evidence against the reports could also be interpreted *expressively*, as a perceived threat towards something of value. Being presented with counterevidence would encourage people to be even more vocal about their original views so as to protect their values from being undermined.

A similar analysis has been convincingly applied by Marianna Bergamaschi Ganapini to the sharing of fake news: 'Some members share stories to show full commitment. Sharing fake stories demonstrates their loyalty to a certain group as it can rescind their ties with out-group members' (Bergamaschi Ganapini 2023). Here the role of sharing a story is for us to signal our commitment to a group we already belong to or we want to join. Again, the observation of how the signalling works reveals some apparently paradoxical behaviour. The more outlandish the fake story is, the better, because when we commit to something implausible we have more to lose, and thus our commitment to the group is perceived to be stronger (Mercier 2020). To endorse publicly something that is evidently false is a way for aspiring or existing group members to *prove* their loyalty to the group. In some cases, the fake story becomes an integral part of the group narrative and contributes to the identity of the group as a whole.

Strategic beliefs

Making unusual reports can have the same signalling function as sharing fake stories: it can be done to cement group membership. Daniel Williams argues that, when we utter something like 'The Earth is a flat disc surrounded by a 150-ft wall of ice guarded by NASA employees', we may want to join a flat-Earth group or show our commitment to it if we already belong. The absurdity we report is *strategic* and contributes to strengthening our bonds with people who already believe what we claim (Williams 2022). Williams does not conclude from the presence of an expressing or signalling role that our reports are other than beliefs, mere expressions of feelings or rites of passage to ensure affiliation with the desired groups. Instead, for Williams, the reports can be genuine beliefs with an expressing and signalling role, beliefs that may preserve some of their traditional epistemic roles such as representing reality but also play a role in reflecting and contributing to our personal identity and the identity of the groups we affiliate with.

It is tempting to challenge the representational role of some reports or even their belief status on the basis of the fact that they are both implausible and unshakeable. However, how beliefs behave is not conclusive evidence of what their role is. Surely some beliefs fail to fulfil their roles and some beliefs are more successful at fulfilling their roles than other beliefs. That is why there is no reason to deny that the expressing and signalling roles of beliefs can accompany (rather than entirely replace) their representational role. Once the possibility of a plurality of roles is acknowledged, for at least some beliefs, delusional beliefs seem to be a paradigmatic case of beliefs that do not merely represent but also signal and express, thereby reflecting and contributing to our identities.

Indeed, the idea that genuine beliefs (intended as an investment we have in things being in a certain way) can express and signal as well as represent is suggestive of the distinct sets of constraints operating on beliefs. In my view, it is the key to understanding the complexity and importance of delusional beliefs. As representations of reality, beliefs are subject to epistemic norms in that they are supposed to be well-supported by existing evidence, sensitive and responsive to new evidence, and well-integrated with other beliefs to form a coherent and plausible picture of the world. They respond to our need to understand enough of the world around us to be able to navigate it successfully. So, when their role is to represent, beliefs aspire to be well-grounded, flexible and true. But what do beliefs aspire to when their role is to express and signal? As signals and expressions of preferences and values, beliefs are supposed to be attuned to how we feel and what we value. They respond to needs of ours that are not predominantly or exclusively epistemic, but also psychological, such as the need to feel special and unique, to be part of something bigger than ourselves and to exercise some control over the reality surrounding us.

Offering an example of the social role of beliefs, Williams argues that beliefs that express and signal are formed and maintained so that we can get other people to behave in ways that benefit us. For instance, via our beliefs we may get other people to trust us more, do what we ask, cooperate with us and help us achieve our goals. When beliefs succeed in expressing and signalling, the beliefs are *socially adaptive*. Interestingly, the examples of socially adaptive beliefs listed by Williams (2021) include ideological convictions, conspiracy theories and self-aggrandizing beliefs. Some of those are also good examples of delusions – in the broad sense of delusions explored in this book, across clinical and nonclinical contexts.

This discussion offers us an opportunity to examine one answer to the question why delusions matter. As it transpires from the first three chapters, the mystery of delusions is why beliefs that are so implausible are also maintained with sincerity and conviction, and so tenaciously that they become virtually unshakeable. Maybe delusions do not fulfil their representational role well but are great at expressing and signalling. We would not describe clinical delusions as socially adaptive as such, but some everyday delusions, such as optimistically biased beliefs and conspiracy beliefs, fulfil our need for uniqueness, belonging and control. The tight connection between delusional beliefs and identity explains why delusional beliefs are so persistent once they are adopted and why giving them up requires something akin to a conversion. There are many things we can easily change about ourselves but our identity – how we see ourselves and want to be seen by others – is something relatively stable that requires time and effort to shift. If delusions capture our identity, then changing them requires changing ourselves.

Delusions as identity beliefs

The notion of identity can take different meanings depending on who is using it, in what context and for what purpose. Often, we use 'identity' as we use 'self-concept' or 'self-image', as encompassing our beliefs and feelings about ourselves. In political science and in the philosophical and psychological literature, there are two common uses of identity that are both relevant to our present discussion, social and personal identity (see Fearon 1999).

Social and personal identity

Social identity is about the social categories to which we belong – those categories can be characterized by membership rules, attributes and patterns of behaviour. Being Italian, being a mother and being an academic are some of my social identities. Social categories include 'race, ethnicity, religion, language, and culture' (Deng 1995, p. 1) but also gender, sexual preference, age and socio-economic status. Social identities are essentially labels, although the labels can be of two distinct types: they can refer to the roles we play in society (such as being a mother and an academic) or to other characteristics that may be historical or affect our behaviour without being societal roles (such as being Italian).

Personal identity includes those features that acquire a special significance for us for one of the following reasons:

a) we take special pride in them;

b) we feel they are integral to the kind of person we are or want to be;

c) they guide our actions;

d) they are stable – maybe not impossible but certainly difficult to change.

If the features that make up our personal identity were to change, we would be a different person. Some social identities can also become personal identities: if I am proud of being a mother and I feel that is integral to who I am, then being a mother is for me at the same time one of my roles in society and part of my personal identity. Being a feminist is now part of my personal identity – but wouldn't have been for me as a teenager when I had a very vague and imperfect understanding of what feminism was and I did not identify as a feminist. At that time, being a Christian was part of my personal identity, and now it is no longer, or at least not in the same way. Charles Taylor says that personal identity comprises the 'commitments and identifications which provide the frame or horizon within which I can try to determine from case to case what is good or valuable, or what I ought to be done, or what I endorse or oppose' (C. Taylor 1989, p. 27) but it is an open question whether personal identities are always so tightly linked to values.

When we talk about identity *beliefs*, we can refer to beliefs that reflect our social identities and beliefs that convey our personal identities. The sense in which it makes sense to think of delusions as identity beliefs is the latter: delusions need not be beliefs about our belonging to certain social categories but are often beliefs that tell people something about our 'commitments and identifications'. That is part of the reason why we saw delusions as investments in Chapter 1, because delusions are typically beliefs that do not fade in the background but take space (often too much space, at least in the eyes of the interpreter) and make a difference to the person we think or feel we are.

Delusions, I argue, act as *personal identity beliefs*. But they need not be self-related or self-defining. Beliefs are self-related when they are about facts about ourselves or events that happen(ed) to us. Contrary to what the *Diagnostic and Statistical Manual of Mental Disorders* says, that clinical delusions are about *external reality*, delusions often are about ourselves. Recall some of the examples I discussed in previous chapters, the delusion that we have received a message from god, that our life partner is unfaithful, that we are an underestimated genius, that our mother has been replaced by an impostor, that the surrounding houses are inserting thoughts in our heads and so on. All those belief contents involve the self.

However, in the nonclinical context, there are also delusions that tell us about the world, independent of us. Many delusional beliefs are not self-related: climate change denialism and Covid-19 conspiracies are about the world, about how powerful individuals and organizations have an interest in presenting some events as unnecessarily threatening. These events and their interpretations obviously have far-reaching consequences for our lives and the things and people we care about, but the subject matter of denialism and conspiracy theories extends beyond us and our experiences. We may be characters in the stories that those delusions tell, but not the leading characters.

Unrealistically optimistic beliefs have narrower focus and concern our skills and our future prospects: I am exceptionally generous to my friends, my immune system is better than average, I won't get a divorce. So unrealistically optimistic beliefs are typically self-related and they are optimistically biased only in so far they apply to us, our romantic partners, our offsprings or the groups we belong to. Once we consider the virtues, skills and prospects of other people and other groups whose performance does not reflect on us, the optimism quickly dissolves to leave room for more realistic evaluations.

Some of the beliefs that are self-related can be self-defining but not all self-related beliefs are also self-defining. Self-defining beliefs concern aspects of our identity that we consider as central to who we are as an individual or to the kind of person we are. They significantly overlap with personal identity beliefs. Again, they can be about gender, ethnicity, religion, life history, intelligence, health. They may generate strong feelings, and often be on our minds. On the face of it, a delusion about lizard people invading the earth or about the surrounding houses inserting thoughts into our heads is not self-defining. That said, some aspects of the delusional belief may take special or personal significance: we may be the only ones who know about the lizard people or the houses may be inserting thoughts about ourselves, for instance, thoughts about us being bad, as in the example from the memoir by Elyn Saks. We can see then that the delusion acquires the features of a personal identity belief. A delusion about receiving a message from god sounds like the kind of belief that can be self-defining, as it conveys our importance in god's big plan. We are the chosen ones or the true sons or daughters of god. Similarly, our blaming ourselves for the state of the world or for our life partner's infidelity may be indications of our nature, and convey that we are not worthy, that people cannot but deceive us or that we cannot do anything right. Again, in these instances, we may feel that the delusion defines us.

Not all optimistic beliefs about ourselves are obviously self-defining: I may be absolutely confident of my public speaking skills (in an exaggerated or illusory way) and yet refrain from seeing that skill as a central feature of myself. The self-prediction that my romantic relationship will be lasting and satisfactory reflects (positively) on my partner and myself but need not be something that defines me. However, the optimistic beliefs that interpreters are tempted to call delusional are often self-defining: if I believe to be more generous than average, where this is not a realistic evaluation of my character or behaviour, my belief about my above-average generosity can shape how I think of and talk about myself.

Contributions to identity

Whether or not our beliefs are self-related, at the time when the interpreter calls them delusions, they have likely assumed a dominant role in our mental lives and serve as personal identity beliefs. Identity beliefs have certain characteristics (Aguiar and de Francisco 2009). They are *explicit*: in identity beliefs we refer to ourselves, our experiences or our views; and we are disposed to share those beliefs with others unless we fear sanctions (as in 'I am a Christian'). They are *stable*: as previously highlighted, personal identity beliefs do not usually change overnight. When they do evolve, this typically happens via a gradual, transformative process rather than a quick revision (as in 'I am a Marxist'). They are *emotion laden*: we may feel proud of our identity and loyal to those who share it with us, and we may harbour hatred or mistrust towards those who oppose it.

As already seen in several examples throughout the book, delusional beliefs share those features with personal identity beliefs. We have already amply commented on the stability (some would say fixity) of delusional beliefs. But delusions are also explicit and emotion-laden. Interpreters attribute delusional beliefs to people who report them verbally and in these reports the contribution of the content to reflecting and shaping the identity of the speaker is often transparent or easy to infer. In some cases, the delusion has a fairly narrow content but supports a broader identity belief. So, viewing Covid-19 vaccine mandates as part of a conspiracy will make sense to us if we already oppose invasive medical interventions and mistrust healthcare professionals and pharmaceutical companies. When we claim that we are hosting a tea party whereas we are in the cafeteria of a caring facility for people with dementia, the report reflects the image we have of ourselves prior to the illness, of a person who is generous, hospitable and has an active social life (as in the case study described by Hyden and Örulv 2009). When we claim that the police planted little cameras in our garden to monitor our movements, this sense of being under surveillance may fit our prior experience of being shunned for having a relative charged with sexual misconduct (as in a case study examined by Gunn 2018). Denying the role of carbon emissions in climate change may be one manifestation of an overall concern with the influence of the scientific community on political decisions (Maslin 2019).

Another feature of personal identity beliefs found in delusional beliefs is that their grip extends beyond the narrow domain of their content, being often accompanied by strong emotional reactions. Delusions tend to *spill over*. In the case of clinical delusions, one way of making this point is to say that they exert *pressure*: we are usually 'preoccupied and concerned with the expressed delusional beliefs' (Kendler et al. 1983) and the delusion becomes the lens through which we see the world, colouring all of our experiences. Here is an example of how the delusion *spreads*, up to the point where most of what happens to us is interpreted in the light of the delusional belief:

In each rehearsal of the delusion in the present instance, there is a 'monotonous' spreading of the delusion to new experience […] and, as such, it is both fixed and elastic […]. For example, we interviewed a middle-aged schizophrenia patient with the intractable erotomanic delusion that a college acquaintance had fallen in love with her and now controls parts of her life. Whenever she thinks of him, she hears a 'car beep' or 'trips while walking,' i.e., signals intended to inform her that he knows she is thinking about him.

(Mishara and Corlett 2009, p. 531)

In nonclinical delusions, the belief can be seen as a key to a deeper understanding of the world, it might cause preoccupation and it might sustain strong emotions. Covid-19 denialists who reject the idea of germ-based infection have a belief about how diseases are transmitted. But the belief becomes part of how people describe their views and values. The denial of germ-based transmission and the elaboration of an alternative story about the origin of diseases may reveal a particular way of thinking and making choices, a way that presupposes a rejection of the expertise of scientists and medical professionals. Those who reject germ-based transmission may present themselves as promoters of holistic models of health (see for instance the case of Kelly Brogan as described in Ritschel 2020). They see self-help and lifestyle changes as an affirmation of agency and distance themselves from the use of immunization and medication, which are perceived as unnecessary and unwelcome interferences with nature. Not everybody who rejects germ-based transmission also endorses holistic models of health but adopting the belief may lead one to buy into a whole ideology, which spills over to other aspects of their lives. Or the commitment to a certain ideology makes the adoption of the belief more likely, enabling one to integrate new experiences into a pre-existing system of values.

In a paper drawing an analogy between conspiratorial thinking and religious mentality (Franks et al. 2013), the reliance of the conspiracy belief on principles such as 'Do not interfere with nature' is emphasized as an analogous feature to religious belief. Another analogy between some delusions and religious beliefs is the tendency of the belief to turn an unspecified sense of threat into a specific fear that appears as more manageable or easier to understand, thereby partially restoring our sense of control over it. We might not know about how to deal with a new virus that has caused a global pandemic, but we have ideas about how to stop medical professionals from interfering with our natural lives: we can protest against them and refuse to follow their recommendations.

Delusional beliefs both reflect and shape our identities. They are not always self-related but, when they are, they tend to become self-defining. When delusional beliefs are about the world, then they also serve as or turn into personal identity beliefs.

PART II

CHAPTER 5
DELUSIONS AND DYSFUNCTION

In part 1, I focused on predominantly epistemic dimensions of delusionality and argued that reports by a speaker are described as delusional by an interpreter when they appear to be the reports of genuine personal identity beliefs that are both implausible and unshakeable. But the obvious objection to my way of proceeding so far is that the folk notion of delusion cannot be satisfactorily addressed unless we discuss the nature of delusions as *pathological beliefs*. Isn't that the most distinctive feature of delusions? Not only clinical delusions, but also conspiracy theories are often described as pathological, and they are often dismissed in social interactions and political debates on the basis of that (Raab et al. 2013; Sapountzis et al. 2013). In this chapter and the next I will attempt to show that, although it is common for interpreters to associate delusional beliefs with the speakers not being 'in their right minds', there is no good reason to think of delusions as pathological beliefs.

What does it take for a belief to be pathological? An influential conception of disorder in the philosophy of medicine (a version of so-called *normativism*) says that a belief is pathological when it is harmful. Are delusions harmful? That's a question I aim to answer in the next chapter where I review the various costs that delusional beliefs have been claimed to have. Another influential conception of disorder in the philosophy of medicine (a version of so-called *naturalism*) claims that a belief is pathological when it is the output of a dysfunctional process. Are delusions the outputs of dysfunctional processes? That's the question I aim to answer in this chapter.

There is a third, very influential, account (the *harmful-dysfunction* view) according to which a belief is pathological if it is both the output of a dysfunctional process and it is harmful. If I manage to show that neither the dysfunction condition nor the harmful condition are necessary for delusionality, then I will also have shown that the conjunction of those two conditions fails as a criterion of delusionality.

Let me start with the role of dysfunctional processes in the formation and maintenance of delusional beliefs. Coming to a definitive conclusion about whether delusions are the output of dysfunctional processes is difficult given that the science of delusion formation and maintenance has not delivered any unanimous verdicts. Rather, I will express a general scepticism about the possibility of identifying a cognitive dysfunction giving rise to delusions. Such scepticism is also accompanied by a concern about extending the language of disorder and pathology to mental states in isolation from their context and from other relevant information about the person who has those mental states. When we look closely at how delusions are likely to be formed and maintained, it is far from obvious that they are the output of a dysfunctional process in a way that justifies their being characterized as pathological beliefs (Bortolotti 2022a).

Dysfunctional beliefs

When a belief is described as delusional, the implication often is that the belief is pathological: the speakers are not in their right minds or their brains are not working properly (Sakakibara 2016). When conspiracy beliefs are described as delusional, for instance, the intention is to pathologize the person believing the conspiracy theory, with varying levels of success (Veling et al. 2021; Greenburgh and Raihani 2022). One sense of *pathological* that applies to beliefs comes from a naturalist approach to the notion of disorder and suggests that pathological beliefs are produced and sustained by dysfunctional belief formation and maintenance processes.

Naturalism

According to a version of *naturalism* about disorder, a condition is pathological when it is a biological dysfunction. The pathology can be identified by using the resources of science, that is, in a largely value-free way (Boorse 1977). Take coronary heart disease. When we have this disease, fatty plaques narrow or block the coronary artery used by the supply of oxygen-rich blood to reach the heart muscle. When there is no sufficient flow of oxygen-rich blood, the heart muscle cannot contract properly, and we may experience a heart attack. According to naturalism, what makes coronary heart disease a pathology is that some important biological functions are not being carried out as they should: the coronary artery should supply sufficient oxygen to the heart muscle but it does not; the heart muscle should contract enough to supply oxygen to the rest of the body but it does not.

Now consider obesity. When we are obese, excess fat accumulates in our body. This may be due to a combination of factors, both genetic and environmental. On the naturalist account, what makes obesity pathological – just like in the case of coronary heart disease – is that some important biological functions are not being carried out as they should. For instance, food cravings should kick in only when energy is low. If we experience cravings when energy is high, ingesting more food than is necessary for us to sustain ourselves, then excess fat ends up being stored in our bodily cells. And this contributes to obesity.

But how can *a belief* be pathological in a naturalist sense? A sensible thing for a naturalist to say would be that delusions are pathological beliefs if they are the outputs of a cognitive dysfunction affecting belief formation and maintenance processes. There may be different types of dysfunctions impacting how we form beliefs; however, for *the belief* to count as pathological the dysfunction needs to be a cognitive one, that is, in a nutshell, a dysfunction that concerns the way we process information. Cognitive processes include learning, remembering, problem-solving and decision-making.

The harmful-dysfunction account

According to the *harmful-dysfunction* account of disorder, which aims to combine insights from naturalism and normativism, a pathology is a condition that is caused by a biological dysfunction and is also judged to be harmful (Wakefield 1992). On this view, there are two components: a value-free component for which we need to rely on science to determine whether the condition is caused by a biological dysfunction, and a value-laden component for which we need to take into account our interests to determine whether the condition is harmful. So, being caused by a biological dysfunction and being judged as harmful are both necessary and jointly sufficient conditions for a pathology. Coronary heart disease and obesity are pathological conditions because they are caused by a biological dysfunction and they are harmful, posing life-threatening risks for us.

But how can *a belief* be pathological in a harmful-dysfunction sense? A belief can be pathological in this harmful-dysfunction sense if it is the output of a cognitive dysfunction and causes harm to ourselves. It is important to unpack what being harmful may consist of, and I will try and do so in the next chapter, but relevant considerations may be how the belief influences our other beliefs, intentional states, emotions and actions, and whether it adversely affects our well-being and psychological functioning. Delusions are pathological beliefs if they are the outputs of a cognitive dysfunction and cause harm to us (in a way to be further specified). In the existing literature on delusions, an influential account of the pathological nature of delusions is that they are *harmful malfunctioning beliefs*. Such a view is sometimes explicitly endorsed and defended (Miyazono 2015, 2019), and at other time implicitly assumed in discussions of clinical delusions (McKay and Dennett 2009).

For naturalism about disorder, the presence of a cognitive dysfunction is the key criterion for the pathological nature of belief; and for the harmful dysfunction view, it is one of the two key criteria. Do these approaches offer us a promising account of delusions as pathological beliefs? Here I attempt to answer this question by examining the role of cognitive dysfunction in delusions formation and maintenance. It is worth noting that, although the notion of dysfunction is central to the conviction that delusions are pathological beliefs in a naturalist framework and in the harmful-dysfunction one, the details of what count as a dysfunction – which aspects of the belief formation or maintenance processes are compromised – are not part of our lay understanding of delusionality. Interpreters may associate delusions with a pathology of some kind or some damage to the capacity people have to form beliefs that reflect reality, where the dysfunction might explain the implausibility or unshakeability of the delusion. However, most interpreters do not have a clear sense of what aspect of the process is damaged, and, as we shall see, experts also disagree about what the relevant dysfunction is.

Delusion formation

Are there good reasons to believe that delusions are due to a cognitive dysfunction? The answer varies depending on the chosen theory of belief formation and maintenance. Competing theories reach different conclusions about whether a dysfunction is involved and, if so, about where exactly the dysfunction lies. I am going to briefly consider here predictive coding theories, and one- and two-factor theories of the formation and maintenance of delusional beliefs. (I review psychodynamic and motivational accounts in Chapter 7 as not only do they avoid positing a dysfunction, but they also bring to the fore some potentially adaptive or protective role in delusions.)

Although the aetiological accounts I discuss here have been proposed for clinical delusions, they can be – and have been – fruitfully applied also to conspiracy beliefs and other everyday delusional beliefs. One important consideration is that not all the explanations reviewed here as alternative accounts of delusion formation operate at the same explanatory level – some theories offer a *psychological* account of how we form beliefs, asking how agents explain puzzling experience and weigh up evidence. Other theories offer *neurobiological* accounts, referring to the subpersonal processes by which information is acquired and assessed – processes we are often not conscious of and we do not deliberate about. Another thing to keep in mind is that alternative accounts may be compatible (fully or in part) with one another – they may point to distinct factors that in combination contribute to the formation of delusional beliefs. Even theories that present themselves as direct competitors, such as the predictive coding account and the two-factor theory, which I discuss later in this chapter, can be seen as complementary (Miyazono et al. 2014; Miyazono and McKay 2019).

Thirdly, for some delusions it is reasonable to hypothesize that different factors contribute to the person adopting or maintaining the belief. Let me offer one example of a delusion whose formation and maintenance have been explained by reference to both motivational factors and cognitive deficits. In anosognosia (which is the failure to acknowledge the presence of illness), delusions take the form of: 'I am moving my arm', when my arm cannot move; or 'I can climb stairs but I am a little slow' when my leg is paralysed. Anosognosia has been considered as a pathology *of belief* because there is a mismatch between my description of my abilities and the impairment I experience (Aimola Davies et al. 2009). For instance, some patients claim that they are clapping their hands even when one of their arms is paralysed and they cannot perform the action. They insist that they are clapping even if they cannot see their hands moving or hear a clapping sound (Berti et al. 1993). A more recently discovered case of anosognosia has been studied by researchers working on long-Covid (Voruz et al. 2022): people who were infected and hospitalized with the virus lost the capacity to monitor their own cognitive capacities, stating for instance that their memory and concentration were unimpaired whereas their families and co-workers thought otherwise.

It is plausible that anosognosia stems from a combination of neuropsychological factors (e.g., a damage to parietal lobe which compromises belief updating) and motivational factors (e.g., a defence mechanism in place to ensure that we preserve the sense of ourselves we had before the illness, as self-sufficient agents whose capacities are not irremediably impaired). Denying the change brought about by illness can be attributed to the existing brain damage, as the neural networks responsible for integrating current perception and past memories may be disrupted (Langer and Bogousslavsky 2020). But it may also have psychological origins as a coherent sense of self is instrumental to behaving in a stable and predictable manner (Ramachandran 1996). So anosognosia is a good example of a delusion whose formation and maintenance can be explained by a plurality of heterogeneous factors.

Similarly, the belief that immunization may give my child autism can be arrived at and sustained for different reasons. I may have a history of bad experiences with medical professionals in my life that causes me to mistrust the advice provided by my general practitioner and reject invasive medical interventions. I may also have a personality that renders me more suspicious of authorities, and more vulnerable to conspiratorial thinking. In a recent study (Hornsey 2021), vaccine hesitancy was found to correlate strongly with *conspiracy mentality*, that is, the acceptance of a general worldview according to which elite groups and powerful individuals deceive the public by plotting secretly. Another relevant factor was *identity expression*, that is, the sense that we should embrace a view because it coheres well with other views we are committed to and identify with, among which ideologies and political allegiances. As many other beliefs, a certain attitude to vaccines can be an expression of people's identities and become a reason for preserving existing group affiliations or gaining new ones, as we saw in Chapter 4 when we considered delusions as personal identity beliefs.

Biases affecting information processing can also be part of the picture. In a recent attempt to map the cognitive biases that might affect vaccine hesitancy and anti-vaccination beliefs (Azarpanah et al. 2021), three types of biases were examined. Some biases were triggered by information about vaccines. An example would be the *availability bias*. There is plenty of information about vaccines available for us to read, but what may be easier for us to remember and think about is a vivid report in the media of a child dying as a result of a reaction to immunization. The report is likely to influence our decision-making to a greater extent than the copious data about the safety of immunization programmes. There are also biases triggered by the decision about whether to vaccinate. An example would be the *optimism bias*. We might believe that a specific disease is not going to pose a threat to our child even if it poses threats to other people. On the basis of that, we decide that it is not necessary for our child to be immunized against that disease. Finally, there are biases triggered by prior beliefs. An example would be the *confirmation bias* which is the tendency to rely on information that is compatible with existing views. If we already tend to mistrust doctors and are concerned about the risks of medical interventions, we will not be impressed by arguments about the utility and overall safety of vaccines.

This means that both motivational factors and cognitive processes may play a role in explaining why we adopt certain beliefs and make decisions that interpreters find problematic or objectionable.

A response to uncertainty

The explanatory framework of predictive coding has been applied to the adoption and maintenance of delusional beliefs. The predictive coding model does suggest that some dysfunctional process is involved in the formation of delusions. So the question I am going to ask here is whether the dysfunction posited by the predictive coding account is one that can legitimize the idea that delusions are pathological beliefs. In this section, I review some of the ways in which predictive coding theorists have accounted for the formation of clinical and everyday delusions.

Prediction errors

According to predictive-processing theories, delusional beliefs as a whole can be viewed as inferences under uncertainty and, in particular, responses to situations characterized by ambiguity or threat. Belief-updating and learning differences are observed in those who adopt a conspiracy theory or experience delusions. This includes a higher sensitivity to changes in the environment and a tendency to predict uncertain events inflexibly. On the predictive coding view, the delusion is the default explanation for mismatches between our existing model of the world and new inputs that are due to the disruption of prediction-error signals.

The idea behind predictive coding is that our mind is in the business of predicting what comes next.

> [T]he brain is a sophisticated hypothesis-testing mechanism, which is constantly involved in minimizing the error of its predictions of the sensory input it receives from the world. This mechanism is meant to explain perception and action and everything mental in between.
>
> (Hohwy 2014, p. 1)

We form expectations about our experiences in line with our general model of the world, a model we have constructed on the basis of our previous experiences. In this process, our attention is grabbed by events that are unexpected, because those unexpected events may signal that our existing model of the world is incomplete or inaccurate. If our model of the world does not enable us to predict those events, then maybe it needs to be upgraded so that it will be able to predict similar events in the future. On this approach, experiencing unexpected events is considered to be an integral part of how we learn. When our expectations are not met – and thus a prediction error is coded – we have an opportunity to integrate new information in our model. The revised and improved model can then be used for future predictions.

But when prediction-error signalling is disrupted, our attention is grabbed by an event that does not deserve our attention. We are led to make changes to the existing model of the world even if the model is still adequate. This disruption might manifest in our experiencing an event as particularly salient and thus urgently requiring an explanation, when the event should not be seen as salient and could be explained by the resources already available to us. So, we come to think that we need to upgrade our model of the world in the light of the 'special' event, but that is not the case. This happens because the prediction-error signal is unreliable or imprecise: it tells us that something is off, but it does not tell us exactly what needs to be changed.

The prediction-error theory has been applied to the Capgras delusion. Let us suppose that when a young woman sees her father, she does not get the usual autonomic response that she gets when she recognizes other familiar faces. She experiences an unexpected event which gives rise to a prediction error and she comes to think of that event as salient. The reaction to the prediction-error signal is an attempt to explain the unexpected event and the explanation that fits the woman's experience is a delusional hypothesis: 'This person does not feel like my father and thus cannot be my father. It must be an impostor' (see Corlett et al. 2007). Experiencing the unexpected event as salient results in the woman adopting a delusional belief, where the adoption of the delusion can be described as an 'error of learning'. The model of the world has been altered to include the impostor hypothesis, but the impostor hypothesis is false (Fineberg and Corlett 2016).

Which dysfunction?

As we saw, in the explanation of how delusions emerge according to the framework of the prediction-error theory, there is something that does not work as it should and that can be described as a *dysfunction*. The problem seems to lie in the disruption of prediction-error signalling. The prediction-error signal suggests that our model of the world does not match new stimuli and needs to be changed. The delusion is adopted and maintained as the default explanation for the mismatch and future prediction-error signals consolidate the delusion (Corlett 2018). So, when the young woman meets her father again, her experience is still affected by the lack of an autonomic response. She can explain the experience on the basis of the delusional hypothesis she has already formulated and endorsed. This will have the effect of 'confirming' the delusion and explains how resistant the delusional belief can become to counterevidence. Though her family members may insist that the person in front of her is her father, the woman's experience of the face as unfamiliar constitutes a reminder that something is amiss, and the delusional hypothesis is recruited, again and again, as the default explanation. The formulation of the delusional hypothesis constitutes an error of learning, but arguably enables us to remain in vital connection with our environment (Mishara and Corlett 2009) at a time when our experience of the world is unreliable.

How should we understand this claim? Let's consider delusions in schizophrenia as a further example. The experience of radical change and of uncertainty, of not knowing what is happening, is often reported when people with a history of schizophrenia are asked to describe how they felt prior to the delusion forming: 'It was like a lightning bolt hitting my world [...] It was like I couldn't escape from it. I didn't know what was happening as well' (Bögle and Boden 2022). In the early stage of psychosis, people describe a radical change in experience. The predictive coding account might say that we are bombarded by imprecise prediction-error signals which means that we feel like something important is about to happen to us, but we do not know what exactly we should expect. During this period, things may appear different to us, and perceptual experiences may be more intense (e.g., brighter colours) because excessive prediction errors cause increased salience. The processes underlying automated and habitual learning are disrupted as a result of excessive prediction-error signals because the attention that we usually dedicate only to unexpected events is now required by all the events that appear salient to us, and conscious and controlled processes take over. The delusion is formed to put an end to the uncertainty and the sense of unpredictability caused by the imprecise coding of the prediction errors. The stimuli previously experienced as inexplicable and distressing no longer make demands on our attention and an explanation – the delusion – is offered for the salience of the unexpected events. As a result, automated and habitual learning processes can resume.

The delusion is then stamped into our memory and reinforced in the presence of new prediction errors. The claim that delusions help us stay in touch with our environment refers to the fact that delusions enable us to attend to other cues in our environment because the delusion is there to 'neutralize' the salience of the events that were made salient by the imprecise prediction-error signalling.

> [T]he delusion disables flexible, controlled conscious processing from continuing to monitor the mounting distress of the wanton prediction error during delusional mood and thus deters cascading toxicity.
> (Mishara and Corlett 2009, p. 531)

In sum, what is the prediction-error theory's verdict about whether delusions are the output of a cognitive dysfunction? In the process leading up to the fixation of the belief a dysfunction can be identified: prediction errors are produced in excess and they are imprecise. But what seems not to function properly is the way we receive stimuli from the world. Events are coded as unexpected when they should not be, and the unwelcome effect is that automated learning is disabled. Once the prediction-error signal is there, the belief formation process works as it should, providing an explanation (the delusional hypothesis) for the prediction error. The formation of the delusion is a response to the disruption of prediction-error signalling, and a response that can be also seen as adaptive in that it enables automated learning to resume.

Paranoia

An interesting question is whether the prediction-error theory can tell us also something about delusional beliefs that are not associated with a psychiatric diagnosis. Here I will consider briefly conspiracy beliefs at a time of crisis and unrealistic optimism in the presence of a threat as two instances of delusional beliefs that occur in the nonclinical population. Some work has been done on how we experience increasing levels of paranoia when a crisis emerges. During the Covid-19 pandemic, it transpired that 'people who were more paranoid endorsed conspiracies about mask-wearing and potential vaccines and the QAnon conspiracy theories' (Sutharan et al. 2021). Can the prediction-error theory make sense of this?

In general, in a crisis we feel threatened and the way we revise our beliefs changes: perhaps unsurprisingly, during the Covid-19 pandemic, the levels of paranoia and anxiety in self-reports soared as a response to the unpredictability of the world. But paranoia increased much more significantly than anxiety, showing that what changed the most was our attitude towards other people: we became suspicious of their intentions. As conspiracy beliefs are based on blaming some powerful individuals or groups for a negatively valued event, the increase in paranoia can help explain why in critical situations conspiracy theories flourish. However, paranoia and conspiracy beliefs do not overlap perfectly: paranoia is related to personality characteristics such as neuroticism and introversion whereas conspiracy theories are associated with low trust in authorities (Imhoff and Lamberty 2018; Greenburgh et al. 2022).

Unrealistic optimism can also be interpreted as an issue concerning how we update our beliefs, about ourselves rather than the world. We saw that in the prediction-error model a failed prediction can lead to our revision of the current model of the world. Updating beliefs, though, can be asymmetrical (Sharot et al. 2011). If our prediction failed because we overestimated the probability of experiencing an undesirable event (we predicted failing an exam or being rejected by a loved one), then we take on board the error and correct our model of the world accordingly, making a more optimistic prediction. If, however, our prediction failed because we underestimated the probability of experiencing an undesirable event, then we tend to neglect the new evidence and preserve our 'disconfirmed' but more optimistic model of the world (Moutsiana et al. 2015). This asymmetry explains why positive assessments of our future prospects are difficult to abandon and can become unshakeable.

Beliefs about what might happen to us in the future are important because they drive planning and action. For instance, during the early stages of the Covid-19 pandemic, discrepancies between the expert evaluation of the situation and citizens' perception of the risks to their health might have been caused by a biased updating of beliefs in the light of new information:

> While the World Health Organization had declared a public health emergency as early as the 30th of January [2020], and subsequent evidence had highlighted the threat of a global pandemic, it took many more weeks for many governments and individuals to put into place and adopt precautionary measures.
>
> (Bottemanne et al. 2020)

The factors that can affect belief updating in conspiratorial thinking and optimism bias are unlikely to amount to a cognitive dysfunction. Differences in belief updating can give rise to implausible beliefs, and occasionally drive us to make decisions that have harmful consequences for ourselves or others (Jefferson and Bortolotti 2023). But whether our (lack of) sensitivity to prediction errors is adaptive seems to depend on the structure of the environment (e.g., the world becoming more threatening and volatile) and on the contribution that the resulting beliefs (such as 'The government is not to be trusted'; 'I am not going to catch Covid'; 'I can avoid infection by wearing a mask'; 'Bill Gates wants to control me') make to our chances for survival and reproduction.

Deficits and biases

According to the one-factor theory, the formation and maintenance of delusional beliefs can be explained without recurring to a fault in reasoning. According to the two-factor theory, the formation and the maintenance of delusional beliefs can be explained by a fault in reasoning, in addition to an experiential anomaly or, in the case of nonclinical delusions, some other factor – for conspiracy beliefs this could be a general epistemic mistrust towards official sources of information (Pierre 2020). The difference between one-factor and two-factor theories means that their supporters will likely offer different answers to the question whether delusions are pathological beliefs in a naturalist sense or whether delusions satisfy the dysfunction condition of the harmful dysfunction account.

The one-factor theory

For the one-factor theory of delusion formation (Maher 1974, 1988, 1999), no reasoning deficit needs to be postulated to explain the formation or maintenance of delusional beliefs. Thus, for one-factor theorists, the answer to the question whether delusions are the output of a cognitive dysfunction is a straight-forward one. There is no cognitive dysfunction and thus the delusion does not meet the necessary requirement for a pathological belief in the naturalist account of disorder. Indeed, Brendan Maher – who is considered the father of the one-factor theory – is explicit that clinical delusions only appear pathological to an interpreter because the interpreter does not share the same experiences as the speaker who forms the delusion. If the interpreter could share those experiences, the delusions would not appear as puzzling. Maher goes even further and states that not only the cognitive mechanisms responsible for delusion formation are not abnormal, but they are the same mechanisms we depend on when we do science.

Factor one has something to do with an anomalous experience, often due to brain damage from trauma or to a degenerative disease. In the Capgras delusion, as we saw, one hypothesis is that the anomalous experience is due to a problem with the affective route of the face recognition system. In delusions of persecution, when we believe that others are hostile and threatening, ambiguous stimuli (such as a stranger glancing at us from a distance) might be interpreted as signs of hostility, suggesting that we have a somewhat distorted perception of social exchanges (Freeman et al. 2004). Another factor in persecutory delusions may be mood instability: disturbances of mood are often a mediating factor between trauma (such as bullying) and paranoia, leading us to experience the world as unpredictable and unsafe (Broome and Bortolotti 2018).

Two-factor theories

For two-factor theories, the answer to the question whether delusions are the outputs of a cognitive dysfunction is more complicated. That is because two-factor theorists assume that a delusion is due to the combination of anomalous experiential data or another factor such as epistemic mistrust for conspiracy beliefs, and a second factor which amounts to a fault in reasoning. On one version of the two-factor theory, the second factor is a cognitive *deficit* (Coltheart 2007; Coltheart et al. 2010), so delusions are the outputs of a cognitive dysfunction. In the cognitive-deficit version of the two-factor theory, delusions meet the condition for pathological beliefs in a naturalist account or the dysfunction condition for pathological beliefs in the harmful dysfunction account. In addition to a deficit responsible for anomalous experiential data or an underlying epistemic mistrust for conspiracy beliefs, there is also a deficit that can be described as an inability to inhibit implausible hypotheses in the process of adopting a belief or an inability to revise current beliefs on the basis of counterevidence and counterarguments. For instance, Robyn Langdon and Max Coltheart argue that delusions arise 'when the normal cognitive system which people use to generate, evaluate, and then adopt beliefs is damaged' (Langdon and Coltheart 2000, p. 184).

Thinking about clinical delusions, the two-factor theory of delusion formation aspires to make sense of most cases where the first factor explains *where the delusion comes from*, and the second factor explains *why the delusion is not rejected* (Aimola Davies and Davies 2009). As we saw, the first factor usually consists in a neuropsychological deficit resulting in anomalous experience. The second factor consists in an impairment of belief evaluation or belief revision, that is, a problem with the assessment of the evidence for and against the delusional belief. Such a problem then gives rise to the adoption of an implausible hypothesis or to the maintenance of a belief that is disconfirmed by counterevidence and counterarguments. The adoption of an implausible hypothesis is due to the fact that, faced with disconcerting data, we end up endorsing an unusual belief to explain the data, because we lack the capacity to reject the hypothesis on the basis of its implausibility. This explanation of factor two has faced a number of serious objections: for instance, if it is true that our capacity to inhibit implausible hypotheses is permanently disabled, it is not clear why we do not endorse more beliefs that are implausible and limit ourselves to one delusion or a small number of delusional beliefs. This objection explains why some two-factor theorists consider the possibility that the problem may be caused by a cognitive deficit, but they are also open to the possibility that it may be caused by a motivationally biased handling of the evidence (Aimola Davies and Davies 2009).

In a more recent version of the two-factor theory, the deficit is no longer described as a problem with the evaluation of hypotheses. In an interesting twist, the adopted hypothesis is considered to be the best explanation available to the person given the anomalous data, so no cognitive deficit affects *the endorsement of* the delusional hypothesis. A new cognitive deficit is identified in the inability to reject the adopted belief when it encounters strong external challenges. It is no longer problematic that we adopt an unusual hypothesis as a belief, as the hypothesis explains the anomalous data as well as it can. But it is problematic that we maintain the belief even when evidence against it becomes available. The belief that makes sense of the anomalous experience may not be pathological when it is adopted but becomes pathological at a later stage when it is not given up even in the face of powerful counterevidence (Bongiorno and Bortolotti 2019). So, it is *the failure to reject* the hypothesis that constitutes the problem and the cognitive dysfunction lies in the belief maintenance process (Coltheart et al. 2010). There are some problems with the latter way of identifying the second factor as well.

The cognitive deficit is postulated to explain how the delusion resists counterevidence, and this resistance to counterevidence is identified as the key feature of the pathological belief. But this is certainly not a feature unique to clinical delusions, and more economical explanations of it can be offered than to postulate a cognitive deficit dedicated to it. It is not uncommon to refrain from giving up beliefs that are important to how we see the world and ourselves, especially if there are significant costs in adopting alternative beliefs – and accepting an alternative to the delusional belief can have evident psychological costs if it requires the acknowledgement that we have a serious mental illness. What the theory describes as the result of a deficit seems to be a common feature of beliefs, especially identity beliefs, characterizing forms of cognition that are not usually described as either delusional or pathological – such as prejudiced beliefs, motivated beliefs, core beliefs and instances of self-deception and confabulation (McKay et al. 2005). This concern with the two-factor account has inspired and motivated the bias account.

The bias account

For most bias accounts, there may be several factors involved in the adoption of clinical delusions where one of the factors is a cognitive bias or set of biases (McKay 2012). If delusional beliefs are the outputs of biased reasoning, no dysfunction needs to be posited. That is because deficits are responsible for permanent malfunctions, indicating that a process cannot operate in the way in which it should operate. Biases do not need to work that way. The same bias can give rise to rational beliefs in one context and irrational beliefs in another. This feature of biases as opposed to deficits means that biased processes are not always malfunctioning processes. Thus, in the bias version of the two-factor theory, delusions are unlikely to be successful candidates for pathological beliefs. The bias or set of biases constituting factor two, or one of the factors contributing to the adoption of the delusion, is not a dysfunction, but a tendency to process information in a certain way. Such tendency may be accentuated in those of us who are prone to delusion formation but is something that can be observed in everyone, and that has different outcomes depending on the context (Lancellotta and Bortolotti 2020).

In bias versions of the two-factor account, the relevant bias has been described as a tendency to adopt a hypothesis that seem to fit well the phenomenon we need to explain – the anomalous experiential data in the case of some clinical delusions – even when the hypothesis is implausible and does not fit well with other things we believe. Explanatory adequacy can lead us to believe that our spouse is an impostor if our face recognition system is compromised and we find the face of our spouse unfamiliar (resulting in the Capgras delusion); but explanatory adequacy can also lead a scientist to overthrow a well-accepted theory to account for some new recalcitrant data (resulting in scientific progress). The same tendency can give rise to a delusion and trigger a scientific revolution! Where the data to be explained are not anomalous and are the outcome of well-functioning perceptual and inferential processes, explanatory adequacy may lead to the adoption of true beliefs and prompt the revision of a model of the world that actually needs updating. However, where the data are anomalous and are produced by malfunctioning perceptual processes, explanatory adequacy may lead to the adoption of false beliefs.

Within two-factor models, conspiracy beliefs are also explained by a first factor described as epistemic mistrust resulting in the official version of the events being rejected (Pierre 2020). The mistrust in question is generally shared by well-defined social groups and often directed at institutions – such as the press, the experts and the political authorities. As with clinical delusions, the second factor is thought to be predominantly cognitive and is described in terms of reasoning deficits or biases which would explain the implausibility and imperviousness to counterevidence of conspiracy beliefs.

In the case of conspiracy theories, the bias account is the most popular – probably because no psychiatric diagnosis is associated with the adoption of conspiracy beliefs as such. The second factor would consist in a variety of cognitive biases, such as the so-called intentionality bias, proportionality bias and confirmation bias, as well as various forms of motivated reasoning. The intentionality bias is the tendency to interpret other people's behaviour as deliberate (Rosset 2008). We tend to believe that if an event with bad consequences happens, then someone is responsible for it ('Scientists in a lab in Wuhan engineered coronavirus'). The proportionality bias is the tendency to believe that big effects have big causes. We tend to believe that a significant event must be caused by something equally significant ('The assassination of John F. Kennedy cannot be the result of the actions of a mentally unstable person but must be the outcome of a large-scale conspiracy'). The confirmation bias is the tendency to seek information that confirms what we already believe ('This winter is colder than last winter, global warming must be a scam.'). These biases underlie the ways in which we seek to fill the explanatory gap created by the rejection of the official account of the events and build defences for our own claims, contributing to processes of belief formation and maintenance (Pierre 2020; Douglas et al. 2019).

Although such cognitive tendencies may be accentuated in those of us who are prone to accepting conspiracy theories, they do not seem to indicate a distinctive dysfunction and are a way to cope with adverse events, like seeking a causal explanation for a threat, wanting to restore a sense of control or give meaning to distressing circumstances, being willing to defy apparent counterargument in order to hold on to a seemingly satisfactory explanation (Bortolotti and Ichino 2020). These ways of coping, such as the need to feel in control of our environment and the need to assign responsibility for something unpleasant to someone who is not us, can be related to motivational factors, both in clinical delusions and conspiracy beliefs. On one account of delusions of persecution, for instance, poor life outcomes are attributed to the hostility and evil intentions of others as a response to low self-esteem and to preserve a positive sense of self (Bentall 2003).

To sum up: on the naturalist account of disorder, what would count as a reason for delusions being pathological beliefs is their being caused by a belief formation and maintenance process involving a cognitive dysfunction. But I have shown that processes giving rise to the adoption and maintenance of delusional beliefs do not need to involve a cognitive dysfunction. The one account suggesting a role for a reasoning deficit as opposed to a set of reasoning biases, the deficit version of the two-factor theory, is an account that does not have a satisfactory answer to the question why common features of beliefs, implausibility and resistance to counterevidence, are the product of a dysfunction in delusional beliefs but not elsewhere.

CHAPTER 6
DELUSIONS AND HARM

What does it take for a belief to be pathological? In Chapter 5, I described the naturalist approach to pathology according to which a belief is pathological if it is the output of a belief-formation or belief-maintenance process that involves a dysfunction. I ended on a sceptical note. I suggested that there is no good reason to believe that delusions are the outputs of cognitive dysfunctions.

In this chapter, I am considering the normativist view of disorder, according to which a pathology is a condition that brings harm to the person with that condition. Are delusions pathological beliefs because they cause harm? It is difficult to deny that delusions are costly in some way. Delusionality involves the sense that the belief is costly either to the speaker, to a group or to society at large, but the kinds of costliness associated with delusionality do not directly support the idea that delusions are pathological beliefs. For delusions to be pathological beliefs, they need to be the cause of harm to the speaker. But it is not clear whether all delusions are harmful in that way.

Delusions can have considerable costs for speakers and beyond, and their being costly is often implied by the lay concept of delusion. Whether or not delusions count as pathological beliefs according to normativism, in this chapter I will be able to illustrate with some examples what the costliness of delusions amounts to, in terms of both epistemic and psychological disadvantages. Delusional beliefs can contribute to states of affairs that compromise mutual understanding between interpreters and speakers. They can be accompanied by negative emotions and make us feel isolated. They can be the reason why other people stop trusting us or engaging with us. They can disrupt the pursuit of our goals by shifting our attention away from things we used to care about and redirecting it to concerns motivated by our commitment to the delusional content. They can cause us to misidentify threats and see friends as enemies, or enemies as friends.

Harmful beliefs

In the previous chapter, I sketched a view called naturalism about disorders which sees dysfunction as the criterion for pathology. The key aspect of naturalism is that no values need to be involved in establishing whether there is a disorder – if there is a dysfunction and the relevant processes do not work as they should, we are in the presence of a pathology. Normativism departs from this view by identifying disorders with conditions that are *disvalued*.

Normativism

According to *normativism* about disorder, a pathology is a condition judged to be harmful for the person who has that condition. What makes the view a case of normativism is that a pathology cannot be identified independently of a judgement about the condition causing harm. In other words, being judged as harmful is necessary for pathology. Such a judgement is value-laden and dependent on societal standards and human interests: in a society that places great importance on natural reproduction and for a person who has a strong desire to become a parent, infertility may be a great harm. In a society where there is no expectation for people to have their own children and for a person who does not wish to become a parent, infertility may not constitute a harm.

In a very influential paper, Rachel Cooper, who is a normativist, has unpacked the meaning of disease as follows:

> By disease we mean a condition that it is a bad thing to have, that is such that we consider the afflicted person to have been unlucky, and that can potentially be medically treated.
>
> (Cooper 2002, p. 263)

Other normativists may propose a different set of conditions for pathology, but the core of the account is that the person is and is perceived to be worse off because of a problem that can be at least partially addressed by medical practice. Take coronary heart disease. Coronary heart disease is pathological because it can lead to death or disability and we generally believe those to be undesirable prospects. When our heart muscle fails to contract properly due to lack of oxygen, a heart attack may occur and this may be life-threatening for us. Now consider obesity. Obesity is pathological because excess fat in bodily cells can be a risk factor for diabetes, stroke, kidney disease and other serious illnesses that we would generally prefer not to have. This means that obesity represents a serious health threat. But how can *a belief* be pathological in a normativist sense? A belief can be pathological if it causes harm to us *as a belief*, that is, in virtue of how adopting, maintaining or reporting the belief impacts our lives. On this view then, a delusion is a pathological belief if having the belief is harmful for us.

Harm to whom?

In some accounts of the pathological nature of delusions, such as Kengo Miyazono's version of the harmful-dysfunction account, the disadvantage is also characterized as harm but is intended more broadly, as something that can impact other people and not merely the person with the delusion. For instance, the harm may impact the person's immediate social circle (Miyazono 2019). It is true that delusions can be harmful in this broader sense. It is upsetting for the spouse of someone with Alzheimer's disease not to be recognized at all, when the person with Alzheimer's cannot remember ever getting married and believes to be sixty years younger than they are. For the child of a person with anti-vaccination beliefs it is harmful not to be given the opportunity to be immunized against diseases that might lead to complications. However, here I will confine my discussion to normativist views according to which the harm relevant to the pathological nature of the belief is caused to the person with the delusion. That is because is not clear why the harm caused to others should count as a reason for the belief to be pathological as opposed to merely undesirable.

Miyazono relies on the analogy between the delusion and a malfunctioning heart to motivate his view about the nature of delusions as harmful malfunctional beliefs. If the delusion is to a belief what a malfunctioning heart is to a well-functioning heart, then it is a pathology for the person who experiences the delusion. A delusional belief may be a pathology for us because it may cause distress, just like heart failure is a pathology for us because it may cause our heart to stop. Obviously, a malfunctioning heart causing cardiac arrest can bring costs not only to the person whose heart stops, but also to their family and friends who care for the person's health and well-being. However, the person's malfunctioning heart is not a pathology for anybody else but the person whose heart stops beating. Similarly, the delusion can be a belief with undesirable consequences for many but, if pathological, it is a pathology of the person who adopts, maintains and reports the delusional belief.

So, in the next section, I consider whether having a delusion is harmful to the self, encompassing physical injuries and suffering. Obviously, there are other disadvantages of delusions beyond the speaker's physical injuries and suffering, and I address some of those in the rest of the chapter.

Harmful to the self

Let us start with the view that delusions are harmful in the sense that, when we have a delusional belief, it is having that delusional belief that causes us harm. Is harmfulness to the self a promising candidate for a necessary condition for delusionality? The short answer is that harmfulness to the self is not always a feature of delusional beliefs but interpreters often associate delusions with beliefs that are harmful. In some clinical contexts there are cases in which unquestionable harm is associated with believing the delusional content. Some delusions have such upsetting content that having those delusions leads directly to concrete and severe forms of harm. An obvious example is when we inflict self-injuries due to delusions of guilt or feel scared and anxious as a result of having persecutory delusions. It is tempting to endorse the general claim that clinical delusions (differently from many irrational beliefs that are not thought of as symptoms of a mental disorder) negatively affect our well-being, contributing to anxiety and distress, impaired functioning, social isolation and social withdrawal (Garety and Freeman 1999; Bolton 2008). But it is difficult sometimes to pinpoint the exact role of the delusional belief in the causal chain leading to the harm. For instance, in a study on self-harm in the context of early psychotic episodes (Harvey et al. 2008), it was found that in the great majority of cases self-harm was a response to the stress caused by the experienced symptoms overall and not clinical delusions in particular.

Self-injury and suicide

In some cases, it is the delusion itself that causes the person to harm themselves, for instance when a person is commanded to injure themselves in the context of passivity experiences – which are situations in which the person believes that their thoughts or actions are influenced or controlled by someone else. In a more recent study analysing a large dataset (de Cates et al. 2021), delusions were associated with suicidal thoughts and suicidal attempts even after confounders were taken into account, with depression and mood instability often mediating. Although the evidence does not deliver consistent results, it is fair to assume that at least in some cases it is having a delusion with a specific content that makes it more likely for people to either self-harm or plan to terminate their lives. One example is the case of a young woman who died by suicide after a major depressive episode with psychotic features (Hassan et al. 2014). After examining several factors contributing to the woman's state of mind, the authors conclude that her 'perfectionism' influenced her decision to terminate her life: she had beliefs about being incompetent and she was feeling guilty for a number of reasons, for not taking good care of a close relative who was terminally ill, not being good at school and being a burden to her family. In this case, the woman's delusional beliefs (negative beliefs about herself and her alleged incompetence) had a role in making her feel depressed and hopeless and in motivating her to complete suicide. So, the evidence strongly suggests that in some cases clinical delusions are harmful to the self, but that does not apply to all delusions.

One might be sceptical about the existence of delusions that are not harmful to the self. But in the next chapter I turn to some delusions that are empowering and that give a sense of meaningfulness to our lives (Ritunnano and Bortolotti 2022; Fulford and Jackson 1997; Hosty 1992). Believing that god has chosen us for an important mission may be a source of pride in delusions of reference. Believing that a celebrity is in love with us may boost self-esteem in erotomania. Arguably, the illusory nature of the alleged privilege can cause further harms down the line, including creating a rift between us and our immediate social circle. Moreover, the empowering nature of the delusion may be short-lived and in tension with disturbing features of our delusional worldview – as is apparent in some case studies, the delusion can be at the same time a boost for self-esteem and a significant psychological burden (Gunn and Bortolotti 2018). When it comes to clinical delusions, judgements of harmfulness may vary from case to case, which makes it harder to establish whether clinical delusions as a whole fulfil the normativist conditions for pathological beliefs.

Taking risks

What about delusional beliefs outside the clinical context? Can they also be harmful to the self? As seen in recent comparisons between clinical delusions and conspiracy beliefs, the most striking disanalogy seems to be the presence of harm (Bortolotti et al. 2021). While delusions in the clinical context are seen as harmful to the person reporting them, conspiracy beliefs are typically described as harmless if not comforting and uplifting. But some refuse to think that this is the whole story (Douglas 2021). When we endorse conspiracy beliefs, we might be more likely to make health choices that carry risks or have a negative impact on our well-being. Here are some examples: those who believe that birth control in the United States and South Africa is a way to commit genocide by eliminating Black people will refuse contraception; South African citizens who believe in AIDS denialism are less likely to practise safe sex; British citizens endorsing Covid-19 conspiracy theories have a different perception of risk related to the pandemic and do not comply with Covid-19 public guidelines; in general people with health-related conspiracy beliefs tend not to trust medical professionals and use alternative medicine and those who endorse anti-vaccination conspiracy theories are less likely to get protection from potentially deadly diseases (Grebe and Nattrass 2012; Douglas 2021; Hughes et al. 2022). These examples show that at least some conspiracy beliefs contribute to situations, decisions and actions that have negative consequences for the person with those beliefs – where the negative consequences concern people's health prospects and lifestyle. Some caution is needed here too, though: I said that, in order for the beliefs to count as pathological in the normativist framework, the beliefs themselves should be the cause of the harm. While conspiracy beliefs have undesirable effects and they are compatible with taking risky decisions and actions in some contexts, it is not clear whether they are always the source of the problems we experience or the actual reason why we take risks. One alternative hypothesis to consider is that we are disposed to experience problems and take risks independently of the belief, and the belief offers a post-hoc rationalization of those problems and risks.

What causes us to continue smoking twenty cigarettes a day despite the protestations of our family and friends and the advice of our doctor? Is it our optimistically biased belief that we are very unlikely to get lung cancer because our immune system is stronger than average? Maybe we are already inclined to continue smoking independent of the belief, and the belief is how we respond to friends and family who are concerned about the effects of smoking on our health. Arguably a belief that rationalizes risky behaviour and bad habits is just as costly as a belief that causes harm directly, but it is not clear that it is harmful in the sense that a normativist would require for claiming that the belief is pathological.

Clinical delusions are considered symptoms of mental disorders and conspiracy beliefs are often pathologized as well, but it is not uncommon to see both types of belief described as imperfect responses to an existing crisis rather than as the problem causing the crisis. If the delusion emerges as a response to a crisis and is accompanied by the harmful effects of the crisis when it cannot neutralize them all or neutralize them effectively, then the delusion deserves to be considered as a poor response to the crisis. However, it should not be considered as harmful just because it does not successfully extinguish a pre-existing harm. At least for some delusions, such as delusions in schizophrenia and delusions that can be interpreted as playing a defensive function, the delusion seems to emerge to address an existing problem (Bortolotti 2015; Bortolotti 2016). In delusions in schizophrenia, the beliefs relieve the uncertainty caused by puzzling, unusual experience by providing an explanation for our experience that helps manage anxiety (as in Jaspers 1963). In motivated delusions such as erotomania and anosognosia, delusions make it easier for us to manage overwhelming negative emotions that are due to a previous physical or psychological trauma with which we cannot cope effectively. In such cases, delusions are described as defence mechanisms (McKay et al. 2005) or as doxastic shear-pins (McKay and Dennett 2009), as I explain further in Chapter 7. Although such accounts do not entirely redeem delusions, they suggest that delusions can play some positive psychological role, especially in the short term, enabling us to maintain the motivation to interact with the surrounding environment or pursue our goals at a critical time.

Something similar can be said – and has been said (e.g., Jutzi 2020; Van Prooijen 2022) – for conspiracy beliefs. Such beliefs seem to proliferate during circumstances people fear and are concerned about, such as political instability, poverty and financial crises, conflicts and health threats. The conspiracy belief is often a fairly effective way to replace an uncertain threat which causes us considerable anxiety with a better-known threat that we can get our head around and that we can hope to manage more easily (van Prooijen 2011). It may be unsettling to realize that a new virus can infect humans, spread quickly and cause death and destruction before an effective therapy or vaccine can be developed. Somehow, the idea that a political enemy has created the virus to cause havoc is less unsettling: for an American citizen to blame the Chinese for the Covid-19 pandemic has indubitable advantages. We cannot predict when the next virus will give rise a global pandemic, and we cannot blame anybody specific when that happens. But the prospect of stopping the Chinese from experimenting with dangerous viruses in their labs is a concrete course of action that gives us a(n illusory) sense of control. I return to the potential for delusional beliefs to play a positive psychological role in the next chapter.

Social isolation

There are other harms worth considering apart from physical injuries, suicide, negative feelings and health risks: the harms of social isolation and exclusion. Social inclusion is defined as involving a feeling of acceptance and the capacity to participate in social activities, and is hindered by negative stereotypes. Such stereotypes for mental illness include people being considered as dangerous, unpredictable and unintelligent (Hall et al. 2019). Stereotypes are negative beliefs about people belonging to a specific group, and prejudice is the endorsement of those stereotypes, which can give rise to a number of beliefs (e.g., 'People who have delusions are dangerous') and emotions such as fear of people who have delusions. In turn, prejudice can lead to discrimination, which is the behavioural reaction to prejudice: typical behavioural reactions to people against whom there are negative stereotypes include social distance and exclusion – 'I don't want to be with them'; 'They shouldn't be here' – and sometimes, when anger is involved, hostility emerges too (Corrigan and Watson 2002). Discrimination deprives people with delusions of opportunities in many areas of life including housing and employment. There are two forms of stigma: public stigma and self-stigma. In the latter case, we have a negative stereotype about ourselves (e.g., 'I am weak') that is conducive to low self-esteem and affects behaviour as well, preventing us from pursuing valuable opportunities.

In some countries, anti-stigma campaigns and interventions have reduced exclusion by countering negative stereotypes about mental illness. However, stigma is still rife and it is particularly damaging in the case of delusions: for instance, it has been shown that the labels of schizophrenia and psychosis elicit the stereotype of dangerousness – this has very powerful effects leading people to develop strong negative emotions against the person with mental illness and increase social distance (Link et al. 1999; Angermeyer and Matschinger 2003). It is interesting that this is true of schizophrenia and psychosis but does not seem to apply to other diagnostic labels, such as major depression. In popular culture, such as in the depiction of people with mental illness and in particular clinical delusions in films and novels, there are some dominant stereotypes that can be very damaging: one is that the person is *dangerous*, and thus should be avoided or confined; and the other is that the person is *childlike and irresponsible*, unable to make decisions of their own, and thus needs to be taken care of and to be told what to do.

When Todd Phillips's film *Joker* was released, there was an interesting discussion among critics about whether the portrayal of Joker interpreted by Joaquin Phoenix was perpetrating harmful stereotypes about psychotic illness. In the film, Joker has grandiose delusions, as well as other symptoms. A review in the *Guardian* expressed concerns about the effects of the film on attitudes towards mental illness:

> Portrayals of mental illness in film can perpetuate unfounded stereotypes and spread misinformation. One of the more toxic ideas that Joker subscribes to is the hackneyed association between serious mental illness and extreme violence. The notion that mental deterioration necessarily leads to violence against others – implied by the juxtaposition of Phoenix's character Arthur stopping his medication with his increasingly frequent acts of violence – is not only misinformed but further amplifies stigma and fear.
>
> (Driscoll and Husain 2019)

Conspiracy beliefs have also been shown to attract social stigma and researchers point to two distinct sources of prejudice: first, conspiracy theories are considered to be 'invalid knowledge', so they are discredited epistemically and often associated with epistemic vices, gullibility or ignorance; and second, when we endorse a conspiracy theory, we may not be taken seriously due to being perceived as part of a 'social fringe' and not the 'mainstream' (Barkun 2015; Thalmann 2019). A third source of prejudice is the perceived correlation between conspiracy theories and paranoia and the idea that conspiracy beliefs are themselves a sign of mental illness. For a combination of these reasons, when we defend conspiracy theories, we expect to be challenged and socially excluded, but this expectation is reduced when we defend conspiracy theories in interactions with members of our social groups (Lantian et al. 2018).

Do the harms of negative stereotype, prejudice and discrimination derive from believing the content of the delusion? The stigmatization and subsequent social isolation we sometimes experience when we report a delusional belief are an effect of the way in which our social context responds to our nonmainstream belief. When we endorse delusional beliefs, we lose credibility and authority in the eyes of our peers and may attract negative judgements leading to our being silenced or ridiculed.

In a more tolerant environment, endorsing the same beliefs would not have the same damaging effects. Once again, it seems important to distinguish the harm of having the belief, of believing that the world fits the delusional hypothesis, from the harm of reporting the belief in a potentially hostile environment. The harm associated with stigmatization and social isolation is not to be attributed to the delusion itself, or at least not exclusively, but to the attitudes towards neurodivergent behaviour and in general towards behaviour that does not conform to the social and conventional norms that are accepted in society as a whole or in a specific social group.

To sum up, for a belief to be pathological, the belief itself should be harmful. The challenge in claiming that delusions are pathological beliefs in the light of normativism is that often what we know about delusions does not enable us to determine whether the harm is caused by having the beliefs; is caused by something else but ultimately explains why the beliefs are adopted or maintained – as when the beliefs act as post-hoc rationalizations; or happens alongside the adoption, maintenance or reporting of the belief.

The harm-based account fares better than the naturalist account in establishing which beliefs need medical attention: the presence of harm does seem a sufficient reason for seeking help from medical professionals, and this applies both to delusional beliefs and other beliefs associated with experienced harm. However, if the presence of harm is sufficient for the purpose of demarcating what needs medical support, it would appear that we do not need a further judgement that the belief is pathological to justify the appropriateness of medical intervention – especially if the judgement about the pathological nature of the belief depends on identifying with some precision the causal factors responsible for the harm to be experienced, which is a serious challenge given that the relevant factors can be multiple and be related in ways that it is not always possible to disentangle (Bortolotti 2020b).

Having set aside the question about the pathological nature of delusional beliefs, I should ask whether being harmful to the self is a condition for attributions of delusionality. Although being harmful to the self is a common feature of delusions, and interpreters often associate delusional beliefs with dangerousness, harmfulness does not seem to be a feature of all delusions in the narrow sense that I have considered here. Is being harmful in general, including harmful to others, a more promising condition?

Harmful to others

As I discussed in the previous section, it is not straight-forward to establish whether delusional beliefs are harmful to the self in the sense that having the beliefs is *the cause of* the harm. Will it be easier to establish whether delusional beliefs are harmful to other people? Although harmfulness to others is arguably not a condition for being a pathological belief, it is definitely a reason to consider the belief undesirable and costly. So, in this section I am considering whether delusions are harmful to others. Predictably, the answer will be that some are.

Motivating violence

There is a widespread assumption that acts of violence such as mass shootings are driven by the actions of people who have delusional beliefs. This is an oversimplification and does not take into account some of the societal factors that increase the probability of people perpetrating violent acts:

> Certain psychiatric symptoms, such as paranoid delusions with hostile content, are highly nonspecific risk factors that may increase the relative probability of violence, especially in the presence of other catalyzing factors such as substance intoxication. Yet the absolute probability of serious violent acts in psychiatric patients with these 'high risk' symptoms remains low. In general, focusing on individual clinical factors alone leaves too much unexplained, as it tends to ignore the important social contexts surrounding mass shootings and multiple-victim homicides.
>
> (Metzl et al. 2021, p. 82)

As Metzl and colleagues argue, even when the focus remains on the psychological features of the perpetrator, anger and social deviance predict violent acts much more reliably than psychotic symptoms such as the presence of clinical delusions. A very high-profile case that brought to the fore the need to better understand the relationship between mental illness and violence, and in particular the role of delusional beliefs, is that of Anders Breivik (Bortolotti et al. 2014). Breivik – who authored a manifesto for the 'cultural independence of Europe', openly opposing multiculturalism, Islam and feminism – killed seventy-seven people in Norway in July 2011. In his first psychiatric evaluation, he was diagnosed with paranoid schizophrenia and his most implausible beliefs were regarded as bizarre delusions. With a diagnosis of psychosis, Breivik would have not been accountable for his actions, because one cannot be attributed criminal responsibility for action in the Norwegian Criminal Procedure Code if one has psychotic symptoms (such as delusions). Breivik would have been regarded as criminally insane and sentenced to compulsory psychiatric treatment.

However, this first assessment was overruled. A second pair of assessors diagnosed Breivik with a narcissistic personality disorder accompanied by pathological lying. Some commentators like Ingrid Melle (2013) believed that Breivik had schizophrenia all along, but his symptoms were less florid at the time of the second assessment, which occurred several months after the crime. Given the new diagnosis of narcissistic personality disorder, Breivik was held accountable for his actions and he was sentenced to twenty-one years in prison in August 2012. Ten years later he applied for parole, but his bid was rejected on the ground that his views and psychological profile had not changed, and he was still posing a risk to society.

During the first assessment, Breivik reported a number of delusional beliefs (in the broad sense of 'delusional' I am using here). Some delusional beliefs were bizarre and idiosyncratic: he claimed to be the ideological leader of a Knights Templar organization, he said that he would soon become the new regent of Norway, and he believed that he could decide who was to live and die in the nation. He also had beliefs that were shared by extremist groups, such as anti-Islamic beliefs and other beliefs about the dangers of multiculturalism. Both sets of beliefs had the features of delusions I have discussed so far: implausibility, unshakeability and centrality to identity. But was it having those beliefs that led him to murder so many people? In this case, there seems to be a direct link between the content of Breivik's beliefs and his actions, suggesting that the beliefs might have motivated him to act in the way he did. Obviously, it is difficult to exclude the role of cognitive or neuropsychological impairments that might have impacted on his decision to commit the crime, and it is possible that his beliefs had the role of rationalizing his actions in addition to, or instead of, motivating them.

There are other, less high-profile, cases in which violent acts seem to stem directly from the delusional belief and are likely to cause reoffending. John Junginger (2006) reports the case of DJ, a young woman who came to believe that she was the daughter of a famous entertainer who had recently died. Subsequently she also believed that the entertainer was not really dead but had to go underground to round up all his daughters. This had to be done secretly as there were sinister forces (the 'opposition') wanting to prevent the reunion. DJ came to believe that she could recognize members of the opposition. When someone at the till of a gas station where she had refuelled her car asked her whether she had everything she needed, DJ interpreted this as a clue that the person knew about the plans for the reunion and wanted to stop her. So, she attacked him and injured his hand and arm with her car keys, claiming later that she wanted to stop him from reaching the phone and informing the rest of the opposition of her plans. DJ was treated and her delusion seemed to fade for a time, but after she stopped taking medication and engaging with her care team, the delusion returned, and DJ attacked another person who she thought was working for the opposition. According to Junginger, this is an interesting case of a delusion that persists over time and continues to motivate violent actions – and there are some other clinical delusions that present similar features.

In the Breivik case, extremism is bound to have had as much responsibility for motivating his murderous actions as his more idiosyncratic beliefs about being the new regent of Norway. This suggests that delusional beliefs that are not necessarily associated with a psychiatric diagnosis can also give rise to violent actions. A common view is that conspiracy beliefs make extremist violent actions more likely and recent evidence suggests that there is a strong correlation between the two. Rottweiler and Gill (2020) report that, according to the FBI, '[w]idespread and easily assessible fringe political conspiracy theories may drive those with extremist attitudes towards conducting extremist violence'. Based on their study on a German population, they argue that 'stronger conspiracy mentalities lead to increased violent extremist intentions', especially when people score low in self-control, have weak law-relevant morality and score high self-efficacy. The idea is that conspiracy beliefs, by directing attention to a common enemy with evil intentions, justify the use of violence (Bartlett and Miller 2010). There are numerous examples of conspiracy theories leading to objectionable acts, including the role of QAnon in the Capitol attacks in the United States in 2021. The attacks to the Capitol involved assaulting police officers to manifest support for Trump and it is believed that many of the people involved were influenced by QAnon beliefs (Basit 2021).

According to QAnon, President Trump is a hero who aims to shut down a Satan-worshipping network of powerful paedophiles working in politics, business and the media. The conspiracy theory started in 2017 but grew during the pandemic in 2020. QAnon supporters claim that Covid-19 was a stratagem so that people would be distracted and forget about the issue of child sex-trafficking. QAnon is currently very popular in the United States – in 2022 a survey found that 7 per cent of Americans still believed the conspiracy theory. Most of the actions justified by QAnon conspiracy beliefs involve online abuse directed to people who are thought to be part of the paedophile ring. But on some occasions, the conspiracy inspired violent action offline too. For instance, in 2018 a man blocked a bridge over the Hoover Dam in Colorado for 90 minutes, and it was later discovered that he was armed with two assault-style rifles, two handguns and 900 rounds of ammunition. His intentions were not clear, but he pleaded guilty to making a terrorist threat and he used the language of the QAnon conspiracy theory to explain his actions in a letter from prison.

According to Basit, the link between conspiracy theories and violent extremism is not purely coincidental. There are some common elements between them: (1) distrust of institutions and rejection of mainstream narratives; (2) the need to overcome a sense of powerlessness by adopting a simplistic explanation of significant events; (3) an 'us versus them' ideology where the distinction between in-group and out-group is sharp and polarization is intensified; (4) a perception of there being a serious threat that originates in powerful others. That said, according to Basit, violent action is a defining characteristic of extremist ideology but not of conspiracy beliefs, and the adhesion to conspiracy theories is not a necessary condition for violent action. Although conspiracy theories can inspire violence, they are only one of a number of factors leading to it. One suggestion is that for violent extremist groups the use of conspiracy theories is strategic and serves to make certain types of action appealing to a wider public:

> Violent extremists employ CT [conspiracy theories] as a 'rhetorical device' to advance their ideologies, identify scapegoats and legitimise use of (indiscriminate) violence. Violent extremist groups exploit conspiracies which have strong emotional appeal, such as pedophilia, child abduction, freedom struggles and victimhood narratives, to increase their influence and outreach in their immediate societies.
>
> (Basit 2021, p. 4)

Undermining relationships

A popular view is that conspiracy theories damage participation in public life, leading either to political apathy (such as abstention from voting) or to extremist views with the potential for action (such as violent protest). Both apathy and extremism are thought to have the overall effect of undermining the bases for democracy.

The somewhat surprising result of a recent study is that, when we are inclined to believe conspiracy theories, we do not withdraw support from all forms of democratic governance, but we strongly prefer *direct democracy* to *representative democracy* (Pantazi et al. 2022). Electing representatives to make decisions on our behalf seems to increase feeling of mistrust and cynicism whereas directly voting for a policy as via a referendum is a way to enhance the sense that we can actively intervene and leave a mark on the political scene, reducing feelings of powerlessness. One key aspect of direct democracy is that the political elites are invested of less executive power, and citizens are involved in active decision-making.

> [P]eople who believe conspiracy theories do not reject the current democratic system because they resent democratic values; instead, they reject it partly because they consider it insufficiently democratic, and they prefer a different form of democracy that puts the power more directly in the hands of citizens.
>
> (Pantazi et al. 2022)

Another charge levied to conspiracy theories is that they delegitimize those institutions on which we should rely for the production of reliable knowledge. By encouraging us to disdain experts and do without them, conspiracy beliefs are a threat to democracy: 'Insofar as it delegitimates knowledge-producing institutions, conspiracism also incapacitates democratic government' (Rosenblum and Muirhead 2019). But if it is true that when we are attracted to conspiracy theories we are concerned about there being intermediaries (people we do not necessarily trust) between ourselves and the lives we want to build, then the rejection of expertise as a source of power in decision making is not surprising. If we are not the designated experts, we feel excluded and powerless because we think that we do not have a voice. As we do not like the idea of electing representatives to approve policies for us, we may not like the idea that scientists and journalists are there to tell us what to think and what to do. After all, as I suggested in Chapter 4, when we have delusions, we believe that *we* are the experts in the domain of the delusions and we are not likely to defer to others, especially to members of out-groups.

In addition to compromising the effectiveness of forms of government that are based on participation in public life, some interesting studies have shown that the distrust towards institutions typically found in conspiracy beliefs is also responsible for worse interpersonal relationships. In the words of van Prooijen and colleagues (2022), 'when people perceive societal institutions to be of low quality, it also deteriorates the quality of their social relationships.' The first aspect of low trust in institutions affecting interpersonal relationships is the sense of security. If citizens feel that their interests are not safeguarded and they are not protected from exploitation by their institutions, then they will take fewer risks for the benefit of interpersonal cooperation, and stop trusting other citizens for fear of corruption and unfairness. This may result in polarization and conflict between different groups. Indeed, polarization between Republicans and Democrats in the United States and the rise of populism in Europe have been associated with particularly low trust in political leaders. In general, feeling less secure and less protected leads to being more suspicious towards people who behave and think differently, and also to expressing more anger.

The second aspect of low trust in institutions that erodes interpersonal relationships concerns the perceived failure of institutions to serve as role models. Institutional norms are considered as a template for group norms. If citizens believe that their institutions are fair and honest, they will try to reproduce fairness and honesty in their own relationships and groups. But if they come to believe that institutions are unfair and corrupted instead, they will have fewer incentives to adhere to norms of fairness and honesty in their relationships and within their groups (Jefferson and Bortolotti 2023). As a result, low levels of prosocial behaviour and cooperation are experienced.

> [E]xperimentally exposing participants to the conspiracy theory that the British government murdered Princess Diana reduced participants' political engagement (e.g., voting, donating money to political candidates or parties). [...] Exposure to climate change conspiracy theories [...] decreased participants' willingness to reduce their carbon footprints.
>
> (Jolley and Douglas 2014)

Conspiracy beliefs can undermine the perception that institutions are trustworthy and thus be partially responsible for the apathy, anger and suspiciousness I discussed here. However, even the researchers establishing a connection between conspiratorial thinking and lack of participation in public life, and between conspiratorial thinking and the poor quality of interpersonal relationships, recognize that the key element for improving outcomes is to ensure that institutions become more trustworthy so that citizens feel that they can rely on such institutions at difficult times. Some conspiracy theories unfairly represent institutions as being untrustworthy but there are also actual cases of low integrity and corruption that are deeply damaging. According to van Prooijen and colleagues (2022), we should ensure more 'transparency in decision-making, and increased contact between institutional representatives and citizens' to limit the appeal and spreading of conspiracy beliefs and repair our trust in the institutions.

Being costly

In this chapter I have offered reasons to think that, on occasion, delusional beliefs can be harmful to the person who reports the beliefs and to others – although it is possible that in at least some of the situations we discussed delusional beliefs were not the main source of harm. Although not all delusions are harmful to the self or harmful to others, all delusions are perceived as costly by interpreters and their being costly contributes to the judgement that the beliefs are indeed delusional.

Costliness as I intend it here is somewhat a vaguer and less demanding notion than harmfulness. Although the delusion of grandeur that Breivik is the new regent of Norway and has power over who lives and dies may have explained some of his violent actions or might have appeared in his post-hoc rationalizations of his behaviour, it is unlikely to have been the main reason for his committing a mass murder. That does not mean that Breivik's delusion is not costly – attempting to justify an ominous act is objectionable and problematic in its own right. Similarly, the belief that Trump was involved in crushing a paedophile ring was probably not the main reason why his supporters attacked the Capitol in 2021, and yet the belief might have been used to try and persuade some hesitant individuals and groups to join the protests by presenting Trump as a hero for whom some serious risks were worth taking.

Delusions are costly in epistemic and psychological ways, as our discussion in the previous chapters has suggested. In Chapters 2 and 3 I argued that delusional beliefs are implausible and unshakeable and by compromising our understanding of the world around us and of ourselves they present considerable epistemic and psychological costs. When, despite receiving copious negative feedback from friends and family, and remembering accurately the poor outcome of the races in which we participated in the past, we are unable to predict that we will arrive last in the next race, the delusion that this year we can run fast enough to win the race will leave us unprepared for the inevitable disappointment.

In Chapter 4 I explained that we tend to ignore the testimony of others in the area of the delusion because we are convinced that we are the experts in that area. This tells us something interesting about delusions, that they disrupt something we should care about, the division of labour we need to rely on when we want to understand the complex world around us. Epistemically we are worse off if we cannot recognize that we need to trust other people's knowledge in understanding complex situations and making important decisions about our lives. We saw that one of the roles of belief is to help us coordinate and communicate with others (Williams 2022). If delusions are beliefs that play that role badly, and prevent us from interacting with others in a way that would be mutually beneficial, this is by itself a reason to think of them as epistemically costly.

One interesting claim is that, when we have a delusion, we become unable to identify and exploit group alliances around the theme of the delusion that would improve our capacity to make good decisions. In this kind of situation, delusions are costly and maladaptive beliefs because they arise out of, and persevere due to, our inability to work together with other people in gaining and vetting information. Delusions prevent us from interacting with the world or with others in a way that would lead us to fulfil our goals.

CHAPTER 7
DELUSIONS AND MEANING

In Part 1, I considered some epistemic features of delusions and in particular their being implausible and unshakeable identity beliefs. Then, in Chapters 5 and 6, I challenged the common conception of delusions as pathological beliefs, on the basis that delusions are not always the outcome of dysfunctional processes of belief formation and maintenance, and they are not always a source of harm for speakers. However, we saw that delusions are imperfect explanations for significant experiences and life events, often fuelled by biases and motivational factors, and that most delusions have epistemic and psychological costs for speakers and for others.

In this chapter, I consider a potential feature of delusions that has not been discussed as much as the negative features of delusions I reviewed so far. Delusions can be beneficial. This is an important feature: it is by recognizing the advantages of adopting or maintaining delusional beliefs that we can better understand why delusions are so persistent in spite of their implausibility, unshakeability and costliness. We can also make room for a more nuanced assessment of delusions. Although delusions are disruptive, as shown in the previous chapter, they also present some benefits that are not always appreciated when attributions of delusionality are made. An appreciation of the benefits of delusions can assist us in interpreting people whose identity beliefs we do not share: although we may have different experiences, life events, values and goals, we may be able to understand why a delusion is attractive to them.

The implausibility and unshakeability of delusional beliefs are often considered signs of a mind that does not work as it should, and the costliness of the belief is seen as a reason to abandon the belief without regret. But there is a different side to delusions, in line with the old psychoanalytic idea that delusions are restorative, and more recent explorations of the idea that delusions respond to a crisis that is not of their own making. Delusions may be adaptive (Lancellotta and Bortolotti 2019), psychologically (McKay and Dennett 2009), biologically (Fineberg and Corlett 2016) and even epistemically (Bortolotti 2016). Delusions can serve a function and that explains their adoption and their resilience, showing that accounts of delusions as mere outcomes of a dysfunction are overall unsatisfactory (Garson 2022). If delusions are adaptive as well as costly, then maybe the delusional mind is not (just) a defective mind, and caution will be needed when the delusional belief is abandoned. As a result of rejecting the delusion, some of its costs may be foregone, but also its restorative or protective role.

Coping with unpleasant realities

In the previous chapter, I argued that not all delusions cause harm, and some delusions that are harmful also have some benefits. What benefits could delusions possibly have? In the deficit and bias accounts of delusions I discussed in Chapter 5 the premise is that belief formation and maintenance processes work in a suboptimal way. But there are other accounts of delusions aiming at identifying what role delusions play in the overall economy of our mental lives. In psychoanalytic accounts, for instance, delusions serve as a defence and they are an attempt to relieve anxiety and other negative emotions (see discussion in McKay et al. 2005). By presenting a desired reality as the actual reality, some delusions can empower us, and contribute to the sense that our lives are meaningful (check the case study in Ritunnano et al. 2022). In delusions of reference and of grandeur, for instance, we come to think of ourselves as having an important mission or as having a talent that is unfairly dismissed by others. We can feel as if it is in our power to achieve something significant (e.g., Fulford and Jackson 1997; Hosty 1992). On deficit and bias accounts, delusions represent what is weak in human cognition and agency, the distortion of reality and the strenuous resistance to counterevidence that count as epistemic failures. But, on alternative accounts, delusions can also represent what is strong about human cognition and agency, as the distortion of reality and the strenuous resistance to counterevidence are the means by which we manage negative feelings and restore some sense of control over the world around us.

From the point of view of interpreters, the delusion is a speaker's unshakeable identity belief, but it should not be, because it is also implausible and costly. But as speakers with our own unshakeable identity beliefs it may be unsettling to realize that there are interpreters out there who consider our cherished beliefs both implausible and costly. Considering the speakers' perspective when we play our role as interpreters and asking whether there is anything that their delusions offer to them can help make sense of the speakers' behaviour. It can also mend the explanatory gap between interpreters and speakers that gives rise to claims of un-understandability and may lead to prejudice.

Psychodynamic accounts

Although psychodynamic accounts of delusional beliefs are no longer popular, for some time they were the standard explanation for clinical occurrences of delusions. When we have Capgras delusion we come to believe that a person close to us has been replaced by an impostor. The delusion is called 'Capgras' from the name of the French psychiatrist who first described in some detail cases of people affected by this delusion. In one of his published case studies, Capgras defends the view that the delusion may be a way for us to resolve a *psychological conflict* (Capgras and Carette 1924). He discusses the case of a woman with schizophrenia who thought that her father had been substituted. He associates the delusion with the Oedipus complex, that is, sexual desire for a parent of the opposite sex. Capgras assumes that the woman had an erotic interest in her father and hypothesizes that her belief that the man was not her father but an impostor helped her manage her desire or feel less ashamed about it. In a paper published a few years later, Capgras's suggestion was criticized on the basis that the woman's delusion did not involve only her father, but also her brother, uncle and aunt. She came to believe that they had all been substituted (Levy-Valensie 1929).

Although Capgras's suggested explanation did not encounter much favour, other psychodynamic accounts of the delusion became popular. In particular, one influential view was that the Capgras delusion was due to a love-hate conflict with family members. This could be resolved by splitting the relevant family member into two and directing love towards the genuine person and hatred towards the impostor (Enoch and Trethowan 1991). Psychodynamic accounts of this kind were challenged for not offering an adequate basis for making predictions about the course of the illness and for failing to inform suitable treatment (de Pauw 1994). Another common complaint was that our need to manage a love-hate relationship did not seem to be a sufficient explanation for the occurrence of the delusion. What else could explain the surfacing of a belief as bizarre as a belief about a substitution? Contemporary defences of the psychodynamic approach are more modest in their goals in that they do not aspire to offer a complete picture of the causal history of delusions (Martindale and Summers 2013). Rather, they propose a framework in which some aspects of delusions make sense of our experience: in general terms, psychosis is an attempt to conjure a new reality. The new reality replaces the actual reality which is too difficult for us to cope with.

The view is that delusions can help us alter a reality that is undesirable in a number of ways (de Pauw 1994). Delusions may arise out of *denial*, when one aspect of our lives or of ourselves is not acknowledged; *projection*, when one undesirable aspect of ourselves is attributed to something or someone external to us; *splitting*, where positive and negative aspects of a third person are somehow detached from one another, as could be the case with Capgras; *severance of mental connections*, when the link between events in our lives and adverse effects on our well-being are denied; *fragmentation,* when we feel that someone or something is falling apart, either physically or mentally; *manic defence,* when our feelings of inadequacy are turned into the opposite, feelings of empowerment; and *thought disorder,* when we are asked to talk about a situation that is psychologically difficult for us to accept and our language breaks down.

An example of the empowering potential of delusions can be found in passage where Max, who had grandiose delusions and believed he worked for the secret services, described how the delusions made him feel 'strong and powerful and sort of able to do anything'. He said: 'The sort of feeling you get, it makes you feel like you become the person you've always wanted to be or better' (Isham et al. 2021). Bob also had grandiose delusions and believed he could become the next Messiah. He explained that before the delusion he hated who he was. Talking about his delusions, he said: 'I tried to seek some sort of route to escape this depression, which was to again fall into this fantasy world in which I would try to elevate myself, and you can elevate yourself as far as you want in your own fantasy, you can be the next messiah' (Isham et al. 2021).

The basic message of psychodynamic accounts is that delusions have meanings, and it is potentially useful to be able to inquire about the lives of people with delusions to see whether their current beliefs and behaviours are linked to their experiences or previous life events. For psychodynamic approaches, there is no dysfunction at the origin of the delusion. Instead, the delusion plays a positive role. The delusion serves a defensive function and averts an inner catastrophe that is about to happen (McKay et al. 2005).

The phenomenon of the insight paradox also offers some reasons to revisit blanket claims about the harmfulness of delusions (Belvederi Murri et al. 2016) and can be partially explained by the acknowledgement that some distortions of reality can play an important psychological and epistemic role at a critical time. What is the insight paradox? Many people with a history of psychotic symptoms who gradually come to realize the delusional nature of their beliefs can be affected by severe post-psychotic depression. According to psychodynamic accounts, knowledge about the world or about ourselves can cause us low mood. Distortions of reality can help us avoid low mood in the face of adversities (Hingley 1997). Having good insight means being more realistic about ourselves ('these ideas are delusional, after all') at the expense of our self-esteem ('I am ill', or worse 'I am mad') (Amore et al. 2020). The expectation is that we will feel better once we take distance from our delusional beliefs, and that we are on our way to recovery because we have at least partially regained insight.

But we may become severely depressed when we approach reality without the filter of our delusional beliefs. Ceasing after many years to believe that we are working for the secret services or that we are the next Messiah, and starting to accept that we have been unwell instead, can be very disruptive and cause us low self-esteem, potentially leading to suicidal thoughts. Not surprisingly, the insight paradox seems to be a more serious concern for those who internalize mental health stigma and, once insight has been at least partially regained, apply to themselves the negative stereotypes that society associates with people affected by mental illness (Buchman-Wildbaum 2020).

Feelings of shame seem to be a very significant factor leading to self-stigma. Isham and colleagues (2021) report that people sometimes feel embarrassed or lost when they lose conviction in the delusional belief: 'you slip into quite a deep depression after you realise [...] it's not like you go from a feeling of being really important back to where you were before, you go from really important to really unimportant.' When beliefs that play an important psychological and epistemic role for us at a critical time are recognized as delusional and gradually subside, they leave a gap which we need to fill by other means. When we start doubting the content of our delusion, the realization that we have suffered from a mental illness for years and that the world we lived in was illusory may have negative consequences for our self-understanding and self-esteem (Freeman et al. 2004). Rates of suicide are highest in the first few years of a psychotic illness when we try to come to terms with our fear of chronic mental illness (see Drake and Cotton 1986; Clarke et al. 2006).

As Belvederi Murri and colleagues suggest, psychological interventions, such as narrative therapy, can help overcome the feeling that we have become unimportant or have been deceived about reality for so long. This can sometimes successfully address depression. The insight paradox reminds us that, for some people at least, life without the delusion may be difficult in a different way, not always less difficult, than life with the delusion – the delusion may have enabled them to keep at bay some negative feelings that are ready to remerge when the delusion fades if no adequate support is available.

Everyday delusions as defences

Everyday delusions can also be explained in psychodynamic terms or by highlighting mechanisms that are amenable to a psychodynamic interpretation – indeed for the psychodynamic accounts it is not difficult to argue for the continuity between clinical and everyday delusions. Conspiracy beliefs have been thought to arise from *projection*, where the enemy identified in the conspiracy theory is a projection of the self. The thesis has first been proposed in the sixties by Richard J. Hofstadter (1964) and has been influential since: it was recently tested in a study where people's willingness to endorse conspiracy theories was associated with their willingness to conspire (Douglas et al. 2011). Participants were asked whether they endorsed a conspiracy theory (such as 'The AIDS virus was created in a laboratory') and whether they would see themselves conspire in the same context ('If you were a scientist, would you have created the AIDS virus?'). The results confirmed that at the basis of the acceptance of conspiracy theories there are social cognitive processes that are not pathological. It makes sense that, if we believe that we would take part in a conspiracy ourselves ('I would do it!'), then we find it plausible that other people would also have taken part in conspiracies ('They must have done it!').

Another way in which psychodynamic accounts can shed light into the adoption of conspiracy beliefs concerns the role of motivation. In the case of some clinical delusions, such as anosognosia, the desire to see ourselves as we were prior to the trauma we experienced (whole, self-sufficient, nondisabled) plays a role in our lack of acknowledgement that one of our limbs is now paralysed. But what motivation would there be to adopt a conspiracy belief? One powerful motivation is the *need for uniqueness* which can be described as our desire to be special, different from other people (Lantian et al. 2017). One way of affirming our difference is to entertain views that are different from mainstream views.

The conspiracy theory offers the chance of hidden, important, and immediate knowledge, so that the believer can become an expert, possessed of a knowledge not held even by the so-called experts.

(Billig 1987)

Studies have shown that when we have a greater need for uniqueness, and are more likely to agree with statements such as 'I prefer being different from other people', then we are also more likely to endorse conspiracy theories and we believe conspiracy theories more strongly (Lynn and Harris 1997). As with projection, the role of motivation in the adoption of conspiracy beliefs shows that there needs to be no dysfunction or pathology at the origin of the endorsement of a conspiracy theory. The conspiracy belief contributes to our sense that we are special and different from others.

Positive illusions are tendencies to adopt overly optimistic beliefs about ourselves and make overly optimistic predictions about our future. Optimistically biased beliefs have been compared to clinical delusions for their resistance to counterevidence. However, they are so widespread in the nonclinical population that not only we cannot think of them as idiosyncratic, but they count as the statistical norm. Positive illusions have been given, from Freud (1928) onwards, psychodynamic and motivational interpretations. Optimism was characterized by Freud as an illusion, a form of *denial* of reality, and thus seen as an obstacle to good mental health and good psychological functioning. Realism, instead, was thought to be conducive to better health and well-being.

Today the view about the consequences of positive illusions is less straight-forward. Optimistically biased beliefs can have good and bad consequences (Bortolotti and Antrobus 2015; Shepperd et al. 2015). Cardiac patients who believed to be less at risk than average to have another cardiac event were indeed less likely to experience a cardiac event over the following 12 months, showing that positive expectations can promote goals persistence in the form of good lifestyle choices that can reduce the risk of health threats (Hevey et al. 2014). However, excessive optimism in the same domain, health, may cause us to underestimate risks. People who are unrealistically optimistic about their being able to avoid catching the H1N1 virus showed reduced interest in conforming to hand hygiene guidelines (Kim and Niederdeppe 2013). Similar findings could apply to individual and institutional responses to the coronavirus pandemic (Bortolotti and

Murphy-Hollies 2022). For instance, researchers found that university students from Poland, Iran and Kazakhstan were unrealistically optimistic about contracting the virus during the first and second waves of Covid-19 and thus did not take precautionary measures to avoid infection (Wojciech Kulesza et al. 2021). It would be interesting to know whether compliance with health and safety regulations was associated with a more realistic attitude towards the severity of the threat.

Although the perception of optimism as a cognitive distortion has persisted, psychological research has challenged the claim that positive illusions compromise good mental health (Peterson 2000). Indeed, the optimism literature has shown that positive illusions protect from anxiety and depression, and secure well-being in the face of setbacks, fuelling resilience and effective coping, as argued in the work of Shelley Taylor (1989). In addition to its psychological benefits, optimism has been deemed biologically adaptive too, a way for members of our species to think ahead about the future without losing the motivation to pursue their goals at the prospect of obstacles, adversities and ultimately death (Tiger 1979).

As I discuss in the next section, optimistically biased beliefs have been described as *adaptive misbeliefs*, that is, beliefs that are unjustified and likely to be false because they do not reflect the available evidence and yet contribute to the goals of survival and reproduction (McKay and Dennett 2009). This way of thinking about positive illusions suggests that no dysfunction is responsible for optimistically biased beliefs, and that on the contrary they may be a designed feature of our cognition and agency, selected for their biological adaptiveness.

Breaking a shear pin

Psychoanalytic accounts viewing delusions as a defence are no longer the standard explanation for beliefs that fly in the face of reality, but contemporary psychologists invite us not to throw the baby away with the bathwater and to acknowledge that a recognition of the benefits of delusions can be made alongside an investigation of the deficits or biases that may be responsible for delusion formation. The key notion of psychoanalytic accounts we can preserve and further investigate is that 'delusions are viewed as having a palliative function – they represent an attempt (however misguided) to relieve pain, tension, and distress' (McKay et al. 2005).

Maladaptive misbeliefs

According to the 'shear-pin' hypothesis by McKay and Dennett (2009), some false beliefs that prevent a cognitive system from being overwhelmed can count as adaptive. They are called *adaptive misbeliefs* because they are false beliefs that do not successfully fulfil their role of representing reality accurately (*misbeliefs*), but they are also means by which we can increase our chances of survival and reproduction (*adaptive*). Imagine a circumstance in which we experience such a traumatic event that we would succumb to serious depression and even suicidal thoughts if our resulting negative emotions were not somehow managed and controlled. If our reality is something that we can hardly cope with, one option is to believe things to be different from (better than) how they are, so that our anxiety and distress can be at least temporarily relieved.

McKay and Dennett describe this process as the 'doxastic analogue of a shear pin breakage'.

> We envision doxastic shear pins as components of belief evaluation machinery that are 'designed' to break in situations of extreme psychological stress (analogous to the mechanical overload that breaks a shear pin or the power surge that blows a fuse). Perhaps the normal function (both normatively and statistically construed) of such components would be to constrain the influence of motivational processes on belief formation [...] Breakage of such components, therefore, might permit the formation and maintenance of comforting misbeliefs – beliefs that would ordinarily be rejected as groundless, but that would facilitate the negotiation of overwhelming circumstances (perhaps by enabling the management of powerful negative emotions) and that would thus be adaptive in such extraordinary circumstances.
>
> (McKay and Dennett 2009, pp. 501–2)

Adaptive misbeliefs are not an accident, but their adoption is designed to prevent a crisis: when our emotions are overwhelmingly negative because reality is too bleak for us, we come to believe that reality is better than it is and, as a result, stress and anxiety are effectively managed. Motivational influences on belief that are usually thought as an effect of bias – because we believe what we desire to be the case and not what we have evidence for – are not evidence that belief formation is malfunctioning but are designed to keep us alive and help us pursue our biological goals. So, can at least some delusional beliefs count as biologically adaptive? McKay and Dennett argue that typically the extent to which desires are allowed to influence belief formation is excessive in the case of clinical delusions, and the rift between belief and reality is too great for the beliefs to be biologically adaptive. This means that for McKay and Dennett clinical delusions are misbeliefs that are maladaptive overall.

Not everybody agrees with them on this point: Aaron Mishara and Phil Corlett argue that clinical delusions have some biologically adaptive features after all, that can be appreciated by considering their role in enabling the habitual and automated learning system to resume after the disruption caused by prediction-error signalling (Mishara and Corlett 2009). As I described in Chapter 5, according to the prediction-error theory of delusion formation, the delusion emerges as an explanation for the events that are made salient by the inaccurate coding of prediction errors. When prediction errors are recorded, this usually signals that the model of the world we have is no longer accurate, and the processes underlying automated and habitual learning are stopped because more flexible and conscious processes are required. In the case of schizophrenia there may be no mismatch causing the prediction-error signalling and the automated and habitual learning system is disabled for no good reason. Instead of learning automatically, we pay conscious attention to the new data that allegedly do not fit the model. This takes up most of our resources causing a possible disconnection with the world. But the events that appeared unpredictable and puzzling can be accounted for by the newly formed delusion, and as a result the processes underlying automated and habitual learning can resume their normal operations. For Mishara and Corlett this is an indication that delusions play a biologically adaptive role.

The biological adaptiveness of clinical delusions in this context has been called into question: Eugenia Lancellotta observes that, when the adoption of the delusion disables the flexible and conscious learning system, it falls under the control of the habitual and automated learning system (Fineberg and Corlett 2016). The consequence of this is that the delusional belief becomes fixed.

> This is the unavoidable cost of the shear pin break: preserving the overall functionality of the learning system in spite of aberrant perceptions or PEs [prediction errors] has the side effect that the system does not function in an optimal manner. The delusion would

restore the overall functionality of the learning system but at the cost of the delusion being irresponsive to evidence and to reasonable argument to the contrary.

(Lancellotta 2022, p. 55)

This rejoinder is not surprising if we think of the delusion as an imperfect response to a crisis: yes, the delusional belief is an emergency response, but it is *not* an optimal response. It is a response that has both benefits and costs, and often the costs outweigh the benefits.

Adaptive misbeliefs

Positive illusions are considered by McKay and Dennett the only instance of *adaptive* misbeliefs, that is, optimistically biased beliefs are both inaccurate representations of the world and beliefs that promote our physical and mental health and our genetic fitness, contributing to actions that are themselves adaptive. They quote Shelley Taylor (1989) when she says that the healthy mind is a self-deceptive one. One example of the adaptive nature of positive illusions is their facilitating commitment to mates and offspring: among our optimistically biased beliefs are inflated views of our romantic partners and our children. This is evolutionarily important because to guarantee the survival of our children we need to care for them for several years and also ensure that there is someone else who helps provide for them and defend them from predators and other dangers.

The 'love-is-blind' positive illusion seems to be doing exactly that: we tend to overestimate the qualities of our romantic partners and children and, when we get negative feedback about their not fitting the idealized conception we have of them, we are creative with the feedback and take it to be evidence of some other quality we can attribute to them – e.g., 'He is not uninterested in my sister's illness, he doesn't want to ask me about it because he knows that talking about it makes me nervous' (Murray et al. 1996). Alternatively, we explain our partners' objectionable behaviour in a way that amounts to excusing it rather than considering a stable character trait of them

[T]hose in blissful relationships tend to write off their partners' negative behavior with external attributions (e.g., explaining surly behavior with an attribution like suffering stress at work), whereas those in unhappy relationships tend to accept the deleterious implications of negative behavior with internal dispositional attributions (e.g., explaining surly behavior with an attribution like insensitivity).

(Fletcher and Boyes 2008)

One example of an adaptive action motivated by optimistically biased beliefs is the tendency to adopt healthier lifestyles when we believe (often in an illusory way) that we have control over our health and can prevent ourselves from contracting a serious illness. For instance, if we think it is up to us whether breast cancer will return, we will do our very best to eat healthily, exercise and follow the advice of our doctors, because we believe that every little counts. But if we feel helpless and believe that it is not in our power to prevent cancer from returning, then we may not be motivated to engage in the same health-promoting behaviours (Taylor et al. 1984). As McKay and Dennett conclude, 'such doxastic departures from reality – such apparent limitations of veridicality – are not culpable but entirely forgivable: design features, even.' Optimistically biased beliefs seem to be instances of delusional beliefs (in the broad sense I have adopted here) whose benefits outweigh the costs.

For the other delusional beliefs that fail the test for biological adaptiveness, we should remember that, even if they do not contribute to the fulfilment of the evolutionary goals of survival, reproduction, and genetic fitness, this does not mean that they should also be denied *psychological* adaptiveness. In particular, one aspect of the psychological benefits of clinical and everyday delusions I want to consider next is their potential for making our lives more meaningful.

Giving meaning

Delusional beliefs are often portrayed as paradigmatic instances of meaninglessness. This view of delusions is reflected in representations of mental illness in popular culture where poor mental health is the blanket explanation for behaviour that appears as irrational, unpredictable and dangerous. But delusions can be meaningful. In Chapter 2, I argued that, when interpreters realize which experiences speakers have and respond to, they move beyond the apparent bizarreness of the belief and are able to appreciate its meaning and its context. In Chapter 4, I suggested that delusional beliefs can reflect and shape identity, affirming our values and signalling our commitment to the groups we want to belong to.

Here I ask whether delusional beliefs can also enhance the sense that our lives are meaningful (Ritunnano and Bortolotti 2022). We already saw some examples of a grandiose delusion where the believed reality was preferable to the speaker than the actual reality and the delusion was infusing the speaker's life with pride and a sense of self-worth. But grandiose delusions are not the only types of delusions can have this effect. Other delusions that attract the attention of medical professionals can be empowering in some circumstances.

'Successful psychotics'

Good examples of empowering delusions in the literature are the stories of Mr A., Simon and Harry:

> Mr A., a 66-year-old man, was admitted following an accidental fall in which he fractured a femur. Following surgery, he expressed bizarre ideas and was referred for a psychiatric opinion. This assessment revealed a long standing complex delusional system in which he believed he was in constant contact with 'spirits from the other side'. This involved clear auditory hallucinations which occurred frequently and he described the spirits discussing his activities among themselves. He had been having these experiences for over ten years. There was no evidence of persistent mood change nor underlying organic disorder. The illness had begun about five years after his divorce and three years before he retired. He was diagnosed as suffering from late onset or paranoid schizophrenia. Mr A. denied any distressing aspect to his illness and considered himself gifted. He refused to attend for any out-patient follow-up and saw no need for help of any kind. In such cases, which it would seem reasonable to call 'successful psychotics', can intervention be justified?
>
> (Hosty 1992, p. 373)

> Simon was a black, middle-class professional in his forties. He reported a series of 'revelation' experiences conveyed by delusional perceptions and thought insertion. Simon's experiences might suggest a diagnosis of schizophrenia. However, from Simon's perspective, his experiences were spiritual revelations: and consistently with this they were entirely beneficial to his life. His experiences and beliefs, whilst unusual in form and content, essentially enhanced his ability to

function effectively: he won a difficult case thus advancing his career as a lawyer. Framing his experiences positively rather than negatively he avoided contact with doctors and instead integrated the information he (somehow) took from them in fighting and winning his court case.

(Jackson and Fulford 1997, abridged)

Mr Harry is a 33-year-old gentleman who has been complaining of being the target of a worldwide conspiracy for the past 5 years. [...]. When asked further about the challenges of conducting a life under the control of others, Harry replied: 'If I went out one day and I realised that people weren't expecting me to be there, it would be a real shock again ... I would be ... I don't know ... ?! I got so used to people expecting me to be there and lash out with them ... I would feel alone again, which is what everyone else feels, like alone. So people are like a family for me, it's like a safety blanket, they make me feel so comfortable now ... If I found out that they are not watching me and reading my mind, I would feel alone and crazy like everyone else. To feel like I have everyone following me around, whether it's negative or positive, that alone is a force of power ... knowing that you can influence people's minds in the right way, I feel like Jesus (of course I'm not) but why not believe?'.

(Ritunnano et al. 2022, p. 110 abridged)

For Mr. A., Simon and Harry, the delusional experience is not (always) lived as a burden or perceived as generating anxiety but is seen as enlightening. Moreover, the delusional beliefs contribute to reflecting and shaping people's identities. For Mr. A, the contact with the spirits is welcome and seen as a gift that gives rise to no concerns. For Simon as well, the delusions have a connection to his spiritual beliefs. For Harry, the delusions express a sense that he is connected to other people, making him feel less alone and more important. And yet the beliefs Mr A., Harry and Simon report are implausible, unshakeable and idiosyncratic to them. A well-balanced account of delusions can explain the harm that delusions typically cause without ignoring the fact that in some circumstances, and often temporarily, delusions can give meaning to our lives. The three descriptions of 'successful psychotics' stress the role of delusional beliefs in giving a sense of purpose and meaning, downplaying the negative effects on well-being that delusions typically have. This is probably due to the self-enhancing content of the delusions reported where speakers thought of themselves as gifted, having an important role, or being invested with special responsibilities, and the support provided by their immediate social circle.

Besides individual case studies, there have been studies suggesting that delusions, especially elaborated ones that take the form of largely coherent narratives that make sense of the speaker's experiences, increase the sense that the speaker's life is meaningful and are correlated with well-being. Patients with elaborated delusions were found to score higher than patients in remission, rehabilitation nurses and Anglican ordinands in the 'purpose in life' test and the 'life regard' index (Roberts 1991). The purpose in life test and the life regard index are considered as reliable means for measuring important aspects of the sense of meaning and purpose in people's lives. Roberts concludes that 'for some there may be satisfaction in psychosis and that [delusion formation] is adaptive' (p. 19). In another study (Bergstein et al. 2008), elaborated delusions were found to contribute to the *sense of coherence*. What is the sense of coherence?

[A] global orientation that expresses the extent to which one has a pervasive, enduring though dynamic, feeling of confidence that (1) the stimuli deriving from one's internal and external environments are structured, predictable, and explicable; (2) the resources are available to one to meet the demands posed by these stimuli; and (3) these demands are challenges, worthy of investment and engagement.

(Antonovsky 1987, p. 91)

Both sense of coherence and meaningfulness help us cultivate an interest in attaining goals that we find worth pursuing. In first-person accounts of delusional experience conveying a sense of ambiguity and uncertainty about the future, delusions can be accompanied by feelings of anxiety, but the experience can also be described as exciting (Ritunnano and Bortolotti 2022).

Meaningfulness in conspiracy beliefs

There is more to having delusions than misrepresenting the world or adopting hypotheses that are not well-grounded in evidence. The narrow view of delusions as beliefs whose role is simply that of representing reality fails to acknowledge how delusions are linked to our life histories and our experiences of the world, reflecting and shaping our identities, as argued in Chapter 4. Unfortunately, the powerful links between the delusional beliefs and the rest of the speaker's mental lives often remain a mystery for the interpreter who does not have the adequate background knowledge to identify the ways in which delusions have and confer meaning. However, a suitably informed interpreter with the willingness to listen and the resources to understand can find meaning in the speaker's reports.

I have also shown that, in some circumstances, adopting the delusion contributes to our lives having meaning and purpose, and at least temporarily and imperfectly restores an already compromised engagement with our physical and social environment. At least from the speaker's point of view, the adoption of a delusion can contribute to re-establishing a sense of coherence – particularly in the context of previously distressing life events. So far, I have looked for evidence for meaningfulness in the clinical delusions literature, but a number of benefits have been identified in conspiracy beliefs (Douglas 2021). In particular, the benefits that have been studied include benefits for the speakers, including the opportunity for those whose views are marginalized to find some support within a sympathetic community; benefits for public life, as the presence of conspiracy beliefs enables the political debate to represent a variety of viewpoints and not merely mainstream views; and benefits for society, by promoting accountability and transparency in official organs of information and encouraging social change.

Let me focus on benefits for speakers here. According to several studies on the consequences of believing conspiracy theories, adopting a conspiracy belief is often motivated by the need to belong and to restore a sense of control, but there is no evidence suggesting that the conspiracy belief is successful at achieving those goals (Van Prooijen 2022). Often speakers are stigmatized as a result of endorsing conspiracy beliefs, and believing in powerful enemies plotting in the shadows makes them feel anxious and unsafe. The real benefit for speakers consists in the belief enhancing meaningfulness.

> Although conspiracy beliefs may not reduce anxiety or help them maintain social relationships, they do stimulate a sense of meaning and purpose in a specific way that is psychologically rewarding.
>
> (van Prooijen 2022)

Three benefits are identified: conspiracy beliefs (1) make us feel important, (2) help us rationalize our behaviour and (3) have entertainment value. When I introduced the sense of coherence, I talked about the idea that there is something out there that is worth examining and that we have the capacity to make progress with it and discover what it is. Conspiracy beliefs play a similar role to clinical delusions in that adopting them means that a significant event that puzzles other people is no longer a mystery to us. We are able to provide a satisfactory explanation for the event and this makes us feel special and unique. Moreover, we feel connected to other people who share the same explanation of the event and the sense of superiority we have for ourselves is also something that we project on our in-group. In the same way as we are special and unique among other people, more knowledgeable than other people in the specific domain of the conspiracy, so members of our in-group are special and unique with respect to members of out-groups.

The adoption of conspiracy beliefs is associated with behaviours that are perceived as nonmainstream and sometimes appear as harmful and disruptive to other people, such as refusing vaccination or protesting against the government. In this context, it is not completely clear whether the conspiracy belief motivates anti-social behaviour or whether it is anti-social behaviour that leads us to adopting conspiracy beliefs so that we can offer a post-hoc justification for our actions. But it is very plausible that the conspiracy belief is used as a rationalizing tool. As Van Prooijen says, people use conspiracy theories to rationalize their beliefs and actions. Confabulation plays an important role in this rationalization project.

> [I]ndividuals want to provide an explanation which, although it may not be strictly accurate, meets other needs for them. They are motivated by the need to have a causal understanding of themselves and the circumstances they are in (Coltheart 2017). They want to signal to other people that they are rational, competent, and trustworthy (Bergamaschi Ganapini 2020) and so they are motivated to provide explanations which present themselves positively and protect positive self-concepts (Sullivan-Bissett 2015, p. 552). Other, perhaps more accurate explanations such as 'I just felt like it' or 'I did it at random' put them at risk of looking foolish or unkind. So, individuals want to provide explanations which paint good pictures of themselves.
>
> (Murphy-Hollies 2022)

Murphy-Hollies's account of the role of confabulation in justifying behaviour can be usefully applied to how we use conspiracy beliefs to defend decisions and actions that others may perceive as problematic. An additional contribution of conspiracy beliefs to meaningfulness is the capacity that conspiracy beliefs have to present reality as more exciting and entertaining than it is. It is not coincidental that many conspiracy theories involve celebrities and are associated with radicalization, the belief in supernatural forces and low tolerance to boredom. The explanations of significant events provided by conspiracy theorists are usually more exciting and have more entertainment value than the official accounts.

Rachel Fraser provides some additional reasons to think that what attracts us to conspiracy theories is that we do not want to miss the interesting and exciting explanation, and, if it there is a chance that the explanation turns out to be true, then we want to be the ones believing it first. She applies the concept of FoMO (fear of missing out) to the case of conspiracy beliefs. 'Fear of missing out' is the phrase used to denote the tendency people have to worry if they are not aware of the latest developments on social media, also defined as the 'desire to stay continually connected with what others are doing' (Gupta and Sharma 2021). Fraser argues that there is an epistemic version of this tendency: if an interesting hypothesis potentially explaining a significant fact has some likelihood to be true, we want to be the ones to endorse it.

> The contemporary conspiracist has a horror not of false belief– about that they are relatively relaxed – but of missing out on true ones. The prospect of falsely believing the royal family killed Princess Diana is unconcerning. What vexes the conspiracist is the prospect of failing to believe that the royals killed Diana if such a claim turns out to be true.
>
> (Fraser 2020)

In conclusion, in this chapter I argued that, far from being conceptualized as the output of a dysfunctional process, in psychodynamic accounts delusional beliefs are perceived as having a positive role, of protection and defence against an undesirable reality. Although psychodynamic accounts have been long out of favour, contemporary psychological research has sought to integrate bias and deficit accounts with a recognition of the potential adaptiveness of delusions. In particular, I considered the possibility that delusions can enable contact with the physical and social environment at critical times, and in some cases also confer some special meaning or purpose to our lives. This coheres well with a feature of delusions I discussed in Chapter 4, their capacity to reflect and shape our identity.

CHAPTER 8
DELUSIONS AND AGENCY

In the last three chapters, I have shown a different side to delusions: they are neither obviously the outcome of a dysfunctional process nor always a source of harm, but they can be conceived as an imperfect response to unusual events and act as a coping mechanism.

Delusional beliefs have an interesting effect on agency, as they are often at the same time disabling and empowering. In this chapter I want to ask what we should do about delusional beliefs in the light of this. First, I discuss how competing models attempt to capture what causes delusional beliefs and what the best remedial strategies are. If we think that delusional beliefs are a problem that needs to be addressed, who is responsible for this problem and what reasonable steps can we take to stop the disabling effects of delusions without necessarily losing their empowering function? How should we exchange ideas with other people when we find their identity beliefs both implausible and unshakeable? Can we create an epistemic environment where delusions do not constitute an obstacle to mutual understanding?

Second, I propose to revisit the triangulation model of interpretation we started with and ask what approach an interpreter should take to a speaker who reports a belief deemed as delusional. Attributions of delusionality are often made in an attempt to strip the speaker of their agency or have as a consequence an inevitable downgrading of the speaker's agency. I suggest this attitude is not well justified given what we know about delusions, and it is not productive if our aim is to promote understanding. Rather, we should ask interpreters to adopt an agential stance towards speakers and remain curious and empathetic throughout. Only by recognizing each other's agency despite the many challenges we face can we work together to respond to personal or societal crises, even when we do not share the same values.

Responsibility for delusional beliefs

In the course of the previous chapters, I sketched a number of different ways to account for the adoption and persistence of delusional beliefs. Some models of delusions are individualistic and focus on the person who has or reports the delusional belief, and some models are social, including considerations about the relationship between the person and their social environment. In the former case, the implication is that there is something wrong with the speakers that explains the formation and maintenance of delusional beliefs; in the latter, it is the situation as a whole, the social context in which speakers find themselves, that explains delusion formation and maintenance. Another relevant distinction is whether the delusion is seen as something akin to a pathology, something to be prevented, treated and ultimately eradicated, or whether the delusion is seen as a way of life that has advantages and disadvantages depending on the personal and social context of the speaker. An individualistic approach goes hand in hand with the medicalization of delusionality, whereas a social approach tends to attribute responsibility for features of people's behaviour to systemic factors and treat delusionality not as a disease but as a social issue.

In this section, I am going to caricature three models of how the problem of delusions could be explained and addressed, examining the suggestions they offer about how we can deal with the delusional beliefs in our lives. This exercise will hopefully help us identify some of the complexities surrounding the formation, maintenance and use of delusional beliefs, and make us wary of solutions to the problems that delusionality engenders which ignore that complexity (Bortolotti 2022b).

Individualistic and social models

In *individualistic medical* models, delusional beliefs are pathological states of our minds that are fundamentally thought to be caused by something wrong within us. So, something about us must be changed to address the problem. Having delusional beliefs can be compared to another condition that is seemingly undesirable and potentially costly – I have chosen being overweight but could have chosen any other condition that is often pathologized and stigmatized in our society. The comparison draws out possible explanations and conceptualizations of the target condition (being overweight or having a delusional belief), and strategies for reducing the risks and negative consequences of the condition for the individual who is primarily affected and their social context.

Individualistic medical model of being overweight

When you are overweight, there is something wrong with you and you need to be treated or enhanced to solve the problem. Due to your weight, your cardiovascular health is at risk and you may have a lower life expectancy than people of normal weight. The responsibility for being overweight is yours. Your genes, lifestyle, personality, habits, etc. are what caused the problem. You cannot do much about your genes, but your lifestyle, personality, habits, etc., need to change and you need to follow medical advice to identify the best measures to take such as eat less and better, exercise more and have surgery. The desired outcome is for you to lose weight.

Individualistic medical model of having a delusional belief

When you have a delusional belief, there is something wrong with you and you need to be treated or enhanced to solve the problem. Your understanding of yourself and of the world is compromised. As a result, you make bad decisions, cause harm to yourself and other people, and exert a negative influence on your immediate or wider social circle. The responsibility for having delusions is yours. Your genes, education, reasoning tendencies, habits, personality, etc., are what caused the problem. You cannot do much about your genes, but your education, reasoning tendencies, habits, personality, etc., need to change so your beliefs can be more plausible, less unshakeable and less costly. To avoid adopting or maintaining delusional beliefs, you can go to therapy, learn about critical thinking, listen to experts, stop relying on untrustworthy sources of information, become less intellectually arrogant and more open minded, etc. The desired outcome is for your delusional beliefs to be revised or replaced.

In the *social nonmedical* models, delusional beliefs are the result of our gathering and exchanging information in an epistemically polluted environment. Delusions are not thought to be caused by something wrong within us but by what goes on between us and around us. Society is largely responsible for the proliferation of delusional beliefs and society must be changed to address the problem. The social model explains the distinctive features of delusional beliefs in terms of the effects of an imperfectly structured social environment on us. Once again, we can compare having delusional beliefs to being overweight and see how the conditions can be explained, assessed and ultimately addressed.

Social nonmedical model of being overweight

When you are overweight, there is something wrong with how society is organized that made it more likely for you to become overweight, and thus there is something about society that needs to be changed. Due to your weight, your cardiovascular health is at risk and you may have a lower life expectancy than people of normal weight. Moreover, you lose opportunities to exercise your agency and enjoy life. You might be unable to pursue some of the goals you care about because you weigh more than average: potential life partners won't date you, employers won't hire you, real estate agents won't show you the best apartments, you won't make the netball team, etc. Society has made life hard for you and is prejudiced against you, actively contributing to your being overweight: ads on TV invited you to consume cheap unhealthy food; eating healthy food and having good habits, such as subscribing to a gym, are expensive; there is no comprehensive information about nutrition in school and during the life course, health risks were not explained to you, etc. Society needs to ensure that in your environment information about healthy food and the benefits of exercise is available and accessible, throughout the life course, and it is easier for people like you to take up and maintain good habits. Also, your peers need to stop blaming you for being overweight because the responsibility does not lie with you. Your surrounding social environment needs to create more opportunities for overweight people like you to fight discrimination and fat-shaming.

Social nonmedical model of having a delusional belief

When you have a delusional belief, there is something wrong with how the epistemic environment is structured in your society and this needs to be changed. Your understanding of yourself and of the world is compromised. As a result, you make bad decisions, cause harm to yourself or other people and exert a negative influence on your immediate or wider social circle. Sensible people won't associate with you, employers won't hire you or will fire you, your views will be ridiculed and you will be denied a platform. Society has made life hard for you and is prejudiced against you. Society is responsible for your having delusional beliefs. You did not receive adequate support when you had adverse experiences and you were made to feel inadequate, isolated and marginalized. You were left in a situation where you could trust nobody, encouraged to trust sources of information that were not reliable, and invited to distrust sources that were reliable (due to lack of support, misleading markers of prestige, fake news on social media, etc.). You were not equipped with the means for critically evaluating the information available around you. Society needs to change, in many ways: adequate support must be offered to people who experience the negative consequences of personal and social crises. Valuable information needs to be made available and accessible and good belief outsourcing must be promoted. It must become easier for people like you to gain and critically assess relevant information before making important decisions and to trust experts with good credentials. Also, your peers have to stop blaming or silencing you for having delusional beliefs and opportunities must be created for people like you who already have delusional beliefs to discuss their views, come into contact with alternative views and be taken seriously.

The agency-in-context model

I described two rival accounts, the individualistic medical model and the social nonmedical model, as caricatures of existing models in the literature to bring to the fore their differences. The individualistic model emphasizes the personal dimension of how problems are identified, explained and faced. Ryan McKay's bias account of delusions fits with the individualistic framework (McKay 2012). The person is the focus of the analysis and what matters happens within the physical and mental boundaries of the person. Often an individualistic model is also a medical model in the sense that the problem is identified with a pathology that the person has. In this case, the person does not meet epistemic standards of good believing due to reasoning biases such as explanatory adequacy, leading the person to believe a hypothesis that makes sense of their experience notwithstanding the implausibility of the ensuing hypothesis.

Quassim Cassam's model of conspiracy beliefs, according to which epistemic vices are largely responsible for conspiracism (Cassam 2019), and Kengo Miyazono's model of clinical delusions, according to which clinical delusions are harmful-malfunctional beliefs (Miyazono 2018), both fit this individualistic medical framework for different reasons. There are epistemic vices or deficits that are partly responsible for the person's delusion and need to be addressed for the problems caused by the delusion to disappear. Obviously, none of these models is as black-and-white as my simplified representation of the individual medical models, and the authors do recognize societal influences on belief formation.

The social nonmedical model emphasizes the role of the environment in how we identify, explain and address the problem. Neil Levy's work on bad beliefs is a shining example of the social model. Everything that matters happens at systemic levels (Levy 2021). The problem is that we live in an epistemically polluted environment where individuals and minority groups are not supported in their struggles, the skills needed to evaluate information are not easy to gain and beliefs cannot be reliably outsourced. The solutions need to be systemic too and Levy recommends nudges. The social model is often a nonmedical model, where the problem is not compared to an illness to prevent, eradicate or treated, but is acknowledged as a complex phenomenon with positive and negative implications for individuals and society. The beliefs I have examined in this book as examples of delusions have adaptive and maladaptive features, encompassing epistemic faults at the level of the individual's interaction with the environment, and epistemic benefits at the level of the individual's interaction with their social context, as Dan Williams discusses in some detail (Williams 2021).

There are several models somewhere in-between the caricatures I sketched here, models that aim to integrate some aspects of the individualistic medical model with the increasing appeal of social epistemology. For instance, the models I briefly discussed in Chapter 4, according to which how we use testimony and interact with in-groups and out-groups is key to how we get beliefs, highlight the social aspect *of belief formation*. That said, the way in which delusional beliefs are presented as a problem that needs to be addressed suggests that delusional beliefs are a pathology affecting some individuals due to their characteristics, these being abnormalities or deficits in testimonial practices or coalitional cognition (Bell et al. 2021; Miyazono and Salice 2021).

In contrast, in Levy's account, which is a social and nonmedical model through and through, there is no deficit or abnormality to be talked of. Even biases and epistemic vices are rejected as the main diagnosis of the problem of delusional beliefs. For instance, for Levy, people with conspiracy beliefs merely trust their own judgements and the judgements of like-minded people much more than the judgement of other people. In Levy's model, this is a nonpathological and even rational way to get beliefs. A clear rejection of the individualistic medical model is very attractive in that it does not place blame on the speaker for the delusional belief, but leaves it unclear why delusional beliefs are a problem at all. If the process by which we get them is rational, and they serve our interests at least to some extent, why should we attempt to get rid of them?

I propose a hybrid model that attempts to combine some of the insights of the individualist medical model with insights of the social nonmedical model. I shall call this the *agency-in-context* model because it is central to the model that we can exercise our agency in ways that can be more or less advantageous, but the exercise of our agency is constrained and influenced by the social context. The focus is on the *interaction between agents and their environment* because agents do not believe or act in isolation. For the third time, we can compare having delusional beliefs to being overweight and see how the conditions are explained, assessed and addressed.

Agency-in-context model of being overweight

When you are overweight, there is something wrong within you and something wrong with society, and this means that to improve the situation and prevent other people from becoming overweight, individual and societal changes are both required. Because you are overweight, your cardiovascular health is at risk and you may have a shorter life than people of normal weight. Moreover, because you are overweight, you may be prevented from pursuing and achieving some of the goals that are important to you. Your condition is due to a combination of factors, including aspects of your identity and existing societal pressures. Your genes, lifestyle, personality and habits matter, but so do societal and cultural influences on your life (such as the ads on TV inviting you to consume cheap unhealthy food; taking up good habits such as eating healthily and going to the gym being expensive).

You need to take responsibility for what you can change, with adequate support – for instance, you can be supported to eat more healthily and exercise more frequently. But society has an important part to play too: it needs to promote education about healthy food and exercise throughout the life course, making it easier for people like you to give up bad habits and take up good habits. Also, your peers have to stop blaming you for being overweight and create more opportunities for overweight people like you to fight discrimination and fat-shaming.

Agency-in-context model of having delusional beliefs

When you have delusional beliefs, this shows that you have experienced a crisis which required an emergency response and the delusional beliefs are your response. As a response, your delusional beliefs are to some extent effective, but they are also suboptimal and bring costs with them. The delusion compromises your understanding of yourself and the world around you, leading you to make bad decisions and exert a negative influence on your immediate or wider social circle. Because of your delusion, you may be prevented from pursuing and achieving some of the goals you care about and experience isolation and stigma.

For you to choose the delusion as your response, it must mean that there is something wrong with you and something wrong with society, and to address this both you and society need to change. The adoption and maintenance of delusional beliefs are due to many factors combining aspects of who you are and what your story is (your genes, reasoning biases, personality, lack of scientific literacy, etc.) and aspects of how epistemic practices operate in the society where you live. Societal and cultural influences on your life need to be addressed, including the structure of your epistemic environment. Maybe you were not offered adequate support when you experienced personal or social crises. Or you were encouraged to trust sources that were not reliable and made to distrust reliable sources (due to misleading markers of prestige, fake news on social media, etc.). You need to take responsibility for what you can change, with adequate support – for instance, you can be supported to adopt healthier epistemic habits, renounce epistemic vices and learn to recognize fake news and bad arguments. But the environment surrounding you also needs to be transformed so good believing and reliable belief outsourcing can be promoted, relevant information can be made more available and accessible, and more opportunities created for people with delusional beliefs to participate in public life by destigmatizing delusions.

In the agency-in-context model the proposed solution is complex: you may need to become less intellectually arrogant and more open-minded, but society needs to help you do so, by promoting critical thinking throughout the life course and making epistemic virtues attractive. Your epistemic environment also needs to be conducive to the use of reliable sources of information. Are there any real-life theories or explanations of delusions that adopt an agency-in-context model?

One example of a real-life agency-in-context model could be Uscinski and Parent's account of conspiracy beliefs (Uscinki and Parent 2014), as reconstructed by Moore (2018). There is a distinctive 'blame the system' social approach in their view. The authors recognize that when we are attracted to conspiracy beliefs it is because we have developed suspicion towards official sources of information and mainstream accounts of significant events, but the suspicion we exhibit is something that we have been socialized into. There is also a distinctive individualism in the consideration of the role of individual differences: the appeal of conspiracism is out there, and when we have a certain history and a certain personality, we are more likely to embrace it. After all, it is adaptive for us to think the worst of powerful elites if past wars and elections have never gone in our favour and we have felt, as individuals and groups, under threat for a long time.

Swiss cheese models

The literature on delusional beliefs I discussed in the previous chapters shows that delusions are means by which we respond to uncertainty, manage negative emotions and express our identity, so they are part and parcel of the way in which we exercise our agency. They are means by which we exercise agency because, by offering us a more desirable reality to deal with than the actual reality, they defuse the paralysing effect of threatening or distressing events and restore a sense of control.

At the same time, delusional beliefs also compromise our agency by undermining our understanding of significant events that impact our lives, inviting risk-taking behaviour, and often transforming our social world into a battle between good and evil that is both inaccurate and unnecessarily divisive. In so far as delusional beliefs are a response to a crisis, they are a suboptimal response, and their implausibility, unshakeability and costliness explain the epistemic aversion in those interpreters who encounters speakers' reports and attribute delusionality to them.

How should we deal with delusions then? Let me go on a short digression. In talking about the different ways to attempt to stop infection during the Covid-19 pandemic, some have advocated the 'Swiss cheese model' of respiratory pandemic defence. The model also made it to the *New York Times*. This is how the model is explained:

> Multiple layers of protection, imagined as cheese slices, block the spread of the new coronavirus, SARS-CoV-2, the virus that causes Covid-19. No one layer is perfect; each has holes, and when the holes align, the risk of infection increases. But several layers combined – social

distancing, plus masks, plus hand-washing, plus testing and tracing, plus ventilation, plus government messaging – significantly reduce the overall risk. Vaccination will add one more protective layer.

(Roberts 2020)

What is especially interesting for us is that the different factors are divided into two broad categories: *personal responsibility* (such as keeping physical distance) and *shared responsibility* (such as government's messaging and vaccination campaigns). Closer to home, Leticia Bode and Emily Varga (2021) have applied the Swiss cheese model to the problem of mitigating the effects of misinformation on social media. They observe how the problem is multifaceted, due to illiteracy and epistemic pollution, and so the solution to the problem also needs to be multifaceted. Not one intervention may work on its own but adopting various strategies simultaneously can make a difference. The problem/solution they consider involve public health officials, social media platforms and educators (operating at the social/ shared responsibility level) but also involve the average social media user

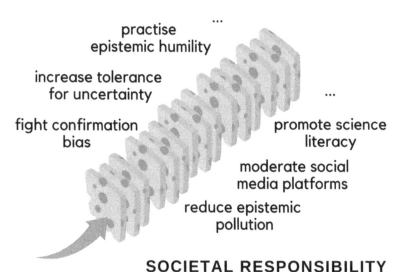

AGENT RESPONSIBILITY

practise epistemic humility

increase tolerance for uncertainty

fight confirmation bias

promote science literacy

moderate social media platforms

reduce epistemic pollution

SOCIETAL RESPONSIBILITY

Figure 1 The Swiss cheese model of responsibility for delusional beliefs, first proposed in Bortolotti (2022b).

(operating at the agent-centred/personal responsibility level). As in the case of the respiratory pandemic, also in the case of the so-called 'infodemic', the claim is that to have the best chances of success, we should engage both institutions and individuals and plan remedial strategies around personal and shared responsibility.

Inspired by Bode and Vraga, my proposal is that we look at the agency-in-context model as a Swiss cheese model. The agency-in-context model does not add anything new to the previous approaches (the individualistic medical model and its rival, the social nonmedical model) but *combines them*. If it is plausible to think that the causes of the spreading of conspiracy beliefs can be analysed in terms of agents' behaviour (e.g., as a response to psychological and epistemic needs) and in terms of systemic issues (e.g., as there being misleading markers of epistemic authority in the space dedicated to public debate), then it is also plausible that remedial strategies should operate at both levels.

Exchanging stories

Delusions support our agency because, by offering us a more desirable reality to deal with than the actual reality, they help us defuse the paralysing effect of unusual experiences and overwhelmingly negative emotions. Delusions also compromise our agency because, by being a suboptimal response to the personal or social crisis that we are experiencing or by boosting our self-esteem and motivation in an illusory way, they constrain the pursuit of our goals, making certain options unavailable to us and altering our interpersonal relationships in a way that invites exclusion and rules out support.

Beyond arguments

It is the tension between what delusions enable and what they prevent that makes delusions interesting and important to how we interact with the world and we relate with one another. In tackling delusions as a problem, the ideal path would be to find a way, at the individual level, to maintain the boost that delusions often offer and get rid of the element of illusion that isolates us epistemically from other agents. The boost can be cashed out in terms of a sense of coherence and a sense that one's life is meaningful, which characterize some delusions and were discussed in Chapter 7. The illusory elements can be captured by the epistemic features of delusions covered in Chapters 2 and 3, their implausibility and unshakeability. It sounds like an impossible feat to reconcile the good and the bad of delusions.

At the social, systemic level more support can be put in place to enable all of us to make better epistemic choices, be in a position to identify genuine expertise, cultivate good habits infused with the epistemic virtues of integrity, open mindedness and humility, and acquire practical skills such as critical thinking and bullshit detection. But more important still, in our epistemic environment authorities should enable us to identify reliable sources of information and ensure that those sources present information in accessible and engaging ways. This is very easy to say and very hard to achieve for some of the reasons already examined in the book: sifting good from bad evidence relies on methodological commitments that are often not shared, so sides must be taken; and for our boredom-averse minds, entertainment value is as important to which view we end up embracing than plausibility, if not more important.

The fact that interpreters do not trust the same methodology as speakers in their evaluation of evidence for and against controversial claims, and the appeal of surprising and engaging narratives in filling gaps in the speaker's knowledge of the world suggest that exchanging reasons may not always be the best way to relate to people whose perspective is different. Well-evidenced arguments satisfy some of the speaker's epistemic needs, but other needs, both psychological and epistemic, can only be satisfied by stories that engage their emotions and speak to their personal experience.

Delusions as stories

When reason fails or falters, we can let our hearts do the talking: this was the advice given by psychologists during the Covid-19 pandemic when families were torn apart by differences about whether the virus was a real threat and what measures it was necessary to take to be safe and keep other people safe. In that context, experts reminded us that arguments do not take us far in conversation with people whose position is radically opposed to ours. First, we need to build a common ground where we can meet and often that ground is not what we already believe but how we feel, what we are concerned about and what we are scared of. We may have very different ideas about how to protect ourselves and the people we love, and we may even have a different answer to what the threat is, but most of us want to avoid pain and death and want our loved ones to do the same. Starting from what we have in common, the minimal, basic things and building from there may help defuse potentially polarized situations.

In *How Minds Change* David McRaney offers an overview of the psychological science aimed at disclosing how people give up beliefs that were very important to them for an extended period of time, beliefs that I called *personal identity* beliefs because they capture some of our values, are laden with emotions, determine our behaviour and are relatively stable. McRaney (2022) is interested in the theory behind the conversions that people experience when they leave a cult or abandon a conspiracy theory. But he is also asking whether the theory can explain the success of some techniques that have been used to get people to distance themselves from their beliefs: deep canvassing and street epistemology among others.

> Deep canvasses are candid, two-way conversations where you ask people to share their relevant, emotionally significant experiences and reflect on them aloud. These conversations typically involve:
> Non-judgmentally soliciting views around an issue and asking follow-up questions to go deeper;
> Sharing narratives about personal experiences with the issue that reinforce values relevant to the issue.
>
> (People's Action Institute 2021)

Deep canvassing is a technique focused on establishing a respectful conversation with a person who seems to have a fixed belief, and finding out about their experiences surrounding the content of the belief. The people involved in the conversation, call them interpreter and speaker, end up sharing *stories* and not *arguments*: this is not because arguments are ineffective. Delusions do not prevent people from joining the game of exchanging reasons, and from playing it well, as we saw in Chapter 3. Moreover, we saw some cases of delusions that were given up after external challenges undermined the speaker's conviction in the delusional beliefs, which means that the arguments are not useless. But arguments do not *typically* change the outcome of the game because they do not necessarily tell interpreters why that belief is so important for the speaker, and thus they do not deepen the background knowledge of the interpreter. Further, one of the effects of exchanging argument, as we saw, may be that the delusion becomes even more ingrained in the speaker's worldview. If the speaker is in the grip of a delusion, they will find ways to elaborate the delusion or dismiss conflicting evidence to preserve their cherished belief.

One thing we learnt is that delusions involve beliefs but are more than just beliefs: we called them investments and maps in Chapter 1, and now we call them stories too. They can stretch like elastic bands, start small and develop into all-encompassing narratives, as convoluted as speakers need them to be in order to make sense of a reality that often slips away. They can inspire and motivate, making people feel powerful and less alone; or they can crush and tear apart, making people feel useless, guilty, helpless. Delusions convey some important aspects of the speakers' identity and signal to others where the speakers belong. So, when a delusion is reported and then defended, it does not just offer a glimpse of the speaker's line of argument at the time, but reveals a lot about speakers, often in the form of a story where speakers are the leading characters or have some important role to play.

Trading stories may be a better strategy than exchanging arguments, because the stories about how speakers grew attached to their delusional beliefs show how the beliefs emerged as reactions to situations that were difficult to manage, and encourage the interpreters to practise curiosity and empathy in finding out more. Although the exchanging of arguments simply invites a cycle of statement, objection and response, the story invites the sharing of personally significant experiences. And where arguments divide, stories unite.

Curiosity and empathy

For curious and empathetic interpreters, delusional beliefs are not mere noise or empty speech acts. They are recognizable attempts to make sense of a confusing reality. Even clinical delusions whose content can initially appear bizarre make sense when interpreters become aware of the unusual experiences that give rise to the delusions. First-person accounts of delusions show us how delusional beliefs in the clinical context do not typically come out of nowhere but are interconnected with past events, feelings, other beliefs and reasons for action.

Curious and empathetic interpreters realize that conspiracy theories, fake stories and implausible political beliefs reflect and shape our identities, enabling us to connect with like-minded others, affirming our values and preferences, and sustaining our sense of control over the world, albeit temporarily and imperfectly.

Delusions as an expression of agency

Attributions of delusionality have been traditionally seen as disempowering because when interpreters say that a belief is delusional they also openly challenge the speaker's agency, that is, the speaker's capacity to intervene in the surrounding physical and social environment, produce and share reliable information with others, identify meaningful goals to pursue, and choose the best means to pursue those goals. The statement: 'You are delusional' is taken to exclude and stigmatize, to mean something along the lines of: 'It is a waste of time to talk to you about this'.

But by now we have moved away from the conception of delusion as a negation of the speaker's agency. We saw that delusions can be meaningful for speakers because they make sense of their experiences and motivate them to keep engaging with the world at critical times. Delusionality is an expression of agency: Interpreters who recognize this do not consider delusions as mere 'glitches in the brain', pseudo-beliefs that evade a proper folk-psychological explanation, but see them as (imperfect) outputs of a belief formation system whose aim is to make sense of an uncertain world in such a way as to enable speakers to at least partially interact with that world. At times, what the delusion needs to do in order to enable the speaker's continued interaction with the world is to present reality as different from what it is, as in the shear-pin cases. At other times, delusions merely relieve the anxiety caused by the uncertainty surrounding unusual events and experiences. In both cases, delusional beliefs can confer meaning to speakers' lives and empower them, albeit in an illusory or temporary way.

> Delusion formation can be seen as an adaptive process of attributing meaning to experience through which order and security are gained, the novel experience is incorporated within the patient's conceptual framework, and the occult potential of its unknownness is defused.
>
> (Roberts 1992, pp. 304–5)

In the light of the complex picture that the agency-in-context model recommends, what is the best way to relate to people who report delusional beliefs? If we are interpreters facing speakers who report implausible and unshakeable identity beliefs, how can we build a bridge and pursue mutual understanding? If we are speakers meeting interpreters' incredulous stares or stigmatizing smirks, how do we react? The agency-in-context model suggests a risk-averse strategy: we should do a bit of everything that feels right. A curious interpreter treats each belief as an investment and a discovery. An empathetic interpreter won't necessarily share the speaker's belief but will ask how the belief came about and consider the possibility that, as implausible as it may sound, the belief offers some protection to the speaker and thus is valuable.

The agential stance

A clue about how to manage exchanges involving attributions of delusionality comes from some interesting literature on conversations in clinical encounters. In what we may want to describe as *bad* conversations between clinicians and people with clinical delusions, when the person shares their delusional belief, the mental health practitioner shows embarrassment, does not look at the person directly, provides minimal verbal feedback and avoids answering the person's direct questions.

> Patients with psychotic illness actively attempted to talk about the content of their symptoms during routine consultations. [...] they clearly attempted to discuss their psychotic symptoms and actively sought information during the consultation about the nature of these experiences and their illness. When patients attempted to present their psychotic symptoms as a topic of conversation, the doctors hesitated and avoided answering the patients' questions, indicating reluctance to engage with these concerns.
>
> (McCabe et al. 2002, p. 1150)

In what we may consider as *good* conversations, mental health practitioners show interest in the content of the person's delusional beliefs and ask more details about the beliefs, in order to understand the symptoms better.

> Psychiatrists commonly asked questions to elicit the content (and sometimes evidence) of the delusional experience, explored the impact of the symptoms on the patients' behaviour and functioning, and also questioned the validity of the beliefs by directly challenging them or offering alternative explanations.
>
> (Zangrilli et al. 2014, p. 6)

The different approaches to delusions in the studies on patient communication really bring home the importance of becoming curious and empathetic interpreters who listen and ask before dismissing the other person's contribution to the conversation. No matter how implausible and unshakeable the speaker's belief seems to be, it offers an insight into how the speaker sees the world that deserves to be taken into account.

In a recent project on how to preserve agency in young people using mental health emergency services, Bergen and colleagues developed a stepped approach to communication in interactions characterized by power imbalances. They called it the *agential stance* (Bergen et al. 2022), and the main point of it is that when an interpreter adopts the agential stance towards a speaker, they commit themselves to seeing the speaker as an agent. Not all the steps of the agential stance may be relevant outside the clinical context, but there are some lessons that can definitely be learnt about how to tackle delusional beliefs without stripping speakers of their agency.

During the conversations between interpreter and speaker, the speaker's agency can be preserved by the interpreter's recognition that the speaker is a subject of experience with a perspective on the world and on themselves, and that their perspective matters. The interpreter who adopts the agential stance acknowledges that the speaker's beliefs reflect the speaker's experiences and perspectives and that the adoption or maintenance of such beliefs can respond to multiple needs and interests. Thus, the interpreter does not exclude the speaker from deliberation and decision-making, and the speaker's participation in the social interactions underlying those processes is valued.

Respecting the speaker's agency in the ways I have outlined does not imply that interpreter and speaker must converge in their beliefs and perspectives on the world and themselves. What is often described as 'validation' is about communicating that the speaker's experiences matter and that the interpreter wants to know about them. Communication techniques contributing to validation include attentive and empathetic listening. Validation rests on showing interest in the person's experience without immediately redescribing, dismissing or challenging it. It can be practically manifested by asking open questions motivated by generous curiosity about the speaker's journey to the delusional belief. So, interpreters can validate a speaker's report without accepting it as true. Responding by saying: 'I want to know more about how you came to believe this' is very different from saying 'I agree with you'. In a way that is not dissimilar from deep canvassing, in the agential stance it is by showing curiosity and empathy that bridges are built.

If we are among the lucky ones who can affect change in society, or among the experts who have a voice and can influence political leadership, how can we help mend the polarization affecting public debates and build a common ground so that people can feel safe enough to share their views? Coherent suggestions emerging from the Swiss cheese model of tackling delusional beliefs will help, starting from the acknowledgement that the most effective changes will be those that are systemic and do not place an excessive burden on the shoulders of individual agents. Effective communicators will make scientific explanations fun and attractive, so they won't pale in comparison with the intriguing and unlikely plots weaved by conspiracists. Leaders will embrace an enlightened paternalism by carefully engineering nudges that can shape speakers' and interpreters' epistemic environments and listen to expert advice. Given that interpersonal relationships are modelled on the conduct of institutions, in public debates opponents should be encouraged to have a genuine opportunity to listen to each other and build common ground as opposed to shouting insults to each other and ignoring middle-ground solutions. This can become a template for more local interactions between interpreters and speakers.

The emphasis on systemic changes does not seem to apply equally well to the delusions that are idiosyncratic and symptomatic of mental disorders. How can we stop the stigmatization and exclusion affecting people with clinical delusions? Curiosity and empathy still help, as the interpreter can identify in the stories the speaker shares the role that the delusion is playing in making the speaker's reality more manageable and less puzzling. Although the delusion is something that can be very costly for the speaker, it is important to recognize its positive contribution to the speaker's mental life. This means that support can be offered to ensure that, when the delusion is given up, either a better coping mechanism takes its place or the speaker's newly gained insight does not turn into low self-esteem, depression or desperation. One common assumption about speakers who report clinical delusions is that they have irremediably lost their grip on reality and their testimony can no longer be trusted. But there is no good reason to think that the presence of a delusional belief compromises the person's capacity to have and express their perspectives on the world and to produce and share knowledge more generally.

In conversation with a new friend, Julie Delpy who plays the character of Celine in the film *Before Sunrise* says:

> I believe if there's any kind of God it wouldn't be in any of us, not you or me but just this little space in between. If there's any kind of magic

in this world it must be in the attempt of understanding someone sharing something. I know, it's almost impossible to succeed but who cares really? The answer must be in the attempt.

This is why delusions matter. Delusions are invoked when the 'attempt of understanding someone sharing something' fails and we feel like we cannot reach the other person, either as interpreters or as speakers. My hope is that a reflection on the importance of delusions, on their capacity to hinder and support agency all at once, can bring back the magic.

BIBLIOGRAPHY

Acar, K., Horntvedt, O., Cabrera, A. et al. (2022). Covid-19 conspiracy ideation is
    associated with the delusion proneness trait and resistance to update of beliefs.
    Nature Scientific Reports, 12: 10352. DOI: 10.1038/s41598-022-14071-7.
Aguiar, F., & de Francisco, A. (2009). Rational choice, social identity, and
    beliefs about oneself. *Philosophy of the Social Sciences*, 39: 547–71. DOI:
    10.1177/0048393109333631.
Aimola Davies, A.M., Davies, M., Ogden, J.A., Smithson, M., & White, R.C. (2009).
    Cognitive and motivational factors in anosognosia. In T. Bayne & J. Fernàndez
    (eds), *Delusions and self-deception: Affective influences on belief-formation*. Hove:
    Psychology Press, pp. 187–225.
Alexander, M.P., Stuss, D.T., & Benson, D.F. (1979). Capgras' syndrome: A
    reduplicative phenomenon. *Neurology*, 29: 334–9. DOI: 10.1212/wnl.29.3.334.
Alicke, M.D., & Sedikides, C. (2009). Self-enhancement and self-protection: What
    they are and what they do. *European Review of Social Psychology*, 20 (1): 1–48.
    DOI: 10.1080/10463280802613866.
Alicke, M.D., & Sedikides, C. (2011). *Handbook of self-enhancement and self-
    protection*. New York, NY: Guilford Press.
Allen, M. (2020). 'Immune to evidence': How dangerous Coronavirus conspiracies
    spread. *Propublica*. Accessed at: https://www.propublica.org/article/immune-to-
    evidence-how-dangerous-coronavirus-conspiracies-spread in June 2022.
American Psychiatric Association (2013). *Diagnostic and statistical manual
    of mental disorders* (5th edn, Text Revision). Washington, DC: American
    Psychiatric Publishing. DOI: 10.1176/appi.books.9780890425596.
Amore, M., Belvederi Murri, M., Calcagno, P. et al. (2020). The association
    between insight and depressive symptoms in schizophrenia: Undirected
    and Bayesian network analyses. *European Psychiatry*, 63. DOI: 10.1192/j.
    eurpsy.2020.45.
Angermeyer, M.C., & Matschinger, H. (2003). The stigma of mental illness: Effects
    of labelling on public attitudes towards people with mental disorder. *Acta
    Psychiatrica Scandinavica*, 108: 304–9. DOI: 10.1034/j.1600-0447.2003.00150.x.
Anonymous (2018). Learning to live with schizoaffective disorder: A transformative
    journey toward recovery. *Schizophrenia Bulletin*, 44 (1): 2–3. DOI: 10.1093/
    schbul/sbx125.
Antonovsky, A. (1987). *Unraveling the mystery of health: How people manage stress
    and stay well*. San Francisco, CA: Jossey-Bass.
Aronson, E. (2019). Dissonance, hypocrisy, and the self-concept. In E. Harmon-
    Jones (ed.), *Cognitive dissonance: Reexamining a pivotal theory in psychology*.

Washington DC: American Psychological Association, pp. 141–57. DOI: 10.1037/0000135-007.

Azarpanah, H., Farhadloo, M., Vahidov, R. et al. (2021). Vaccine hesitancy: Evidence from an adverse event following immunization database, and the role of cognitive biases. *BMC Public Health*, 21: 1686. DOI: 10.1186/ s12889-021-11745-1.

Barkun, M. (2015). Conspiracy theories as stigmatized knowledge. *Diogenes*, 62 (3–4): 114–20. DOI: 10.1177/0392192116669288.

Bartlett, J., & Miller, C. (2010). *The power of unreason: Conspiracy theories, extremism and counter-terrorism*. London: Demos.

Basit, A. (2021). Conspiracy theories and violent extremism: Similarities, differences and the implications. *Counter Terrorist Trends and Analyses*, 13 (3): 1–9. https://www.jstor.org/stable/27040260.

Bayne, T., & Pacherie, E. (2004). Experience, belief, and the interpretive fold. *Philosophy, Psychiatry, & Psychology*, 11 (1): 81–6.

Bayne, T., & Pacherie, E. (2005). In defense of the doxastic conception of delusions. *Mind and Language*, 20 (2): 163–88. DOI: 10.1353/ppp.2004.0034.

BBC (2014). These things shall pass: Delusions and how to survive them. Accessed at: https://www.bbc.co.uk/programmes/articles/3L4NFK4lBTNdzjml9LSnPwz/ these-things-shall-pass-delusions-and-how-to-survive-them in May 2022.

Beck, A.T., & Rector, N.T. (2002). Delusions: A cognitive perspective. *Journal of Cognitive Psychotherapy*, 16–4: 455–68. DOI: 10.1891/jcop.16.4.455.52522.

Begby, E. (2021). *Prejudice*. Oxford: Oxford University Press.

Bell, V. (2013). You needn't be wrong to be called delusional. *The Guardian*, August 4th. Accessed at: https://www.theguardian.com/science/2013/aug/04/truly-madly-deeply-delusional in January 2023.

Bell, V., Raihani, N., & Wilkinson, S. (2021). Derationalizing delusions. *Clinical Psychological Science*, 9 (1): 24–37. DOI: 10.1177/2167702620951553.

Belvederi Murri, M., Amore, M., Calcagno, P. et al. (2016). The 'Insight Paradox' in schizophrenia: Magnitude, moderators and mediators of the association between insight and depression. *Schizophrenia Bulletin*, 42: 1225–33. DOI: 10.1093/schbul/sbw040.

Bentall, R. (2003). The paranoid self. In T. Kircher, & A. David (eds), *The self in neuroscience and psychiatry*. Cambridge: Cambridge University Press, pp. 293–318. DOI: 10.1017/CBO9780511543708.015.

Bentall, R., & Kaney, S. (1989). Content specific information processing in persecutory delusions: An investigation using the emotional stroop test. *British Journal of Medical Psychology*, 62: 355–64.

Bentall, R., Kinderman, P., & Kaney, S. (1994). Self, attributional processes and abnormal beliefs: Towards a model of persecutory delusions. *Behaviour Research and Therapy*, 32: 331–41. DOI: 10.1111/j.2044-8341.1989.tb02845.x

Bergamaschi Ganapini, M. (2020). Confabulating reasons. *Topoi*, 39: 189–201. DOI: 10.1007/s11245-018-09629-y

Bergamaschi Ganapini, M. (2023). The signalling function of sharing fake stories. *Mind & Language* 38 (1), 64–80. DOI: 10.1111/mila.12373.

Bergen, C., Bortolotti, L., Tallent, K., Broome, M., Larkin, M., Temple, R., Fadashe, C., Lee, C., Lim, M.C., & McCabe, R. (2022). Communication in youth mental health clinical encounters: Introducing the agential stance. *Theory & Psychology*, 32 (5): 667–90. DOI: 10.1177/09593543221095079.

Bergstein, M., Weizman, A., & Solomon, Z. (2008). Sense of coherence among delusional patients: Prediction of remission and risk of relapse. *Comprehensive Psychiatry*, 49: 288–96. DOI: 10.1016/j.comppsych.2007.06.011.

Berti, A., Spinazzola, L., Pia, L., & Rabuffetti, M. (1993). Motor awareness and motor intention in anosognosia for hemiplegia. In P. Haggard, Y. Rossetti, M. Kawato (eds), *Sensorimotor foundations of higher cognition*. Oxford: Oxford University Press, pp. 163–81.

Billig, M. (1987). Anti-semitic themes and the British far left: Some social-psycho-logical observations on indirect aspects of the conspiracy tradition. In C.F. Graumann, & S. Moscovici (eds), *Changing conceptions of conspiracy*. New York, NY: Springer, pp. 115–36.

Bode, L., & Vraga, E. (2021). The Swiss cheese model for mitigating online misinformation. *Bulletin of the Atomic Scientists*, 77 (3): 129–33. DOI: 10.1080/00963402.2021.1912170.

Bögle, S., & Boden, Z. (2022). 'It was like a lightning bolt hitting my world': Feeling shattered in a first crisis in psychosis. *Qualitative Research in Psychology*, 19 (2): 377–404. DOI: 10.1080/14780887.2019.1631418.

Bolton, D. (2008). *What is mental disorder?* Oxford: Oxford University Press.

Bongiorno, F., & Bortolotti, L. (2019). The role of unconscious inference in models of delusion formation. In A. Nes, & T. Chan (eds), *Inference and consciousness*. London: Routledge, chapter 3.

Boorse, C. (1977). Health as a theoretical concept. *Philosophy of Science*, 44 (4): 542–73. http://www.jstor.org/stable/186939.

Bortolotti, L. (2009a). *Delusions and other irrational beliefs*. Oxford: Oxford University Press.

Bortolotti, L. (2009b). The epistemic benefits of reason giving. *Theory & Psychology*, 19 (5): 624–45. DOI: 10.1177/0959354309341921.

Bortolotti, L. (2015). The epistemic innocence of motivated delusions. *Consciousness & Cognition*, 33: 490–99. DOI: 10.1016/j.concog.2014.10.005.

Bortolotti, L. (2016). The epistemic benefits of elaborated and systematised delusions in schizophrenia. *British Journal for the Philosophy of Science*, 67 (3): 879–900. DOI: 10.1093/bjps/axv024.

Bortolotti, L. (2018a). Optimism, agency, and success. *Ethical Theory and Moral Practice*, 21: 521–35. DOI: 10.1007/s10677-018-9894-6.

Bortolotti, L. (2018b). Delusions and three myths of irrational belief. In L. Bortolotti, (eds), *Delusions in context*. Oxford: Palgrave Macmillan. DOI: 10.1007/978-3-319-97202-2_4.

Bortolotti, L. (2020a). *The epistemic innocence of irrational beliefs*. Oxford: Oxford University Press.

Bortolotti, L. (2020b). Doctors without 'Disorders'. *Aristotelian Society Supplementary Volume*, 94 (1): 163–184. DOI 10.1093/arisup/akaa006.

Bortolotti, L. (2022a). Are delusions pathological beliefs? *Asian Journal of Philosophy*, 1: 31. DOI: 10.1007/s44204-022-00033-3.

Bortolotti, L. (2022b). Sharing responsibility for conspiracy beliefs: The agency-in-context model. *Resistances*, 3 (6): e210103. DOI: 10.46652/resistances.v3i6.103.

Bortolotti, L., & Antrobus, M. (2015). Costs and benefits of realism and optimism. *Current Opinion in Psychiatry*, 28 (2): 194–8. DOI: 10.1097/YCO.0000000000000143.

Bortolotti, L., & Broome, M. (2009). A role for ownership and authorship in the analysis of thought insertion. *Phenomenology and the Cognitive Sciences*, 8: 205–24. DOI: 10.1007/s11097-008-9109-z.

Bortolotti, L., & Broome, M.R. (2012). Affective dimensions of the phenomenon of double bookkeeping in delusions. *Emotion Review*, 4 (2): 187–91. DOI: 10.1177/1754073911430115.

Bortolotti, L., & Ichino, A. (2020). Conspiracy theories may seem irrational – but they fulfill a basic human need. *The Conversation*, December 9th. Accessed at: https://theconversation.com/conspiracy-theories-may-seem-irrational-but-they-fulfill-a-basic-human-need-151324 in January 2023.

Bortolotti, L., & Miyazono, K. (2015). Recent work on the nature and the development of delusions. *Philosophy Compass*, 10 (9): 636–45. DOI: 10.1111/phc3.12249.

Bortolotti, L., & Murphy-Hollies, K. (2022). Exceptionalism at the time of COVID-19: Where nationalism meets irrationality. *Danish Yearbook of Philosophy*, 55 (2): 90–111. DOI: 10.1163/24689300-bja10025.

Bortolotti, L., & Stammers, S. (2020). When the personal becomes political: How do we fulfil our epistemic duties relative to the use of autobiographical stories in public debates? In S. Stapleford, & K. McCain (eds), *Epistemic duties: New arguments, new angles*. New York: Routledge, chapter 16.

Bortolotti, L., & Sullivan-Bissett, E. (2019). Is choice blindness a case of self-ignorance? *Synthese*, 198: 5437–54. DOI: 10.1007/s11229-019-02414-3.

Bortolotti, L., Broome, M.R., & Mameli, M. (2014). Delusions and responsibility for action: Insights from the breivik case. *Neuroethics*, 7: 377–82. DOI: 10.1007/s12152-013-9198-4.

Bortolotti, L., Cox, R., & Barnier, A. (2012). Can we recreate delusions in the laboratory? *Philosophical Psychology*, 25 (1): 109–31. DOI: 10.1080/09515089.2011.569909.

Bortolotti, L., Ichino, A., Mameli, M. (2021). Conspiracy theories and delusions. *Reti, Saperi e Linguaggi*, 2: 183–200. DOI: 10.12832/102760.

Bortolotti, L., Sullivan-Bissett, E., & Antrobus, M. (2019). Are optimistically biased beliefs epistemically innocent? In M. Balcerak-Jackson, & B. Balcerak-Jackson (eds), *Reasoning: Essays on theoretical and practical thinking*. Oxford: Oxford University Press, pp. 232–47.

Bottemanne, H., Morlaàs, O., Fossati, P., & Schmidt, L. (2020). Does the Coronavirus epidemic take advantage of human optimism bias? *Frontiers in Psychology*, 11. https://www.frontiersin.org/article/10.3389/fpsyg.2020.02001. DOI: 10.3389/fpsyg.2020.02001.

Bibliography

Breen, N., Caine, D., Coltheart, M., Hendy, J., & Roberts, C. (2000). Towards an understanding of delusions of misidentification: Four case studies. *Mind and Language*, 15: 74–110. DOI: 10.1111/1468-0017.00124.

Bressan, P. (2002). The connection between random sequences, everyday coincidences, and belief in the paranormal. *Applied Cognitive Psychology*, 16: 17–34. DOI: 10.1002/acp.754.

Broome, M., & Bortolotti, L. (2018). Affective instability and paranoia. *Discipline Filosofiche*, XXVIII (2): 123–36.

Buchman-Wildbaum, T., Váradi, E., Schmelowszky, A., Griffiths, M.D., Demetrovics, Z. & Urbán, R. (2020). The paradoxical role of insight in mental illness: The experience of stigma and shame in schizophrenia, mood disorders, and anxiety disorders. *Archives of Psychiatric Nursing*, 34 (6): 449–57. DOI: 10.1016/j.apnu.2020.07.009.

Buzzell, A., & Rini, R. (2022). Doing your own research and other impossible acts of epistemic superheroism. *Philosophical Psychology*. DOI: 10.1080/09515089.2022.2138019.

Campbell, J. (2001). Rationality, meaning, and the analysis of delusion. *Philosophy, Psychiatry, & Psychology*, 8 (2/3): 89–100. DOI: 10.1353/ppp.2001.0004.

Capgras, J., & Carette, J. (1924). Illusion des sosies et complexe d'Oedipe. *Annales Médico-Psychologiques*, 82: 48–68.

Cassam, Q. (2019). *Conspiracy theories*. Cambridge: Polity Press.

Cermolacce, M., Sass, L., & Parnas, J. (2010). What is bizarre in bizarre delusions? A critical review. *Schizophrenia Bulletin*, 36 (4): 667–79. DOI: 10.1093/ schbul/ sbq001.

Chapman, L.J., & Chapman, J.P. (1988). The genesis of delusions. In T.F. Oltmanns & B.A. Maher (eds), *Delusional Beliefs*. New York: Wiley, pp. 167–83.

Clarke, M., Whitty, P., Browne, S., Mc Tigue, O., Kinsella, A., Waddington, J.L., Larkin, C., & O'Callaghan, E. (2006). Suicidality in first episode psychosis. *Schizophrenia Research*, 86 (1–3): 221–25. DOI: 10.1016/j. schres.2006.05.026.

Coady, D. (2006). Conspiracy theories and official stories. In D. Coady (ed.), *Conspiracy theories: The philosophical debate*. Burlington, VT: Ashgate, pp. 115–28.

Coady, D. (2021). Conspiracy theory as heresy. *Educational Philosophy and Theory*, DOI: 10.1080/00131857.2021.1917364.

Coltheart, M. (2007). Cognitive neuropsychiatry and delusional belief. *Quarterly Journal of Experimental Psychology*, 60 (8): 1041–62. DOI: 10.1080/17470210701338071.

Coltheart, M. (2017). Confabulation and conversation. *Cortex*, 87: 62–8. DOI: 10.1016/j.cortex.2016.08.002.

Coltheart, M., Langdon, R., & McKay, R. (2011). Delusional belief. *Annual Review of Psychology*, 62: 271–98. DOI: 10.1146/annurev.psych.121208.131622.

Coltheart, M., Menzies, P., & Sutton, J. (2010). Abductive inference and delusional belief. *Cognitive Neuropsychiatry*, 15 (1): 261–87. DOI: 10.1080/13546800903439120.

Conrad, K. (1958). *Die beginnende Schizophrenie. Versuch einer Gestaltanalyse des Wahns*. Stuttgart: Thieme.

Cooper, R. (2002). Disease. *Studies in History and Philosophy of Science* Part C: *Studies in History and Philosophy of Biological and Biomedical Sciences*, 33 (2): 263–82. DOI: 10.1016/S0039-3681(02)00018-3.

Corlett, P. (2018). Delusions and prediction error. In L. Bortolotti (ed.), *Delusions in context*. Cham: Palgrave Macmillan, pp. 35–66.

Corlett, P., Murray, G.K., Honey, G.D., Aitken, M.R.F., Shanks, D.R., Robbins, T.W., Bullmore, E.T., Dickinson, A., & Fletcher, P.C. (2007). Disrupted prediction-error signal in psychosis: Evidence for an associative account of delusions. *Brain*, 130 (9): 2387–400. DOI: 10.1093/brain/awm173.

Corrigan, P.W., Watson, A.C. (2002). Understanding the impact of stigma on people with mental illness. *World Psychiatry*, 1: 16–20.

Costabile, K.A., Shedlosky-Shoemaker, R., & Austin, A.B. (2018). Universal stories: How narratives satisfy core motives. *Self and Identity*, 17 (4): 418–31. DOI: 10.1080/15298868.2017.1413008.

Cross, K.P. (1977). Not can, but will college-teaching be improved. *New Directions for Higher Education*, 17: 1–15.

Currie, G., & Ravenscroft, I. (2002). *Recreative minds: Imagination in philosophy and psychology*. Oxford: Oxford University Press.

Cuttler, C., & Ryckman, M. (2019). Don't call me delusional: Stigmatizing effects of noun labels on people with mental disorders. *Stigma and Health*, 4 (2): 118–25. DOI: 10.1037/sah0000132.

Davidson, D. (1973). On the very idea of a conceptual scheme. *Proceedings and Addresses of the American Philosophical Association*, 47: 5–20. DOI: 10.2307/3129898.

Davies, M., & Coltheart, M. (2000). Introduction: Pathologies of belief. *Mind and Language*, 15: 1–46. DOI: 10.1111/1468-0017.00122.

Davies, M., Coltheart, M., Langdon, R., & Breen, N. (2001). Monothematic delusions: Towards a two-factor account. *Philosophy, Psychiatry & Psychology*, 8 (2/3): 133–58. DOI: 10.1353/ppp.2001.0007.

de Cates, A.N., Catone, G., Marwaha, S., Bebbington, P., Humpston, C.S., & Broome, M.R. (2021). Self-harm, suicidal ideation and the positive symptoms of psychosis: Cross-sectional and prospective data from a national household survey. *Schizophrenia Research*, 233: 80–8. DOI: 10.1016/j.schres.2021.06.021.

de Pauw, K.W. (1994). Psychodynamic approaches to the capgras delusion: A critical historical review. *Psychopathology*, 27: 154–60. DOI: 10.1159/000284864.

de Pauw, K., & Szulecka, T. (1988). Dangerous delusions: Violence and the misidentification syndromes. *British Journal of Psychiatry*, 152 (1): 91–6. DOI: 10.1192/bjp.152.1.91.

De, S., Bhatia, T., Thomas, P., Chakraborty, S., Prasad, S., Nagpal, R., Nimgaonkar, V.L., & Deshpande, S.N. (2013). Bizarre delusions: A qualitative study on Indian schizophrenia patients. *Indian Journal of Psychological Medicine*, 35 (3): 268–72. DOI: 10.4103/0253-7176.119484.

Deng, F.M. (1995). *War of visions: Conflict of identities in the Sudan*. Washington, DC: Brookings.

Douglas, K. (2021). Are conspiracy theories harmless? *The Spanish Journal of Psychology*, 24: E13. DOI: 10.1017/SJP.2021.10.

Douglas, K.M., & Sutton, R.M. (2011). Does it take one to know one? Endorsement of conspiracy theories is influenced by personal willingness to conspire. *British Journal of Social Psychology*, 50: 433–552. DOI: 10.1111/j.2044-8309.2010.02018.x.

Douglas, K.M., & Sutton, R.M. (2015). Climate change: Why the conspiracy theories are dangerous. *Bulletin of the Atomic Scientists*, 71 (2): 98–106. DOI: 10.1177/0096340215571 9.

Douglas, K.M., Sutton, R.M., & Cichocka, A. (2017). The psychology of conspiracy theories. *Current Directions in Psychological Science*, 26 (6): 538–42. DOI: 10.1177/0963721417718261.

Douglas, K.M., Uscinski, J.E., Sutton, R.M., Cichocka, A., Nefes, T., Ang, C.S., & Deravi, F. (2019). Understanding conspiracy theories. *Political Psychology*, 40: 3–35. DOI: 10.1111/pops.12568.

Drake, R.E., & Cotton, P.G. (1986). Depression, hopelessness and suicide in chronic schizophrenia. *The British Journal of Psychiatry: The Journal of Mental Science*, 148: 554–59. DOI: 10.1192/bjp.148.5.554.

Driscoll, A., & Husain, M. (2019). Why Joker's depiction of mental illness is dangerously misinformed. *The Guardian*, October 21st. Accessed at: https://www.theguardian.com/film/2019/oct/21/joker-mental-illness-joaquin-phoenix-dangerous-misinformed in January 2023.

Enoch, M.D., & Trethowan, W. (1991). *Uncommon psychiatric syndromes*, 3rd edn. Oxford: Butterworth-Heinemann.

Fearon, J.D. (1999). What is identity (as we now use the word)?" Stanford, CA: Stanford University Department of Political Science. Accessed at: https://web.stanford.edu/group/fearon-research/cgi-bin/wordpress/wp-content/uploads/2013/10/What-is-Identity-as-we-now-use-the-word-.pdf in June 2022.

Feyaerts, J., Henriksen, M.G., Vanheule, S., Myin-Germeys, I., & Sass, L.A. (2021). Delusions beyond beliefs: A critical overview of diagnostic, aetiological and therapeutic schizophrenia research from a clinical-phenomenological perspective. *Lancet Psychiatry*, 8 (3): 237–49. DOI: 10.1016/S2215-0366(20)30460-0.

Fineberg, S., & Corlett, P. (2016). The doxastic shear pin: Delusions as errors of learning and memory. *Cognitive Neuropsychiatry*, 21 (1): 73–89. DOI: 10.1080/13546805.2015.1136206.

Flanagan, O. (2009). 'Can do' attitudes: Some positive illusions are not misbeliefs. *Behavioral and Brain Sciences*, 32 (6): 519–20. DOI: 10.1017/S0140525X09991439.

Fletcher, G.J., & Kerr, P.S. (2010). Through the eyes of love: reality and illusion in intimate relationships. *Psychological Bulletin*, 136 (4): 627–58. DOI: 10.1037/a0019792.

Fletcher, G.J.O., & Boyes, A.D. (2008). Is love blind? Reality and illusion in intimate relationships. In J. P. Forgas, & J. Fitness (eds), *Social relationships: Cognitive, affective, and motivational processes*. Hove: Psychology Press, pp. 101–14.

Flores, C. (2021). Delusional evidence-responsiveness. *Synthese*, 199: 6299–330. DOI: 10.1007/s11229-021-03070-2.

Franks, B., Bangerter, A., & Bauer, M. (2013). Conspiracy theories as quasi-religious mentality: An integrated account from cognitive science, social representations theory and frame theory. *Frontiers in Psychology*, 4. https://www.frontiersin.org/articles/10.3389/fpsyg.2013.00424.

Fraser, R. (2020). Epistemic FOMO. *Cambridge Humanities Review*, 17. https://cambridgereview.cargo.site/Dr-Rachel-Fraser.

Freeman, D. (2018). A history of delusions: Cotard, the 'walking corpse delusion'. *BBC Radio*, 4. https://www.bbc.co.uk/sounds/play/m0001f0r.

Freeman, D., Garety, P.A., Fowler, D., Kuipers, E., Bebbington, P.E., & Dunn, G. (2004). Why do people with delusions fail to choose more realistic explanations for their experiences? An empirical investigation. *Journal of Consulting and Clinical Psychology*, 72 (4): 671–80. DOI: 10.1037/0022-006X.72.4.671.

Freud, S. (1928). *The future of an illusion*. London: Hogarth.

Fulford, K.W.M., & Jackson, M. (1997). Spiritual experience and psychopathology. *Philosophy, Psychiatry, & Psychology*, 4 (1): 41–65. DOI: 10.1353/ppp.1997.0002.

Gallagher, S. (2009). Delusional realities. In M.R. Broome, & L. Bortolotti (eds), *Social relationships: Cognitive, affective, and motivational processes*. Oxford: Oxford University Press, pp. 245–68.

Garety, P.A., & Freeman, D. (1999). Cognitive approaches to delusions: A critical review of theories and evidence. *The British Journal of Clinical Psychology*, 38 (2): 113–54. DOI: 10.1348/014466599162700.

Garety, P., & Hemsley, D. (1994). *Delusions: Investigations into the psychology of delusional reasoning*. Hove: Psychology Press.

Garety, P., Hemsley, D., & Wessely, S. (1991). Reasoning in deluded schizophrenic and paranoid patients. *Journal of Nervous and Mental Disease*, 179: 194–201. DOI: 10.1097/00005053-199104000-00003.

Garety, P., Kuipers, E., Fowler, D., Freeman, D., & Bebbington, P. (2001). A cognitive model of the positive symptoms of psychosis. *Psychological Medicine*, 31: 189–95. DOI: 10.1017/s0033291701003312.

Garson, J. (2022). *Madness: A Philosophical Exploration*. New York: Oxford University Press.

Gelfert, A. (2018). Testimony. *Routledge Encyclopedia of Philosophy*. DOI: 10.4324/0123456789-P049-2. Accessed at: https://www.rep.routledge.com/articles/thematic/testimony/v-2 in January 2023.

Gerrans, P. (2001). Refining the explanation of Cotard's delusion. *Mind & Language*, 15 (1): 111–22. DOI: 10.1111/1468-0017.00125.

Gerrans, P. (2014). *The measure of madness*. Cambridge, MA: MIT Press.

Gerrans, P. (2022). A vessel without a pilot: Bodily and affective experience in the Cotard delusion of inexistence. *Mind & Language*, 1–22. DOI: 10.1111/mila.12441.

Gilleen, J., & David, A. (2005). The cognitive neuropsychiatry of delusions: From psychopathology to neuropsychology and back again. *Psychological Medicine*, 35 (1): 5–12. DOI: 10.1017/S0033291704003976.

Gopnik, A. (2000). Explanation as orgasm and the drive for causal knowledge: The function, evolution and phenomenology of the theory formation system. In J.C. Keil, & R.A. Wilson (eds), *Explanation and cognition*. Cambridge, MA: MIT Press, pp. 299–323.

Grebe, E., & Nattrass, N. (2012). AIDS conspiracy beliefs and unsafe sex in cape town. *AIDS and Behavior*, 16: 761–73. DOI: 10.1007/s10461-011-9958-2.

Greenburgh, A.G., & Raihani, N. (2022). Paranoia and conspiracy thinking. *Current Opinion in Psychology*, 47: 101362. DOI: 10.1016/j.copsyc.2022.101362.

Greenburgh, A.G., Liefgreen, A., Bell, V., & Raihani, N. (2022). Factors affecting conspiracy theory endorsement in paranoia. *Royal Society Open Science*, 9 (1). DOI: 10.1098/rsos.211555.

Gunn, R. (2018). Delusion and affective framing. University of Birmingham. Ph.D. Available at: https://etheses.bham.ac.uk/id/eprint/8117/.

Gunn, R., & Bortolotti, L. (2018). Can delusions play a protective role? *Phenomenology and the Cognitive Sciences*, 17 (4): 813–33. DOI: 10.1007/s11097-017-9555-6.

Gunn, R., & Larkin, M. (2020). Delusion formation as an inevitable consequence of a radical alteration in lived experience. *Psychosis*, 12 (2): 151–61. DOI: 10.1080/17522439.2019.1690562.

Gupta, M., & Sharma, A. (2021). Fear of missing out: A brief overview of origin, theoretical underpinnings and relationship with mental health. *World Journal of Clinical Cases*, 9 (19): 4881–9. DOI: 10.12998/wjcc.v9.i19.4881. PMID: 34307542; PMCID: PMC8283615.

Hall, T., Kakuma, R., Palmer, L. et al. (2019). Social inclusion and exclusion of people with mental illness in Timor-Leste: A qualitative investigation with multiple stakeholders. *BMC Public Health*, 19: 702. DOI: 10.1186/s12889-019-7042-4.

Hannon, M. (2021). Disagreement or bad-mouthing? The role of expressive discourse in politics. In E. Edenberg, & M. Hannon (eds), *Political epistemology*. Oxford: Oxford University Press, pp. 297–318.

Harford, T. (2022). The conspiracy theorist who changes his mind. *Cautionary Tales*. Accessed at: https://timharford.com/2022/10/cautionary-conversations-the-conspiracy-theorist-who-changed-his-mind/ in November 2022.

Harvey, S., Dean, K., Morgan, C., Walsh, E., Demjaha, A., Dazzan, P., … Murray, R. (2008). Self-harm in first-episode psychosis. *British Journal of Psychiatry*, 192 (3): 178–84. DOI: 10.1192/bjp.bp.107.037192.

Hassan, S., Flett, G.L., Ganguli, R., & Hewitt, P.L. (2014). Perfectionistic self-presentation and suicide in a young woman with major depression and psychotic features. *Case Reports in Psychiatry*, 901981. DOI: 10.1155/2014/901981.

Hemsley, D. (2004). Disorders of perception and cognition in schizophrenia, *European Review of Applied Psychology*, 54 (2): 109–17. DOI: 10.1016/j.erap.2003.12.005.

Herrig, E. (1995). First person account: A personal experience. *Schizophrenia Bulletin*, 21 (2): 339–42. DOI: 10.1093/schbul/21.2.339.

Hevey, D., McGee, H.M., Horgan, J.H. (2014). Comparative optimism among patients with coronary heart disease (CHD) is associated with fewer adverse clinical events 12 months later. *Journal of Behavioral Medicine*, 37 (2): 300–7. DOI: 10.1007/s10865-012-9487-0.

Hingley, S.M. (1997). Psychodynamic perspectives on psychosis and psychotherapy I: Theory. *The British Journal of Medical Psychology*, 70: 301–12. DOI: 10.1111/j.2044-8341.1997.tb01908.x.

Hofstadter, R. (1964). *The paranoid style in American politics and other essays.* Cambridge, NY: Harvard University Press.

Hohwy, J. (2014). *The predictive mind.* Oxford: Oxford University Press.

Hornsey, M. (2021). The psychology of the anti-vaccine movement. *The Biochemist*, 43 (4): 52–4. DOI: 10.1042/bio_2021_162.

Hosty, G. (1992). Beneficial delusions? *Psychiatric Bulletin*, 16 (6): 373. DOI: 10.1192/pb.16.6.373.

Hughes, J.P., Efstratiou, A., Komer, S.R., Baxter, L.A., Vasiljevic, M., & Leite, A.C. (2022). The impact of risk perceptions and belief in conspiracy theories on COVID-19 pandemic-related behaviours. *PLoS ONE*, 17 (2): e0263716. DOI: 10.1371/journal.pone.0263716.

Hughes, T. (2007). Delusions are not necessarily false. *British Medical Journal*. Rapid responses. Accessed at: https://www.bmj.com/content/335/7610/91/rapid-responses in May 2022.

Huggins, D. (2022). Paranoia, voices, sleeplessness. What my psychotic break felt like. *Washington Post*, November 13th. Accessed at: https://www.washingtonpost.com/wellness/2022/11/13/bipolar-manic-episode/ in November 2022.

Humpston, C. S., & Broome, M. R. (2016). The spectra of soundless voices and audible thoughts: Towards an integrative model of auditory verbal hallucinations and thought insertion. *Review of Philosophy and Psychology,* 7 (3): 611–29. DOI: 10.1007/s13164-015-0232-9.

Hyden, L.C., & Örulv, L. (2009). Narrative and identity in Alzheimer's disease: A case study. *Journal of Aging Studies*, 23: 205–14. DOI: 10.1016/j.jaging.2008.01.001.

Ichino, A. (2020). *The imaginative mind.* Milano: Mimesis.

Ichino, A., & Raikka, J. (2020). Non-doxastic conspiracy theories. *Argumenta*, 1–18. DOI: 10.14275/2465-2334/20200.ich.

Imhoff, R., & Lamberty, P.K. (2017). Too special to be duped: Need for uniqueness motivates conspiracy beliefs. *European Journal of Social Psychology*, 47: 724–34. DOI: 10.1002/ejsp.2265.

Imhoff, R., Lamberty, P.K. (2018). How paranoid are conspiracy believers? Toward a more fine-grained understanding of the connect and disconnect between paranoia and belief in conspiracy theories. *European Journal of Social Psychology*, 48: 909–26. DOI: 10.1002/ejsp.2494.

Ingram, J., & Shutz, B. (2019). The dangerous delusions of climate change denial. *iPolitics*, August 11th. Accessed at: https://www.ipolitics.ca/news/the-dangerous-delusion-of-climate-change-denial in January 2023.

Isham, L., Griffith, L., Boylan, A.M., Hicks, A., Wilson, N., Byrne, R., Sheaves, B., Bentall, R.P., & Freeman, D. (2021). Understanding, treating, and renaming grandiose delusions: A qualitative study. *Psychology and Psychotherapy*, 94 (1): 119–40. DOI: 10.1111/papt.12260.

Jadeja, J. (with A. Carrier) (2021). I left QAnon in 2019. But I'm still not free. *Politico*, 11th December. Accessed at: https://www.politico.com/news/magazine/2021/12/11/q-anon-movement-former-believer-523972 in November 2022.

Jaspers, K. (1963). *General Psychopathology*. Chicago: University of Chicago Press.

Jefferson, A., & Bortolotti, L. (2023). On the moral psychology of the pandemic agent. In E. Barbosa (ed.), *Moral Challenges in a Pandemic Age*. London: Routledge, chapter 2.

Jefferson, A., Bortolotti, L., & Kuzmanovic, B. (2017). What is unrealistic optimism? *Consciousness and Cognition: An International Journal*, 50: 3–11. DOI: 10.1016/j.concog.2016.10.005.

Jolley, D., & Douglas, K.M. (2014). The social consequences of conspiracism: Exposure to conspiracy theories decreases intentions to engage in politics and to reduce one's carbon footprint. *British Journal of Psychology*, 105 (1): 35–56. DOI: 10.1111/bjop.12018.

Jolley, D., Meleady, R., & Douglas, K.M. (2020). Exposure to intergroup conspiracy theories promotes prejudice which spreads across groups. *British Journal of Psychology*, 111 (1): 17–35. DOI: 10.1111/bjop.12385.

Jonas, E., Schulz-Hardt, S., Frey, D., & Thelen, N. (2001). Confirmation bias in sequential information search after preliminary decisions: An expansion of dissonance theoretical research on selective exposure to information. *Journal of Personality and Social Psychology*, 80: 557–71. DOI: 10.1037//0022-3514.80.4.557.

Jones, P. (1999). Beliefs and identities. In J. Horton, & S. Mendus (eds), *Toleration, identity and difference*. Cham: Palgrave Macmillan.

Junginger, J. (2006). "Stereotypic" delusional offending. *Behavioral Sciences & the Law*, 24 (3): 295–311. DOI: 10.1002/bsl.682. PMID: 16773647.

Jutzi, C.A., Willardt, R., Schmid, P.C., & Jonas, E. (2020). Between conspiracy beliefs, ingroup bias, and system justification: How people use defense strategies to cope with the threat of COVID-19. *Frontiers in Psychology*, 11. https://www.frontiersin.org/articles/10.3389/fpsyg.2020.578586. DOI: 10.3389/fpsyg.2020.578586.

Kaney, S., & Bentall, R. (1989). Persecutory delusions and attributional style. *British Journal of Medical Psychology*, 62: 191–8. DOI: 10.1111/j.2044-8341.1989.tb02826.x.

Kendler, K.S., & Campbell, J. (2014). Expanding the domain of the understandable in psychiatric illness: An updating of the Jasperian framework of explanation and understanding. *Psychological Medicine*, 44 (1): 1–7. DOI: 10.1017/S0033291712003030.

Kendler, K.S., Glazer, W.M., & Morgenstern, H. (1983). Dimensions of delusional experience. *American Journal of Psychiatry*, 140 (4): 466–9. DOI: 10.1176/ajp.140.4.466. PMID: 6837787.

Kim, H.K., & Niederdeppe, J. (2013). Exploring optimistic bias and the integrative model of behavioral prediction in the context of a campus influenza outbreak. *Journal of Health Communication*, 18 (2): 206–22. DOI: 10.1080/10810730.2012.688247.

Kinne, P., & Bhanot, V. (2008). I've been abducted by aliens. *Current Psychiatry*, 7 (7): 82.

Kiran, C., & Chaudhury, S. (2009). Understanding delusions. *Industrial Psychiatry Journal*, 18 (1): 3–18. DOI: 10.4103/0972-6748.57851.

Kuhn, T. (1962). *The structure of scientific revolutions*. Chicago: University of Chicago Press.

Kulesza, Wojciech et al. (2021). We are infected with the new, mutated virus uo-COVID-19. *Archives of Medical Science*, 17 (6): 1–10. DOI: 10.5114/aoms.2020.99592.

Lancellotta, E. (2022). Is the biological adaptiveness of delusions doomed? *Review of Philosophy and Psychology*, 13: 47–63. DOI: 10.1007/s13164-021-00545-6.

Lancellotta, E., & Bortolotti, L. (2019). Are clinical delusions adaptive? *WIREs in the Cognitive Sciences*, 10 (5): e1502. DOI: 10.1002/wcs.1502.

Lancellotta, E. and Bortolotti, L. (2020). Delusions in the two-factor theory: pathological or adaptive? *European Journal of Analytic Philosophy*, 16 (2): 37–58. DOI: 10.31820/ejap.16.2.2

Langer, K.G., & Bogousslavsky, J. (2020). The merging tracks of anosognosia and neglect. *European Neurology*, 83 (4): 438–46. DOI: 10.1159/000510397.

Langdon, R., & Coltheart, M. (2000). The cognitive neuropsychology of delusions. *Mind and Language*, 15 (1): 184–218. DOI: 10.1111/1468-0017.00129.

Lantian, A., Muller, D., Nurra, C., & Douglas, K.M. (2017). 'I know things they don't know!': The role of need for uniqueness in belief in conspiracy theories. *Social Psychology*, *48* (3): 160–73. DOI: 10.1027/1864-9335/a000306.

Lantian, A., Muller, D., Nurra, C., Klein, O., Berjot, S., & Pantazi, M. (2018). Stigmatized beliefs: Conspiracy theories, anticipated negative evaluation of the self, and fear of social exclusion. *European Journal of Social Psychology*, 48: 939–54. DOI: 10.1002/ejsp.2498.

Lebelo, L.T., & Grobler, G.P. (2020). Case study: A patient with severe delusions who self-mutilates. *The South African Journal of Psychiatry*, 26: 1403. DOI: 10.4102/sajpsychiatry.v26i0.1403.

Levy, N. (2019). Is conspiracy theorising irrational? *Social Epistemology Review and Reply Collective*, 8 (10): 65–76. https://wp.me/p1Bfg0-4wW.

Levy, N. (2021). *Bad beliefs*. Oxford: Oxford University Press.

Levy-Valensie, J. (1929). L'illusion des sosies. *Gaz Hôp*, 55: 1001–03.

Li, D., Law, S., Andermann, L. (2012). Association between degrees of social defeat and themes of delusion in patients with schizophrenia from immigrant and ethnic minority backgrounds. *Transcultural Psychiatry*, 49 (5): 735–49. DOI: 10.1177/1363461512464625.

Link, B.G., Phelan, J.C., Bresnahan, M, Stueve, A, & Pescosolido, B.A. (1999). Public conceptions of mental illness: Labels, causes, dangerousness, and social distance. *American Journal of Public Health*, 89 (9): 1328–33. DOI: 10.2105/ajph.89.9.1328.

Bibliography

Loftus, E.F., Coan, J., & Pickrell, J.E. (1996). Manufacturing false memories using bits of reality. In L.M. Reder (ed.), *Implicit memory and metacognition*. Mahwah, NJ: Lawrence Erlbaum.

Lynn, M., & Harris, J. (1997). The desire for unique consumer products: A new individual differences scale. *Psychology and Marketing*, 14: 601–16. DOI: 10.1007/978-3-319-11806-2_96.

Maher, B. (1974). Delusional thinking and perceptual disorder. *Journal of Individual Psychology*, 30: 98–113.

Maher, B. (1988). Anomalous experiences and delusional thinking: The logic of explanations. In T.F. Oltmanns & B.A. Maher (eds), *Delusional beliefs*. New York: Wiley, pp. 15–33.

Maher, B. (1999). Anomalous experience in everyday life: Its significance for psychopathology. *The Monist*, 82 (4): 547–70. DOI: 10.5840/monist199982428.

Martindale, B., & Summers, A. (2013). The psychodynamics of psychosis. *Advances in Psychiatric Treatment*, 19 (2): 124–31. DOI: 10.1192/apt.bp.111.009126.

Maslin, M. (2019). The five corrupt pillars of climate change denial. *The Conversation,* November 28th. Accessed at: https://theconversation.com/the-five-corrupt-pillars-of-climate-change-denial-122893 in November 2022.

McCabe, R., Skelton, J., Heath, C., Burns, T., & Priebe, S. (2002). Engagement of patients with psychosis in the consultation: Conversation analytic study. *BMJ*, 325: 1148. DOI: 10.1136/bmj.325.7373.1148.

McKay, R.T. (2012). Delusional inference. *Mind & Language*, 27 (3): 330–55. DOI: 10.1111/j.1468-0017.2012.01447.x.

McKay, R.T., & Cipolotti, L. (2007). Attributional style in a case of cotard delusion. *Consciousness and Cognition*, 16 (2): 349–59. DOI: 10.1016/j.concog.2006.06.001.

McKay, R.T., & Dennett, D.C. (2009). The evolution of misbelief. *Behavioral Brain Science,* 32 (6): 493–510; discussion 510-61. DOI: 10.1017/S0140525X09990975.

McKay, R.T., & Kinsbourne, M. (2010). Confabulation, delusions and anosognosia. Motivational factors and false claims. *Cognitive Neuropsychiatry*, 15 (1): 288–318. DOI: 10.1080/13546800903374871.

McKay, R.T., Langdon, R., & Coltheart, M. (2005). 'Sleights of mind': Delusions, defences, and self-deception. *Cognitive Neuropsychiatry*, 10 (4): 305–26. DOI: 10.1080/13546800903374871.

McKelvey, T. (2020). Coronavirus: Why are Americans so angry about masks? *BBC News*, July 20th. Accessed at: https://www.bbc.co.uk/news/world-us-canada-53477121 in January 2023.

McRaney, D. (2022). *How minds change*. London: OneWorld Publications.

Meechan, C.F., Laws, K.R., Young, A.H., McLoughlin, D.M., & Jauhar, S. (2022). A critique of narrative reviews of the evidence-base for ECT in depression. *Epidemiology and Psychiatric Sciences*, 31: e10. DOI: 10.1017/S2045796021000731.

Mercier, H. (2020). *Not born yesterday*. Princeton, NJ: Princeton University Press.

Metzl, J.M., Piemonte, J., McKay, T. (2021). Mental illness, mass shootings, and the future of psychiatric research into American gun violence. *Harvard Review of Psychiatry*, 29 (1): 81–9. DOI: 10.1097/HRP.0000000000000280.

Mishara, A.L., Corlett, P. (2009). Are delusions biologically adaptive? Salvaging the doxastic shear pin. *Behavioral and Brain Sciences*, 32 (6): 530–1. DOI: 10.1017/S0140525X09991464.

Miyazono, K. (2015). Delusions as harmful malfunctioning beliefs. *Consciousness and Cognition*, 33: 561–73. DOI: 10.1016/j.concog.2014.10.008.

Miyazono, K. (2018). *Delusions and beliefs*. London: Routledge.

Miyazono, K., Bortolotti, L., & Broome, M. (2014). Prediction-error and two-factor theories of delusion formation: Competitors or allies? In N. Galbraith (ed.), *Aberrant beliefs and reasoning*. Hove: Psychology Press, pp. 34–54.

Miyazono, K., & McKay, R.T. (2019). Explaining delusional beliefs: A hybrid model. *Cognitive Neuropsychiatry*, 24 (5): 335–46. DOI: 10.1080/13546805.2019.1664443.

Miyazono, K., & Salice, A. (2021). Social epistemological conception of delusion. *Synthese*, 199: 1831–51. DOI: 10.1007/s11229-020-02863-1.

Moore, A. (2018). Conspiracies, Conspiracy Theories and Democracy. *Political Studies Review*, 16 (1): 2–12. DOI: 10.1111/1478-9302.12102.

Moritz, S., & Woodward, T.S. (2004). Plausibility judgment in schizophrenic patients: Evidence for a liberal acceptance bias. *German Journal of Psychiatry*, 7 (4): 66–74.

Moutsiana, C., Charpentier, C.J., Garrett, N., Cohen, M.X., & Sharot, T. (2015). Human frontal-subcortical circuit and asymmetric belief updating. *Journal of Neuroscience* 35: 14077–85. DOI: 10.1523/JNEUROSCI.1120-15.2015.

Murphy, D. (2012). The folk epistemology of delusions. *Neuroethics*, 5 (1): 19–22. DOI: 10.1007/s12152-011-9125-5.

Murphy-Hollies, K. (2022). Political confabulation and self-regulation. In A. Jefferson, O. Palermos, P. Paris, & J. Webber (eds), Values and Virtues for a Challenging World. *Royal institute of philosophy supplement*. Cambridge: Cambridge University Press.

Murray, S.L., & Holmes, J.G. (1994). Storytelling in close relationships: The construction of confidence. *Personality and Social Psychology Bulletin*, 20 (6): 650–63. DOI: 10.1177/0146167294206004.

Murray, S.L., Holmes, J.G., & Griffin, D.W. (1996). The benefits of positive illusions: Idealization and the construction of satisfaction in close relationships. *Journal of Personality and Social Psychology*, 70 (1): 79–98. DOI: 10.1037/0022-3514.70.1.79.

National Health Service (2019). Symptoms – psychosis. Accessed at: https://www.nhs.uk/mental-health/conditions/psychosis/symptoms/ in May 2022.

Pantazi, M., Papaioannou, K., & van Prooijen, J.W. (2022). Power to the people: The hidden link between support for direct democracy and belief in conspiracy theories. *Political Psychology*, 43: 529–48. DOI: 10.1111/pops.12779.

Parnas, J., Urfer-Parnas, A., & Stephensen, H. (2021). Double bookkeeping and schizophrenia spectrum: Divided unified phenomenal consciousness. *European Archives of Psychiatry and Clinical Neuroscience*, 271: 1513–23.

Payne, R. (1992). First person account: My schizophrenia. *Schizophrenia Bulletin*, 8 (4): 725–28.

People's Action Institute (2021). Deep canvassing. Accessed at: https://deepcanvass.org in November 2022.

Peterson, C. (2000). The future of optimism. *American Psychologist*, 55 (I): 44–55. DOI: 10.1037//0003-066X.55.1.44.

Pierre, J. M. (2020). Mistrust and misinformation: A two-component, socio-epistemic model of belief in conspiracy theories. *Journal of Social and Political Psychology*, 8 (2): 617–41. DOI: 10.5964/jspp.v8i2.1362.

Puddifoot, K. (2021). *How stereotypes deceive us*. Oxford: Oxford University Press.

Raab, M.H., Ortlieb, S.A., Auer, N., Guthmann, K., & Carbon, C.C. (2013). Thirty shades of truth: Conspiracy theories as stories of individuation, not of pathological delusion. *Frontiers in Psychology*, 4: 406. DOI: 10.5964/jspp.v8i2.1362.

Radden, J. (2010). *On delusion*. Abingdon: Routledge.

Ramachandran, V.S. (1995). Anosognosia in parietal lobe syndrome. *Consciousness & Cognition*, 4 (1): 22–51. DOI: 10.1006/ccog.1995.1002.

Ramachandran, V.S. (1996). The evolutionary biology of self-deception, laughter, dreaming and depression: Some clues from anosognosia. *Medical Hypotheses*, 47 (5): 347–62. DOI: 10.1016/S0306-9877(96)90215-7.

Ramsey, F.P. (1931) Truth and probability. In Braithwaite, R.B., (ed.), *The foundations of mathematics and other logical essays*. New York: Harcourt, Brace and Company, pp. 156–98.

Ratcliffe, M., & Wilkinson, S. (2015). Thought insertion clarified. *Journal of consciousness Studies: Controversies in Science & the Humanities*, 22 (11–12): 246–69.

Remski, M. (2020). Inside Kelly Brogan's COVID-denying, vax-resistant conspiracy machine. *GEN Medium*, September 16th. Accessed at: https://gen.medium.com/inside-kelly-brogans-covid-denying-vax-resistant-conspiracy-machine-28342e6369b1 in November 2020.

Ritschel, C. (2020). Goop expert says coronavirus doesn't exist: 'There is potentially no such thing'. *The Independent*, March 24th. Accessed at: https://www.independent.co.uk/life-style/goop-coronavirus-kelly-brogan-expert-contributor-md-deaths-covid-19-a9421476.html in January 2023.

Ritunnano, R., & Bortolotti, L. (2022). Do delusions have and give meaning? *Phenomenology and the Cognitive Sciences*, 21: 949–68. DOI: 10.1007/s11097-021-09764-9.

Ritunnano, R., Humpston, C., & Broome, M. (2022). Finding order within the disorder: A case study exploring the meaningfulness of delusions. *BJPsych Bulletin*, 46 (2): 109–15. DOI: 10.1192/bjb.2020.151.

Roberts, G. (1991). Delusional belief systems and meaning in life: A preferred reality? *The British Journal of Psychiatry*, 159: S19–28.

Roberts, S. (2020). Multiple layers improve success. *New York Times*, 5th December. Accessed at: https://www.nytimes.com/2020/12/05/health/coronavirus-swiss-cheese-infection-mackay.html in November 2022.

Romano, A. (2020). Conspiracy theories explained. *Vox*, November 18th. Accessed at: https://www.vox.com/21558524/conspiracy-theories-2020-qanon-covid-conspiracies-why in January 2023

Rosenblum, N.L., & Muirhead, R. (2019). *A lot of people are saying: The new conspiracism and the assault on democracy*. Princeton: Princeton University Press.

Rosset, E. (2008). It's no accident: Our bias for intentional explanations. *Cognition*, 108 (3): 771–80. DOI: 10.1016/j.cognition.2008.07.001.

Rottweiler, B., & Gill, P. (2020). Conspiracy beliefs and violent extremist intentions: The contingent effects of self-efficacy, self-control and law-related morality. *Terrorism and Political Violence*. DOI: 10.1080/09546553.2020.1803288.

Sakakibara, E. (2016). Irrationality and pathology of beliefs. *Neuroethics*, 9: 147–57 DOI: 10.1007/s12152-016-9256-9.

Saks, E. (2007). *The center cannot hold*. Westport, Connecticut: Hyperion Books.

Sapountzis, A., & Condor, S. (2013). Conspiracy accounts as intergroup theories: Challenging dominant understandings of social power and political legitimacy. *Political Psychology*, 34 (5): 731–52. http://www.jstor.org/stable/43783733.

Sedikides, C. (2021). Self-construction, self-protection, and self-enhancement: A homeostatic model of identity protection. *Psychological Inquiry*, 32 (4): 197–221. DOI: 10.1080/1047840X.2021.2004812.

Sharot, T., Korn, C., & Dolan, R. (2011). How unrealistic optimism is maintained in the face of reality. *Nature Neuroscience*, 14: 1475–9. DOI: 10.1038/nn.2949.

Shearman, D. (2018). Climate Change Denial Is Delusion, and the Biggest Threat to Human Survival, *ABC News*, December 6th. Accessed at: https://www.abc.net.au/news/2018-12-07/climate-change-denialismholocaust-david-attenborough-coal/10585744 in January 2023.

Shepperd, J.A., Waters, E., Weinstein, N.D., & Klein, W.M. (2015). A primer on unrealistic optimism. *Current Directions in Psychological Science*, 24 (3): 232–7. DOI: 10.1177/0963721414568341.

Shou, N. (2009). *Kill the messenger: How the CIA's crack-cocaine controversy destroyed journalist Gary Webb*. New York: Bold Type Books.

Silva, A.J., Ferrari, M.M., Leong, G.B., & Penny, G. (1998). The dangerousness of persons with delusional jealousy. *Journal of American Academic Psychiatry and Law*, 26 (4): 607–23.

Sims, A. (2013). *Symptoms of the mind. An introduction to descriptive psychopathology*. London: Elsevier.

Sowmya, A.V., Gupta, N., Dhamija, S., Samudra, M., Chaudhury, S., & Saldanha, D. (2021). Erotomania: A case series. *Industrial Psychiatry Journal*, 30 (Suppl 1): S249–S251. DOI: 10.4103/0972-6748.328821.

Stanton, B., & David, A. (2000). First-person accounts of delusions. *Psychiatric Bulletin*, 24 (9): 333–6. DOI: 10.1192/pb.24.9.333.

Stapleford, S. (2012). Epistemic duties and failure to understand one's evidence. *Principia*, 16 (1): 147–77. DOI: 10.5007/1808-1711.2012v16n1p147.

Stone, T., & Young, A. (1997). Delusions and brain injury: The philosophy and psychology of belief. *Mind and Language*, 12: 327–64. DOI: 10.1111/j.1468-0017.1997.tb00077.x.

Sullivan-Bissett, E. (2015). Implicit bias, confabulation, and epistemic innocence. *Consciousness and Cognition*, 33: 548–60. DOI: 10.1016/j.concog.2014.10.006.

Bibliography

Sullivan-Bissett, E. (2020). Unimpaired abduction to alien abduction: Lessons on delusion formation. *Philosophical Psychology*, 33 (5): 679–704. DOI: 10.1080/09515089.2020.1765324.

Sunstein, C.R., & Vermeule, A. (2008). Conspiracy theories. *Law and Economics Working Papers*. 387.

Suthaharan, P., Reed, E.J., Leptourgos, P., Kenney, J.G., Uddenberg, S., Mathys, C.D., Litman, L., Robinson, J., Moss, A.J., Taylor, J.R., Groman, S.M., & Corlett, P.R. (2021). Paranoia and belief updating during the COVID-19 crisis. *Nature Human Behaviour*, 5 (9): 1190–202. DOI: 10.1038/s41562-021-01176-8.

Taylor, C. (1989). *The sources of the self: The making of the modern identity*. Cambridge, MA: Harvard University Press.

Taylor, S.E. (1989). *Positive illusions: Creative self-deception and the healthy mind*. New York: Basic Books.

Taylor, S.E., Lichtman, R.R., & Wood, J.V. (1984). Attributions, beliefs about control, and adjustment to breast cancer. *Journal of Personality and Social Psychology*, 46: 489–502. DOI: 10.1037//0022-3514.46.3.489.

Thalmann, K. (2019). *The stigmatization of conspiracy theory since the 1950s*. Abingdon: Routledge.

The Week (2020). Strange conspiracy theories: From 5G to Meghan Markle. Accessed at: https://www.theweek.co.uk/tags/conspiracy-theories in May 2022.

Thomson, H. (2013). Mindscapes: First interview with a dead man. *New Scientist*. Accessed at: https://www.newscientist.com/article/dn23583-mindscapes-first-interview-with-a-dead-man/#ixzz6ZcFJTnXK in January 2023.

Tiger, L. (1979). *Optimism: The biology of hope*. New York: Simon & Schuster.

Tilner, A., Schumpe, B.M., & Erb, H.P. (2022). *The need for uniqueness – A motor for social change*. London: Routledge. DOI: 10.4324/9780367198459-REP RW108-1.

Uscinski, J.E. (ed.) (2018). Conspiracy theories for journalists: Covering dubious ideas in real time. In J.E. Uscinski (ed.), *Conspiracy theories and the people who believe them*. New York: Oxford University Press, chapter 31.

Uscinski, J.E., & Parent, J.M. (2014). *American conspiracy theories*. Oxford: Oxford University Press.

Van Prooijen, J.W. (2011). Suspicions of injustice: The sense-making function of belief in conspiracy theories. In E. Kals, & J. Maes (eds), *Justice and conflicts*. Berlin, Heidelberg: Springer, pp. 121–32. DOI: 10.1007/978-3-642- 19035-3_7.

Van Prooijen, J.W. (2022). Psychological benefits of believing conspiracy theories. *Current Opinion in Psychology*, 47: 101352. DOI: 10.1016/j. copsyc.2022.101352.

Veling, W., Sizoo, B., van Buuren, J., van den Berg, C., Sewbalak, W., Pijnenborg, G.H.M., Boonstra, N., Castelein, S., & van der Meer, L. (2021). Zijn complotdenkers psychotisch? Een vergelijking tussen complottheorieën en paranoïde wanen [Are conspiracy theorists psychotic? A comparison between conspiracy theories and paranoid delusions]. *Tijdschrift voor psychiatrie*, 63 (11): 775–81.

Vines, G. (2007). The Santa Delusion. *New Scientist*, December 18th. Available at: https://www.newscientist.com/article/mg19626351-500-the-santa-delusion/.

Voruz, P., Allali, G., Benzakour, L., Nuber-Champier, A., Thomasson, M., Jacot de Alcântara, I., Pierce, J., Lalive, P.H., Lövblad, K.O., Braillard, O., Coen, M.,

Serratrice, J., Pugin, J., Ptak, R., Guessous, I., Landis, B.N., Assal, F., Péron, J.A. (2022). Long COVID neuropsychological deficits after severe, moderate, or mild infection. *Clinical and Translational Neuroscience,* 6 (2): 9. DOI: 10.3390/ctn6020009.

Wakefield, J. C. (1992). The concept of mental disorder: On the boundary between biological facts and social values. *American Psychologist,* 47 (3): 373–88. DOI: 10.1037/0003-066X.47.3.373.

Wang, E. (2019). *The collected schizophrenias.* Minneapolis: Graywolf Press.

Weiner, S.K. (2003). First person account: Living with the delusions and effects of schizophrenia. *Schizophrenia Bulletin,* 29 (4): 877–9. DOI: 10.1093/oxfordjournals.schbul.a007054.

Wilkinson, S. (2020). Expressivism about delusion attribution. *European Journal of Analytic Philosophy*, 18 (1). DOI: 10.31820/ejap.16.2.3.

Williams, D. (2021). Socially adaptive belief. *Mind & Language*, 36 (3): 333–54. DOI: 10.1111/mila.12294.

Williams, D. (2022). Signalling, commitment, and strategic absurdities. *Mind & Language*, 37 (5): 1011–29. DOI: 10.1111/mila.12392.

Young, A. (1999). Delusions. *The Monist*, 82: 571–89. DOI: 10.5840/monist199982421.

Young, D. (2020). I was a conspiracy theorist, too. *Vox*, May 15th. Accessed at: https://www.vox.com/first-person/2020/5/15/21258855/coronavirus-covid-19-conspiracy-theories-cancer in November 2022.

Zangrilli, A., Ducci, G., Bandinelli, P.L. et al. (2014). How do psychiatrists address delusions in first meetings in acute care? A qualitative study. *BMC Psychiatry*, 14: 178. DOI: 10.1186/1471-244X-14-178.

Zell, E., Strickhouser, J.E., Sedikides, C., & Alicke, M.D. (2020). The better-than-average effect in comparative self-evaluation: A comprehensive review and meta-analysis. *Psychological Bulletin*, 146 (2): 118–49. DOI: 10.1037/bul0000218.

INDEX

Index